Wontner's Guide to
Land Registry Practice

AUSTRALIA
Law Book Co.
Sydney

CANADA and USA
Carswell
Toronto

HONG KONG
Sweet & Maxwell Asia

NEW ZEALAND
Brookers
Auckland

SINGAPORE and MALAYSIA
Sweet & Maxwell Asia
Singapore and Kuala Lumpur

Wontner's Guide to
Land Registry Practice

Twenty-first Edition

Patrick Timothy LLB
Land Registrar

Alison Barker MA
Assistant Land Registrar

THOMSON

™

SWEET & MAXWELL

First Published 1928
Twenty-first edition 2005

Published in 2005 by
Sweet & Maxwell Ltd, 100 Avenue Road,
Swiss Cottage, London NW3 3PF
http://www.sweetandmaxwell.co.uk

Typeset by J.P. Price, Chilcompton, Somerset
Printed in Great Britain by MPG Books Ltd, Bodmin, Cornwall

No natural forests were destroyed to make this product;
only farmed timber was used and replanted.

A CIP catalogue record for this book is available from the
British Library

ISBN 0421 900 407

Editors' Note

Throughout this work (unless otherwise indicated) references to "the Act" and to section numbers relate to the Land Registration Act 2002; references to "the Rules" and to individual rules relate to the Land Registration Rules 2003; and references to "the current Fee Order" relate to the Land Registration Fee Order 2004, a copy of which is set out in Appendix IV.

"Conveyancer" has the same meaning as in the Rules (as amended by the Land Registration (Amendment) Rules 2005), *i.e.* a solicitor, a licensed conveyancer, within the meaning of s.11(2) of the Administration of Justice Act 1985, a fellow of the Institute of Legal Executives or a duly certificated notary public.

The expression "the appropriate office" is used throughout in place of the statutory words "the proper office" being the office designated under s.100(3) for the receipt of applications or a specified description of application.

Acknowledgment

Forms on the CD-ROM are reproduced with kind permission of HM Land Registry.

Preface

When the 1st edition of this book was printed in 1928 land registration in England and Wales was in its infancy. Conveyancers were just coming to terms with the major changes brought about by the Law of Property Act 1925 and supporting legislation. For all but a few, land registration was a distant prospect and Wontner produced his book as a guide for those who came into contact with it.

In 2003, after all conveyancers had become familiar with the law and practice of registered titles, we had another major change which recognised that registration was the norm and unregistered titles were becoming increasingly rare. Indeed one of the major aims of the Land Registration Act 2002 was to encourage registration of title in line with the Land Registry's published strategic aim of completing the Land Register by 2012.

The basic framework of the system was not changed by the new legislation. We still have a register and title plan, albeit now held almost exclusively electronically, the register is divided into three parts and there are four possible classes of title. But there were major changes in almost all areas. Land and charge certificates were abolished along with cautions against dealings and inhibitions. Registration extended to new interests such as profits à prendre in gross and leases for more than seven years became compulsorily registrable. A new method of determining boundaries was introduced. The Registry's records were made more open but there was a new category of exempt information document which contains information which is normally not open to inspection. Objections which cannot be resolved by agreement are now referred outside the Registry to an independent Adjudicator. And, perhaps the best publicised reform, the way in which title can be obtained by adverse possession is completely new and unique to registered land.

The 20th edition was rewritten to reflect the position as at October 13, 2003, the date when the new legislation came into force. Since then, practitioners have been familiarising themselves with a multiplicity of new terms, forms and procedures and Land Registry practice has been evolving. This 21st edition has been comprehensively updated to include information on areas where there have been further developments and changes and we have sought to build into this edition points arising from our experience of the operation of the changes in practice since October 2003. We hope that practitioners will continue to find it useful as they navigate the registration process.

Many thanks to our spouses, Anne and Jonathan, without whose patience and support this book would not have been written.

Patrick Timothy and Alison Barker

Contents

Table of Cases

Table of Statutes

Table of Statutory Instruments

Chapter 1

General Features

Introduction

Her Majesty's Land Registry is a government agency. Its main **1-001** purpose is to register title to land in England and Wales and to record dealings, *e.g.* sales and mortgages, with registered land.

Its published mission is to provide "the world's best service for guaranteeing ownership of land and facilitating property transactions" and its vision is "making property transactions easier for all".

Land registration is carried out under the authority of the Land Registration Act 2002 ("the Act") and the Land Registration Rules 2003 ("the Rules").

Transitional arrangements

The Act replaced existing legislation principally the Land Regis- **1-002** tration Act 1925 with effect from October 13, 2003. Schedule 12 to the Act contains transitional provisions.

Paragraph 1 of Sch.12 to the Act confirms the validity of entries in the register as at the date the new Act came into force.

What interests can be registered?

The Act covers registration of title to legal estates which are **1-003** interests of any of the following kinds:

(1) an estate in land. "Land" includes buildings and other structures, mines and minerals (whether or not held with the surface) and land covered with water including the sea-bed up to the territorial limits of England and Wales

(ss.132 and 130). Manors are not included in the definition and they can no longer be registered and s.119 allows manors registered under earlier legislation to be de-registered. In addition s.90 prohibits the registration of public-private partnership leases relating to transport in London;

(2) a rentcharge (see Chapter 14);

(3) a franchise — a right granted by the Crown, *e.g.* to hold a market or fair;

(4) a profit à prendre in gross which is a right, such as hunting and fishing, which is not attached to land;

(5) any other interest or charge which subsists for the benefit of, or is a charge on, a registered interest; and

(6) interests capable of subsisting at law which are created by a disposition of an interest the title to which is registered.

Who may apply for first registration?

1–004 Subject to the exceptions below, a person may apply to be registered as the proprietor under its own title of an unregistered legal estate in:

(1) land;

(2) a rentcharge;

(3) a franchise; or

(4) a profit à prendre in gross,

if it is vested in him or if he is entitled to require it to be vested in him (but not where he has contracted to buy under a contract) (s.3(1), (2) and (6)).

Section 79 contains provisions under which Her Majesty may grant a freehold estate out of demesne land to Herself and may register that estate.

No application can be made to register a leasehold estate vested in the applicant as a mortgagee where there is a subsisting right of redemption (s.3(5)).

An application to register a lease may only be made if it was granted for a term of which more than seven years are unexpired unless the right to possession under the lease is discontinuous when an application can be made whatever the length of the term (s.3(3) and (4)). An example of a discontinuous term would be a term granted under a timeshare lease.

If a person holds both:

(1) a lease in possession; and

(2) a lease of the same land to take effect in possession on, or within a month of, the end of the lease in possession,

in the same capacity, the leases are treated as creating one continuous term (s.3(7)).

Under s.118 the Lord Chancellor may by order, after appropriate consultation, reduce the length of a leasehold term which may be the subject of an application for registration, but it is not, currently, proposed that he should do so.

Other interests and charges cannot be registered under their own title but may only be registered for the benefit of or charged on a title which is being or has already been registered.

Classes of titles

Registration may be with: **1–005**

(1) Absolute title;

(2) Possessory title;

(3) Qualified title,

and additionally for leaseholds only,

(4) Good leasehold title (ss.9 and 10).

The reasons why the registrar will approve a particular class of title and the effect of registration with that class are explained in Chapter 4.

The circumstances in which title can be upgraded are explained in Chapter 21.

The register of title

Rules 2 and 3 contain provisions as to how the register is to be **1–006** held and how individual registers may be amalgamated or divided. The register is now almost entirely held in electronic form.

Individual registers of title must have a distinguishing number, or series of letters and numbers, known as the title number and must consist of:

(1) a property register;

(2) a proprietorship register; and

(3) where necessary, a charges register (r.4(1) and (2)).

An entry in a register may be made by reference to a plan or other document; in which case the registrar must keep the original or a copy of that document (r.4(3)).

Whenever the registrar considers it desirable in relation to an individual register he may open a new edition showing only the existing entries, rearrange the entries or alter the title number (r.4(4)).

The *property register* contains a description of the registered property by reference to a plan based on the Ordnance Survey map and known as the title plan (except in the case of profits à prendre in gross and certain franchises) and details of other matters, *e.g.* the exclusion of mines and minerals and benefiting easements, rights and privileges (r.5). In addition the property register of a leasehold estate must contain sufficient particulars of the registered lease to enable that lease to be identified and, if the lease contains a provision prohibiting or restricting dispositions, an entry stating that all estates, rights, interests, powers and remedies arising on or by reason of a disposition made in breach of that prohibition or restriction are excepted from the effect of registration (r.6). In the case of a rentcharge, franchise or a profit à prendre in gross the property register must, if the estate was created by an instrument, also contain sufficient particulars of the instrument to enable it to be identified (r.7).

The *proprietorship register* includes, where appropriate, the class of title, the name of the proprietor, the proprietor's address for service (see Chapters 4 and 9), restrictions, bankruptcy entries, details of positive and indemnity covenants and of modification of covenants (see Chapter 7) (r.8(1)). In the case of a possessory title it will contain the name of the first proprietor (r.8(1)(i)). Whenever practicable the proprietorship register will also include details of the price paid or value declared and that entry will remain until there is a change of proprietor, or some other change in the register of title which the registrar considers would result in the entry being misleading (r.8(2)).

The *charges register* contains, where appropriate, details of leases, charges, and any other adverse interests; any dealings with or affecting the priority of those interests, which are capable of being noted; the name and address for service of the proprietor of any registered charge and any restrictions and bankruptcy entries in relation to a registered charge (r.9).

Indices (s.68 and rr.10 and 11)

The *index of proprietors' names* shows for each individual **1–007**
register the name of the proprietor of the land and of the
proprietor of any registered charge together with the title
number. Until every register is kept electronically the index
need not contain the name of any corporate or joint proprietor
of land or of a charge registered as proprietor prior to May 1,
1972. Chapter 8 explains the procedure under which a search of
this index can be made.

An *index map* from which it can be established whether any
parcel of the land is registered, or in the process of being
registered and from which the title number can be identified and
a separate verbal *index of relating franchises and manors* are
kept. Further details including an explanation of how searches
of these indices can be made are contained in Chapter 2.

The day list (r.12)

The day list is a record of the date and time at which every **1–008**
pending application was made and of every application for an
official search with priority. Notice of an application for an
official search with priority remains on the day list until the
priority period allowed by the search comes to an end (see
Chapter 8). For this purpose pending application does not
include an application under Pt 13 of the Rules, which covers
"Information etc", except an application to designate a document an exempt information document under r.136.

If the registrar proposes to alter the register without having
received an application he must enter his proposal on the day
list and, when it is so entered, it will have the same effect as if it
were an application made at the date and time of its entry.

Delivery and priority of applications

Land Registry's office at Lincoln's Inn Fields, London, is an **1–009**
administrative head office. The day to day work of registration is
carried out at the other offices listed in Appendix I. Unless
lodged electronically, all applications and correspondence
should therefore be delivered to the appropriate office, which
can be identified from Appendix II which contains a list of areas
of local government in England and Wales and the offices
serving them.

An application is received when it is delivered:

(1) to the appropriate office; or

(2) in accordance with a written arrangement as to delivery made between the registrar and the applicant or his conveyancer; or

(3) electronically where that is authorised (r.15(3)).

An application received on a business day is taken as made at the earlier of:

(1) the time of the day that notice of it is entered in the day list; or

(2) midnight marking the end of:

    (a) the day it was received if the application was received before 12 noon; or

    (b) the next business day after the day it was received if the application was received at or after 12 noon (r.15(1)).

An application received on a day which is not a business day is taken as made at the earlier of:

(3) the time of a business day that notice of it is entered in the day list; or

(4) midnight marking the end of the next business day after the day it was received (r.15(2)).

A "business day" is a day on which the Registry is open to the public (r.217(1)). At the moment the Registry is normally open to the public daily except for Saturdays, Sundays and bank holidays (see r.216(1)). But the registrar may in the future arrange for the Registry to be open on Saturdays and if he does he must give at least eight weeks notice of his decision (r.216(2) to (4)).

Entries made on the register on first registration (see Chapter 4), on the registration of a disposition required to be completed by registration (see Chapter 9) or entries made in, removed from or altered as a result of any other application have effect from the time the application is made (s.74 and r.20).

Where two or more applications relating to the same registered title are taken as made at the same time the order in which they should rank in priority as between each other is determined in accordance with the provisions of r.55.

See Chapter 8 as to the deemed times of delivery of applications for official searches of the register and as to the priority conferred on applications for registration by official certificates of search.

Forms (rr.206 to 212)

A document affecting a registered title must refer to the title **1–010** number (r.212(3)).

Prescribed Forms which will cover most transactions are set out in Sch.1 to the Rules. Forms of execution are contained in Sch.9 to the Rules.

The registrar also publishes Welsh language versions of the Forms and of forms of execution and when they are published they are to be regarded as if they were contained in Sch.1 or Sch.9 to the Rules.

The registrar may permit a person to make an application relying on a document that is not the relevant scheduled form, if that person cannot obtain and lodge the relevant scheduled form or it is only possible to do so at unreasonable expense, if he is satisfied that neither the rights of any person nor the keeping of the register are likely to be materially prejudiced by allowing the alternative document to be relied upon.

Any application or document in one of the Sch.1 Forms must:

(1) be printed on durable A4 size paper;

(2) be reproduced as set out in the Schedule as to its wording, layout, ruling, font and point size;

(3) contain all the information required in an easily legible form; and

(4) if it consists of more than one sheet of paper, or refers to an attached plan or a continuation sheet, be securely fastened together.

If (other than on Form DL) the necessary information will not fit in the panel provided, the panel must be continued on a continuation sheet in Form CS.

Where a Form is produced electronically:

(a) the depth of a panel may be increased or reduced to fit the material to be comprised in it, and a panel may be divided at a page break;

(b) instructions in italics may be omitted;

(c) inapplicable certificates and statements may be omitted;

(d) the plural may be used instead of the singular and the singular instead of the plural;

(e) panels which would contain only the panel number and the panel heading may be omitted, but such omission must not affect the numbering of subsequent panels;

(f) "X" boxes may be omitted where all inapplicable statements and certificates have been omitted;

(g) the sub-headings in an additional provisions panel may
be added to, amended, repositioned or omitted;

(h) "Seller" may be substituted for "Transferor" and
"Buyer" for "Transferee" in a transfer on sale;

(i) the vertical lines which define the left and right boundaries of the panel may be omitted.

If no Form is prescribed the document must be in such form
as the registrar may direct or allow.

Fees

1–011 Fees are prescribed by the Land Registration Fee Order 2004,
referred to in this book as "the Fee Order". The text of the Fee
Order is set out in Appendix IV.

Fees are normally required to be paid on delivery of the
application to which they relate by means of a cheque or postal
order crossed and made payable to the Land Registry (Fee
Order, art.13).

Where a fee is paid by a cheque which is not honoured the
application may be cancelled (r.16(4)).

Any person or firm, if authorised by the Registry, may use a
credit account for payment of fees on applications and services
of such kinds as the registrar may direct (Fee Order, art.14).
Certain services are only available to credit account holders *e.g.*
the telephone search service.

Applicants who have made prior arrangements may pay fees
for substantive applications by direct debit. Information about
setting up such an arrangement can be obtained from Accounts
Section, Land Registry, Plumer House, Crownhill, Plymouth
PL6 5HY.

When two or more instruments relating to the same land are
delivered for registration as parts of the same application, a
separate fee is payable in respect of each; but when a sale and a
sub sale are effected by one instrument of transfer only one fee,
assessed on the price paid by the buyer or the sub-buyer,
whichever is the greater is payable (Fee Order, art.3).

Requisitions raised by the Registry (rr.16 and 17)

1–012 If an application appears to the registrar to be substantially
defective, he may reject it on delivery or he may cancel it at any
time thereafter.

If an application is not in order the registrar may raise such requisitions as he considers necessary and specify a period (being not less than 20 business days) within which the applicant must comply with the requisitions. If the applicant fails to comply with the requisitions within the specified period, the registrar may cancel the application or may extend the period when this appears to him to be reasonable in the circumstances.

If he considers it necessary or desirable, the registrar may refuse to complete or proceed with an application until further documents or evidence are supplied or notice is given.

If it will not be possible to reply to requisitions in the time specified an extension must be requested. The request should:

(1) state the reason for the delay;

(2) explain what is being done to resolve the problem; and

(3) say when it is expected that a full reply to the requisition can be supplied.

If such a request is made supported by a proper reason an extension will be allowed but if no request is made the application will be cancelled.

The Registry's Practice Guides 49 and 50 contain full details of their policy and practice on the rejection of defective applications and on requisitions and cancellation.

Stamp duty land tax ("SDLT") and stamp duty

SDLT replaced stamp duty for most land transactions on 1 **1–013** December 2003.

Applications for the registration or noting of a land transaction must (see s.79(1) of the Finance Act 2003) be accompanied by either:

(1) a Land Transaction Return certificate; or

(2) a self certificate in form SDLT60; or

(3) a letter explaining why neither certificate is required.

No covering letter is required in the case of a legal or equitable charge, a discharge of a charge or a contract for sale which are exempt transactions.

Where a Land Transaction Return certificate is required, unless it is covered by an outline application (see Chapter 9), the application will be rejected if lodged without it unless at least 20 working days have passed since completion. If the certificate is not by then available the application can be lodged but it must be accompanied by a clear statement that the Land Transaction Return has been sent to Inland Revenue. The application will not be cancelled provided that the Land Registry is asked, in response to requisitions or reminders, to extend the time because Inland Revenue has not provided the certificate. Failure to respond to the Land Registry requisitions or enquiries will result in cancellation.

There are still a few transactions on which stamp duty is payable. These will mainly be based on pre-July 11, 2003 contracts. Where a document is lodged which is endorsed with stamp duty and, if appropriate, with a "produced" stamp, no query will be raised and no covering letter is necessary. A transfer for value (not relating to a share) dated after November 30, 2003 on which stamp duty would still be payable but which is below the stamp duty threshold should be lodged with a Form L(A)451 and a covering letter of explanation.

Land and charge certificates

1–014 Before October 13, 2003 in nearly all cases a land certificate or a charge certificate was issued on completion of first registration and dealings applications. The exception was where certain lenders had agreed to dispense with the need for a charge certificate when a charge in their favour was registered. Since October 13, 2003, land and charge certificates have no longer been issued or required. It is now not necessary to lodge an existing land or charge certificate in connection with any application. If a certificate is lodged it will be destroyed.

Title Information Document

1–015 Although it is not required by the Rules, as a matter of practice the Registry issues a Title Information Document whenever there is a change of proprietorship. The document contains:

(1) the title number;

(2) a verbal description of the land;

(3) the class of title and whether it is freehold or leasehold;

(4) if it is leasehold, short particulars of the lease;

(5) the name and address of the proprietor; and

(6) guidance about how to obtain an official copy of the register and other information.

It is envisaged that the conveyancer will pass this document on to his client.

Retention and return of documents (rr.203 to 205)

Subject to the delivery of any certified copies required, the **1–016** registrar must comply with any request made by an applicant or his conveyancer, with an application, for the return of all or any of the documents accompanying that application. Except on an application for first registration, a person making such a request must deliver with the application certified copies of the documents which are the subject of the request. On an application for first registration, a person making a request for the return of any statutory declaration, subsisting lease, subsisting charge or the latest document of title must deliver with the application certified copies of such documents as are the subject of the request, but is not required to deliver copies of any other documents.

Otherwise on completion of any application the registrar may retain all or any of the documents that accompanied the application.

The registrar may destroy any document which he retains if he is satisfied that he has made and retained a sufficient copy of the document or further retention of the document is unnecessary.

For a period of five years from October 13, 2003, any person who either:

(1) delivered a document to the registrar on which any entry in the register of title is, or was, founded; or

(2) is the current registered proprietor, where the person who delivered the document was at that time the registered proprietor, or applying to become the registered proprietor,

may request the return of that document.

If, at the date of such a request, the document is kept by the registrar he must return it to the person making the request unless he receives more than one request in respect of the same document, when he may either retain the document or, in his discretion, return it to one of the persons making a request.

At the end of the five-year period, if there is no outstanding request in relation to the document, the registrar may destroy any document if he is satisfied that he has retained a copy of the document, or further retention of the document is unnecessary.

The registrar may release any document retained by him upon such terms, if any, for its return as he considers appropriate.

Land Registry Direct

1–017 Land Registry Direct, and its predecessor Direct Access, which is available to Registry account holders only, allows on-line access to registers, title plans and the day list, on-line ordering of official copies and searches and the lodging on-line of some "no fee" applications.

More information can be obtained from: Land Registry Direct, Touthill Close, City Road, Peterborough, PE1 1XN. Tel: 0870 0100299. E-mail: *admin@landregistrydirect.gov.uk*.

Electronic conveyancing

1–018 The Act contains provisions which authorise the establishment of a Registry network to facilitate a system of e-conveyancing (ss.91 to 95 and Sch.5 to the Act). A consultation exercise on such a system was carried out by the Registry in 2002. The roll-out of the system is expected to start in 2007/2008.

In the meantime a number of electronic registration services are being developed in advance of the full system. The first new service to come on stream was electronic discharges which allows lenders to electronically signal the discharge of a legal charge, direct to the Registry, machine to machine. Following electronic validation checks, the discharge is reflected on the register automatically. Up to date information is available at: *www.landregistry.gov.uk/e-conveyancing*.

Information

Inquiries

1–019 Inquiries as to Registry practice may be made in writing, by telephone or by personal visit to the Customer Information Centre at any office which in the case of an inquiry relating to a specific title should be at the appropriate office.

Registry website

1–020 Up to date information about Registry practice and procedure and copies of Forms can be obtained from the Registry's website at *www.landregistry.gov.uk*.

Land Register Online
Land Register Online is an online service, aimed at the **1–021**
general public, enabling a search to be made for
registers and title plans that can be identified by an address.
Copies of registers and title plans found can be downloaded, for
a fee of £2 each, payable by credit/debit card. It can be found at
www.landregisteronline.gov.uk.

Chapter 2

Plans, Maps and Boundaries

Title plans

The property register of each title contains a description of the **2–001**
registered land which refers to a plan based on the Ordnance
Survey map which is called the title plan (r.5). Each title plan is
filed in the Registry's computer system under the unique title
number for the title to which it relates.

The title plan is prepared from:

(1) the plans and verbal descriptions in the title deeds;

(2) an inspection survey of the land where necessary; and

(3) the result of any further inquiries made by the registrar
to establish the identity of the property.

An applicant for first registration must provide sufficient
information by plan or by verbal description to enable his land
to be identified clearly on the Ordnance Survey map
(r.24(1)(a)).

If the extent of land to be included in the title cannot clearly
be related to the features shown on the Ordnance Survey map
an inspection survey will be carried out. This will be done by the
Registry's surveyor or by the Ordnance Survey at the request of
the Registry.

If, as is normally the case, the extent of the land to be
registered can be identified on the Ordnance Survey map from
the information supplied the title plan will be prepared without
a survey.

As all the Registry's plans are based on the Ordnance Survey
map they must not be reproduced without a paper map copying
licence from the Ordnance Survey. If you are intending to make
copies of any of the Registry's maps or plans you should first
make the necessary arrangements by applying to: Customer

Contact Centre, Ordnance Survey, Romsey Road, Southampton, SO16 4GU.

What does the title plan show?

2–002 A title plan shows:

- The title number of the registered property.

- The extent of the land in the registered title, normally with general boundaries (see below), marked by red lines. Sometimes the description of the land in the register will contain information clarifying the extent. For example if the title relates to a first floor flat there will be a note in the property register to explain this.

- Other colours, which are explained in notes on the title plan or in the register, to identify, for example, land affected by easements or restrictive covenants. If land is coloured green it is not included in the title but is surrounded by land which is in the title. If it is edged green it has been removed from the title and it is now registered under a new title number which may be shown in green on the plan.

- Black lines, which represent boundary features such as walls, hedges, fences or buildings taken from the Ordnance Survey map on which the title plan is based.

- The scale to which the plan is drawn. Most plans are at the scale of 1/1250 which is used for land in urban areas, and for developing building estates, small houses, single building plots and so on. 1/2500 scale is used for land in predominantly rural areas such as farms and other medium sized units that are unlikely to be developed in the near future. 1/10560 or 1/10000 is sometimes used for the registration of mountain, moorland and marshland, and similar areas that are most unlikely ever to be developed or actively cultivated. Only the 1/2500 scale Ordnance Survey map shows Ordnance Survey parcel numbers and areas. Where a title plan is based on an extract from the 1/2500 scale map on which the numbers and areas are shown, they will not be deleted, except where only part of a parcel is included in the title. It is important to be aware that the numbers and areas shown on one edition of an Ordnance Survey map may differ from those shown on another.

- Dimensions may be shown to tie the positions of unfenced boundaries or otherwise to clarify extents of land but the fact that such measurements are shown does not mean that the position of the boundary has been determined.

Enlargements are sometimes provided to clarify detail beyond the scope of the normal Ordnance Survey scales, *e.g.* to show small juts in boundary walls and sometimes different floor levels. Supplementary plans can be annexed to title plans for example to show parts of buildings at different floor levels or to carry complicated reference markings that would cause confusion if shown on the title plan itself.

General boundaries

Every property, whether or not it is registered, has exact legal **2–003** boundaries — lines separating the land owned by one person from that owned by their neighbour. But deeds rarely identify these legal boundaries precisely and often the owners do not know where they are. Trying to fix the boundaries at the time of registration would involve a great deal of expense for the adjoining owners and could cause a dispute that would not otherwise have occurred. For that reason title plans normally show general boundaries (s.60).

Registration with general boundaries means that, even though the title plan may show the red edging drawn along a particular wall, hedge, fence or other feature on the ground it does not show the exact line of the legal boundary. As a result the title plan does not define whether the boundary:

- runs somewhere within the feature on the map; or

- runs along one particular side of the feature; or

- runs beyond the near side or the far side of the feature; or

- includes all or any part of an adjoining roadway or stream.

Title plans are based on the Ordnance Survey map and are limited by the precision with which such maps are prepared. As with any map, Ordnance Survey maps are subject to some limitations which depend upon the scale of the map and the accuracy of the surveying techniques used. These limitations are likely to result in some variation between what is shown on the map and what exists on the ground and as a result, title plans cannot be used to establish the precise position of features on the ground simply by scaling from the title plan. In some cases the nature of particular features on the ground can add to the uncertainty. For example, a mature hedge can be several metres wide, so that it can be difficult to relate it to the single line which represents it on the map.

Determined boundaries

2–004 Under the old legislation a title could be registered with fixed boundaries. The applicant had to bear the cost of this expensive process, and there was no guarantee that it would be possible, as a result of the investigations made, to fix the boundaries. In practice applications for fixed boundaries were almost unknown.

Section 60 contains provisions under which the exact line of a boundary may be determined.

An application by a registered proprietor for the exact line of his boundary or part of his boundary to be determined must be made in Form DB accompanied by:

(1) a plan, or a plan and a verbal description, identifying the exact line of the boundary claimed and showing sufficient surrounding physical features to allow the general position of the boundary to be drawn on the Ordnance Survey map; and

(2) evidence to establish the exact line of the boundary (r.118).

If the registrar is satisfied that:

(a) the plan, or plan and verbal description, supplied identifies the exact line of the boundary claimed;

(b) the applicant has shown an arguable case that the exact line of the boundary is in the position shown on the plan, or plan and verbal description; and

(c) he can identify all the owners of the land adjoining the boundary to be determined and has an address at which each owner may be given notice (r.119),

he must give the owners of the land adjoining the boundary to be determined (except the applicant) notice of the application, and of the fact that the exact line of the boundary will be determined if an objection is not received within the notice period.

But the registrar need not give notice of the application to an owner of the land adjoining the boundary where the evidence supplied includes an agreement in writing as to the exact line of the boundary made with that owner (r.119(2)).

The notice period is 20 business days or such longer period as the registrar may decide before the issue of the notice. If before the notice period has expired a request setting out why an extension should be allowed is received by the registrar he may extend the notice period. Any such extension will be for such period as the registrar thinks fit which does not have to be the period requested. In deciding whether to extend the notice period the registrar will take account of all relevant matters including, if he thinks it appropriate, the views of the applicant (r.119(3), (4) and (5)).

If no objection is received within the notice period the registrar must make entries in the register and on the title plans of any titles affected stating that the exact line of the boundary has been determined and giving particulars of that line (r.120).

If an objection is received and it cannot be disposed of by agreement it must be referred to the Adjudicator (see Chapter 22).

Where, when registering a transfer or lease of part of a registered title, the registrar has sufficient evidence to determine the exact line of a boundary between the land transferred or leased and land which at the date of the transfer or lease was owned by the transferor or lessor he may do so (r.122).

A fee in accordance with the current Fee Order is payable. Note that the registrar can charge an additional fee if the cost of the work involved substantially exceeds the fee paid.

Deed plans

Use to clarify title plans
In cases of overlapping floors or party walls, for example, where **2–005** a surveyor or architect has prepared detailed plans on larger scales the Registry will consider referring to those plans as an adjunct to the title plan.

Plan containing a statement of disclaimer
Plans which bear a statement of disclaimer, for example: "Note: **2–006** This plan is for reference only and although believed to be correct, its accuracy is in no way guaranteed and it is expressly excluded from any contract" or "For identification only" are not acceptable.

Reduced copy plans used in original deeds
The Registry will reject any dealing of part or lease application **2–007** which contains plans that have been reduced from their original scale but which still bear the original scale endorsement.

Where it is clear that the plan contained in a deed or copy deed is a reduced copy of the original, it is only acceptable if:

(1) the original scale has been deleted; or

(2) it has been endorsed with a statement to the effect that it is a reduced copy (or in the case of a copy deed, a reduced copy of the plan to the original deed); or

(3) the actual scale is stated in place of the original scale.

If the scale on a layout plan is drawn (by reference to metres or feet) the reduced image of the drawn scale that appears on the reduced copy plan will satisfactorily indicate the scale of the reduced plan; but an endorsement should always appear on the reduced copy plan.

Discrepancy between Ordnance Survey map and transfer plan

2–008 Although registration is normally with general boundaries, the Registry relates the boundaries as accurately as possible to the physical features, including fences, hedges and walls shown on the Ordnance Survey map. Where a transfer plan shows detail which does not correspond with that actually existing on the ground, the Registry may require the transfer plan to be altered so that it corresponds with the position on the ground.

If the plan is to be altered the Registry will if possible avoid the need to prepare a formal deed of rectification. So, for example, the parties concerned may be asked to remove the defective plan, and substitute and sign a new plan or to sign a new plan, under a statement that it correctly represents their intentions, and to sign an appropriate endorsement (referring to the new plan) on the defective plan.

Limitation of title extent

2–009 Where part of the land in an application clearly falls outside the occupied extent of the property which is being registered, as shown on the latest Ordnance Survey map, and it appears to be occupied by another owner or where part of the land in the application is already registered under another ownership the Registry may prepare the title plan to exclude the land in question and send a letter to the applicant explaining that the extent registered is different from the deeds and why. It is open to the applicant to account for the discrepancy, *e.g.* by producing evidence of a licence or tenancy, or, in appropriate circumstances, to apply for alteration of the title plan of an adjoining property (see Chapter 22).

Ownership of fences and walls: 'T' marks

The Registry will make an entry on the property register in **2–010** respect of a declaration as to ownership of fences and other boundary features contained in a transfer of registered land or identified on examination of title on first registration of land about to be registered.

Where 'T' marks are referred to in positive covenants that are set out on the register (because they are intermingled with restrictive covenants — see Chapter 7) explanatory notes are added as necessary, but it is usually unnecessary to reproduce the 'T' marks on the title plan. 'T' marks may appear on the plan to a deed which contains no fencing covenant or other provision which refers to them. If in such a case the applicant for registration specifically asks for the 'T' marks to be reproduced on the title plan, the Registry will usually comply with the request.

It is important to remember that where the register mentions ownership of walls, fences, hedges and other boundary features, these may have changed. For example, new boundary features might have been built and the neighbours at that time might have agreed who was responsible for them. Regardless of any information given on the register it is best if you discuss with your neighbours and agree who owns a fence, hedge, *etc.* before doing anything to it.

Boundary disputes

Except in those rare cases where the boundary has been fixed or **2–011** determined, the Registry cannot decide where the legal boundary between two areas of land lies.

If the legal line of the boundary has to be established this can only be done:

(1) by the adjoining owners reaching agreement; or

(2) judicially.

If it is at all possible, an agreement is the best way of bringing a dispute about the line of the boundary to an end. If an agreement is reached and there are significant changes that ought to be recorded, it is normally best to set the terms of the agreement down in a formal document and arrange for it to be noted on the registers of titles affected.

Although the Registry cannot impose a solution it can sometimes help the parties to reach agreement by providing information which it holds and by offering guidance about land registration practice.

What if there is an error in a title plan?

2–012 If a proprietor thinks his title plan, or someone else's title plan which affects that proprietor and his land, is wrong in some way he should inform the Registry. The Registry will look in to it and say if it agrees. If the Registry does not agree it will say why. Where the title plan is wrong the Registry will correct it if possible. If another registered proprietor is affected by the error or would be affected by the action needed to correct it he will need to be informed about the error. He can either agree that his title plan can be corrected or explain why he objects. Where the registered proprietor is in possession of land it is not normally possible to remove that land from his title without his consent (paras.3(2) and 6(2) of Sch.4 to the Act and see Chapter 22).

If there is an objection there will be a dispute which can only be resolved by agreement or by a judge or the Adjudicator (see Chapter 22).

Anyone who suffers financial loss as a result of an error in a title plan, may be entitled to be indemnified (see Chapter 22). If there is a possibility that there is an error which may lead to costs being incurred the Registry must be approached before incurring any costs. Normally indemnity against costs cannot be paid unless the registrar has consented to those costs being incurred (see Chapter 22).

Indices of registrations

The index (s.68 and r.10)
2–013 An index map is kept by reference to which it can be established whether any parcel of land is registered. From this index it is possible to identify any title number which affects that land and the estate or interest, *e.g.* freehold, leasehold, rentcharge, profit à prendre in gross or caution against first registration registered under that number. The index also shows whether the land is affected by a pending application for registration.

A separate verbal index of registered relating franchises and registered manors arranged by administrative area and identifying their title numbers is also kept.

Searches of the indices
2–014 Both indices are open to inspection. A search is made either:

- by delivering a Form SIM (search of the index map) or Form SIF (search of the index of relating franchises and manors) to the appropriate office;

- by telephone or fax if an account holder; or

- by direct access to the register if an account holder and Land Registry Direct subscriber.

Description of the property to be searched
An application for a search of the index map must fully and **2–015** clearly describe the land to which it relates. The description should include the postal number or description, the road name, the locality, the town, the district or London borough, the administrative county and the post code and/or Ordnance Survey map reference.

If the search is in respect of a particular flat in a block of flats, this should be made clear in the description.

If the registrar requires the applicant must provide a copy of an extract from the Ordnance Survey map on the largest published scale showing the land to which the application relates (r.145(3)).

If a search of a large area is required applicants are requested to contact the appropriate office in advance so that special arrangements may be made to eliminate unnecessary work.

Fees
Fees are payable in accordance with the current Fee Order. A **2–016** credit account can be used for payment of fees on such searches. The Fee Order provides for additional fees in special cases but in such a case the applicant must be notified of the additional fee and given a chance to withdraw his application without fee if he so elects.

Certificate of result of search (r.145(4) and Pt 1 of Sch.6 to the Rules)
The result of an official search of the index map will include the **2–017** following information:

(1) The date and time of the official search certificate;

(2) A description of the land searched;

(3) The reference (if any) of the applicant or the person to whom the search is being sent;

(4) Whether there is:

    (a) a pending application for first registration (other than for a relating franchise);

(b) a pending application for a caution against first registration (other than in respect of a relating franchise);
(c) a registered estate in land;
(d) a registered rentcharge;
(e) a registered profit à prendre in gross;
(f) a registered affecting franchise; or
(g) a caution against first registration (other than in respect of a relating franchise),

and, if there is such a registered estate or caution, the title number.

Where, on a search of a routine nature, the result of the search reveals that part of the land searched is unregistered or is affected by more than one registered title, the Registry will issue a plan illustrating the properties as shown on the Index Map.

These plans are illustrative and do not define the extent of the land in a title. If more specific information is required about a title then the applicant must inspect the register and title plan (see Chapter 8).

There is currently no fee payable for the provision of such a plan. But for the service to operate efficiently it is restricted and such plans are not provided when the search relates to a large area or an area of complex registrations.

The result of an official search of the index of relating franchises and manors will contain the information set out in Pt 2 of Sch.6 to the Rules.

Chapter 3

Cautions Against First Registration

Who can apply?

Subject to the exception set out in this paragraph a caution **3–001** against first registration may be registered by a person who claims to be the owner of or entitled to an interest affecting the land to which the caution relates and which is:

(1) an estate in land;

(2) a rentcharge;

(3) a franchise; or

(4) a profit à prendre in gross.

Because one of the aims of the Act is to encourage registration of title the owner of an unregistered freehold estate or of an unregistered leasehold estate held under a lease of which more that seven years are unexpired is not, except for the transitional period mentioned below, allowed to protect his interest by the registration of a caution against first registration (s.15(3)). The proper way to protect such an interest is to register it.

For a transitional period of two years such an owner was allowed to register a caution against first registration but any such caution ceases to have any effect after October 12, 2005 (para.14 of Sch.12 to the Act).

Existing cautions against first registration, even if registered to protect a claim to an unregistered freehold estate or to an unregistered leasehold estate held under a lease of which more that seven years are unexpired, continued to have effect from October 13, 2003, but they are now subject to the provisions for alteration, withdrawal and cancellation set out below (paras. 1 and 16 of Sch.12 to the Act).

Effect

3–002 A caution against first registration entitles the cautioner to be given notice of an application for first registration of a legal estate to which the caution relates and gives the cautioner the right to object to that application (s.16(1)). But a caution against first registration neither guarantees the validity of the interest which it purports to protect nor confers priority on that interest (s.16(3)).

Method of application

3–003 Application for a caution against first registration must be on Form CT1 accompanied by a plan or other sufficient description to enable the land to which it relates to be identified on the Ordnance Survey map (r.42).

The application must be supported by a statutory declaration made by the applicant or a certificate given by a conveyancer on his behalf setting out details of the interest claimed. Documents proving the interest must not be lodged with the application nor should they be exhibited to the declaration or attached to the certificate. The form of statutory declaration and certificate are incorporated in Form CT1.

The application may be accompanied by consent which must be in writing (r.47).

A fee in accordance with the current Fee Order is payable. But under s.117(2) no fee is payable where the application is to protect an interest which will cease to be an overriding interest on October 12, 2013 (see Chapters 4 and 9).

The cautions register

3–004 A separate register of cautions against first registration is kept (s.19) with an individual register for each caution.

Each individual caution register has its own caution title number and is in two parts:

(1) The caution property register containing a description of the legal estate to which it relates and of the interest claimed. The description will normally refer to a caution plan based on the Ordnance Survey map.

(2) The cautioner's register containing:

(a) the name of the cautioner including, where the cautioner is a company registered under the Companies Acts, or a limited liability partnership incorporated under the Limited Liability Partnerships Act 2000, its registered number;

(b) an address for service (see below and r.198); and

(c) details of any person consenting to the lodging of the caution.

The cautions register is open to inspection (see Chapter 8).

Alteration of the cautions register
The court may make an order for alteration of, or the registrar **3–005**
may alter, the cautions register to:

(1) correct a mistake; or

(2) bring the register up to date (ss.20 and 21).

If the court makes such an order the registrar must give effect
to it when it is served on him (s.20(2)).

If, in any proceedings, the court decides or if on application
the registrar is satisfied that the cautioner does not own the
relevant interest, or only owns part, or that such interest either
wholly or in part did not exist or has come to an end, the court
must make an order for alteration of or, as the case may be, the
registrar must alter, the cautions register (rr.48 and 49).

An application to the registrar to alter the cautions register
must be made in form AP1 and must include written details of
the alteration required and of the grounds on which it is made,
and any supporting document. Before the registrar makes the
alteration he must, unless he is satisfied that it is unnecessary,
serve notice on the cautioner (r.50).

A person who claims that the whole of the relevant interest
described in an individual caution register is vested in him as
successor to the cautioner may apply for the register to be
altered to show him as cautioner (r.51(1)). If the registrar does
not serve notice, because he is satisfied that it is unnecessary, or
if the cautioner does not object within the time specified in the
notice, the registrar must give effect to such an application
(r.51(2)).

If any objection to alteration cannot be disposed of by
agreement it must be referred to the Adjudicator (see Chapter
22).

Where an alteration is made by the registrar he has a
discretion to make a payment in respects of costs reasonably
incurred in connection with the alteration (s.21(3)).

A fee calculated under the current Fee Order is payable.

Withdrawal (r.43)
An application to withdraw a caution against first registration **3–006**
must be made in Form WCT signed by the cautioner or his
conveyancer. If the application affects only part of the land to
which the caution relates, it must contain sufficient details, by
plan or otherwise, to identify that part clearly on the Ordnance
Survey map.

Note that only the cautioner may apply to withdraw the caution. If the cautioner has died the personal representative must first apply to be registered in place of the cautioner (r.51).

No fee is payable.

Cancellation

3–007 The owner of the legal estate to which a caution against first registration relates, or the owner of a legal estate derived out of that estate, may apply for cancellation of the caution (s.18(1) and r.45). But where the caution was lodged with his consent, or with the consent of a person from whom he derives title, the applicant must prove either that the relevant interest has come to an end, or consent was induced by fraud, misrepresentation, mistake or undue influence or given under duress (s.18(2) and r.46).

The application must be in Form CCT and, if the application affects only part of the land to which the caution relates, it must include sufficient details, by plan or otherwise, to identify that part clearly on the Ordnance Survey map (r.44(1) and (2)). It must be accompanied by evidence to satisfy the registrar that the applicant is entitled to apply (r.44(3)).

The registrar must give the cautioner notice of an application for cancellation (s.18(3)). If the cautioner does not object to the application before the end of the notice period, the registrar must cancel the caution (s.18(4)).

If any objection to cancellation cannot be disposed of by agreement it must be referred to the Adjudicator (see Chapter 22).

No fee is payable.

Chapter 4

First Registration

Duty to apply for first registration

There is a duty to apply for registration (s.4) on:

4–001

(1) the transfer, whether by conveyance, assignment, transfer or otherwise, of a "qualifying estate":

    (a) for valuable or other consideration (including a negative value); or

    (b) by way of gift; or

    (c) in pursuance of an order of any court; or

    (d) by means of an assent;

(2) the grant out of a "qualifying estate" of a term of years absolute of more than seven years from the date of the grant:

    (a) for valuable or other consideration (including a negative value); or

    (b) by way of gift; or

    (c) in pursuance of an order of any court;

[Transfer or grant under (1) or (2) above does not include a transfer or grant which creates a bare trust or transfers or grants land from a bare trustee to a beneficiary (s.4(7)).]

(3) the grant of an estate in land of a term of years absolute out of a "qualifying estate" to take effect in possession after the end of the period of three months beginning with the date of the grant;

(4) the creation of a first legal mortgage protected by deposit of documents of a "qualifying estate" — the mortgagee is entitled to apply for registration in the name of the mortgagor whether or not the mortgagor consents (r.21);

(5) the grant of a lease (regardless of the term of the lease) out of an unregistered legal estate in land pursuant to a tenant's right to buy or right to acquire on rent to mortgage terms or right to acquire from a registered social landlord under the Housing Act 1985 (ss.118(1) and s.143(1) (as substitued by the Leasehold Reform, Housing and Urban Development Act 1993) and the Housing (Right to Acquire) Regulations 1997;

(6) the transfer or lease of an unregistered legal estate in land where the right to buy is preserved under s.171A of the Housing Act 1985 (s.171A inserted by the Housing and Planning Act 1986, s.8; Sch.2 para.2).

A "qualifying estate" is an unregistered legal estate which is:

- a freehold estate in land; or

- a leasehold estate in land for a term which at the time of transfer, grant or creation has more than seven years to run (s.4(2)).

"Land" does not include mines and minerals held apart from the surface.

The duty to apply does not arise on:

(a) a transfer by operation of law to which (1) above would otherwise apply, *e.g.* the vesting of unregistered land in a new trustee under s.40 of the Trustee Act 1925 (s.4(3)); or

(b) the assignment of a mortgage term (s.4(4)(a)); or

(c) the assignment or surrender of a lease to the owner of the immediate reversion where the term is to merge in that reversion (s.4(4)(b)); or

(d) the grant of an estate to a person as mortgagee (s.4(5)).

Time limit for application

4–002 The estate owner or his successor in title must apply for first registration within two months of the date on which the event which gives rise to the duty to apply occurs (s.6). If this is not done, the transfer, lease or mortgage will become void as to the grant of a legal estate (s.7(1)). When the application for registration is made after the two months has elapsed a request, giving a written explanation of the failure to register in time, for an order of the registrar extending the time for registration must be made. If a good reason for the delay is given, an extension will be granted and the application will be treated as if s.7(1) had not applied.

No fee is payable for such an order.

Voluntary first registration
An application for the registration of the title to an unregistered **4–003**
legal estate which may be registered (see Chapter 1) may be
made voluntarily at any time.

*Before completion of an application which will result in a duty to
apply*
When an application for first registration must be made when **4–004**
the transaction is completed there is no special procedure to be
adopted before completion. The transaction proceeds in the way
unregistered interests are normally dealt with. The abstract of
title is delivered and perused, requisitions on title are raised and
answered and the transfer, conveyance, assignment, lease or
mortgage is prepared and completed. Besides the usual local
and land charges searches, an application should always be
made for an official search of the index map, as explained in
Chapter 2, to discover whether any interests in the land are
already registered.

Care should be taken to see that the extent of the land to be
registered is accurately defined by reference to boundary walls
or fences or to other physical features on the ground; and that
the transfer, lease or mortgage accurately identifies the land to
be registered in relation to the Ordnance Survey map (r.24). It is
inadvisable to describe the land by reference to a plan to an
earlier document of title unless the plan is known to correspond
with the modern physical boundaries.

The land should be inspected both to ascertain the boundaries, and to discover, so far as this can be done by careful
inspection, any unregistered interests to which it is subject. Any
persons in occupation of the land should be asked to disclose
the nature of their rights and to whom rent (if any) is paid (see
para.4–014 below).

Particular care is required in the case of certain types of
property. Examples are where a garden is separated from the
house to which it belongs by a passage or road, where rooms or
parts of rooms extend into an adjoining property or over a
passageway or where the boundaries are not fully defined by
features on the ground. A conveyancer should always ensure
that such cases are identified by discussing the layout of the
property with the client and the facts should be brought to the
attention of the Registry, preferably by means of a plan, when
lodging the application for registration.

If, while a person is subject to a duty to make an application
to be registered as proprietor of an estate there is a dealing with
that estate, that dealing is treated as if it had taken place after

the date of first registration. The registration of any such dealing delivered for registration with the application for first registration has effect from the time of the making of that application (r.38).

The application for first registration

4–005 An application for first registration is made by submitting a completed application Form FR1 (r.23) with the appropriate fee and (r.24):

(1) sufficient details, by plan or otherwise so that the land can be identified clearly on the Ordnance Survey map. The land to be identified on an application to register a rentcharge, franchise or profit à prendre in gross is the land affected by that estate;

(2) in the case of a leasehold estate, the lease, if in the possession or control of the applicant, and a certified copy;

(3) all deeds and documents relating to the title that are in the possession or control of the applicant. If the title deeds are unavailable see Chapter 5. Deeds and documents which are in the custody of a mortgagee under a mortgage or in respect of which the applicant has only a right to production are not regarded as being under the applicant's control but the applicant should lodge a sufficient marked abstract or certified copy. The registrar has the power to order the production of documents (s.75) but in practice it is rarely necessary for this power to be exercised; and

(4) a list in duplicate in Form DL of all the documents delivered.

Where appropriate the following should also be lodged:

(5) form DI (see para.4–016 below);

(6) a Land Transaction Return certificate or a self certificate in form SDLT60 or a letter explaining why neither certificate is required (see Chapter 1);

(7) any mortgage or charge by the applicant; and

(8) certified copies of any statutory declaration, subsisting lease, subsisting charge or latest document of title which the applicant has requested be returned to him under r.203(2). The latest document of title is the document by which the applicant or, if vesting was by operation of law,

the applicant's predecessor acquired the estate which is being registered (r.203(8)). The registrar is not obliged to return all or any of the documents lodged with the application unless the applicant requests him to do so (r.203(1)). But if the applicant makes such a request on first registration he is not required to lodge certified copies of any documents other than those specified in this paragraph (r.203(4)).

Completing the application form FR1
When completing the Form FR1 the following points should be **4–006** borne in mind:
Address: If the property to be registered has a postcode always include it.
Land Registry fees: On first registration of land a fee is payable calculated in accordance with the current Fee Order. See Chapter 1 as to the methods of payment of fees. Attention is directed to the fact that:

(1) the fee is assessed on the present value of land and buildings whether or not the application is based on a recent purchase; and

(2) there are special provisions made for large scale applications.

Expedition: If you want the application to be expedited, a written request should be made. This can be done by endorsing the application form prominently, "Please expedite".
Class of title sought: The box identifying the class of title which is being applied for should be clearly marked with an "X".
Instructions regarding documents: It is essential that the relevant panels are completed correctly to ensure that documents are issued to the persons entitled to have them.
Address for service (r.198): At least one and not more than three addresses for service to which all notices and other communications to the proprietor by the registrar will be sent, must be provided.

One address for service must be a postal address, whether or not in the United Kingdom. If any additional addresses for service are supplied they must be either a postal address, whether or not in the United Kingdom, a box number at a United Kingdom document exchange or an electronic mail address. *It is very important that addresses for service are up to date.* In the case of an ordinary householder who on completion of the purchase moves to the property being registered, the address to be entered on the register will usually be the full postal address of that property.

Certificate and other statements as to the title: It is important that these boxes are understood and carefully completed. Failure to complete the form honestly and carefully may mean that the applicant will not be protected if a mistake is made on the register.

Signature of form: The Form FR1 should be signed by the applicant or the conveyancer in the name of the firm.

Registration of mines and minerals (r.25)

4–007 Applications for registration of title to mines and materials apart from the surface must be accompanied by:

(1) a plan of the surface under which they lie;

(2) any other sufficient details by plan or otherwise so that they can be identified clearly; and

(3) full details of rights incidental to their working.

Registration of cellars, flats, tunnels, etc. (r.26)

4–008 Unless all of the land above and below the surface (except where only mines and minerals are excluded) is included the applicant must provide a plan of the surface on, under or over which the land to be registered lies, and sufficient information to define the vertical and horizontal extents of the land which is to be registered.

Official examination of title

4–009 In examining title the registrar may have regard to any examination by a conveyancer prior to the application and to the nature of the property (r.29).

The registrar may (r.30):

(1) make searches and enquiries and give notices to other persons;

(2) direct that searches and enquiries be made by the applicant; and

(3) advertise the application but this is very unusual.

Absolute freehold or good leasehold title may be approved if the registrar is of the opinion that the title is one which a willing buyer could properly be advised to accept by a competent professional adviser (ss.9(2) and 10(2) and (3)). For absolute leasehold title the registrar must also approve the lessor's title to grant the lease (s.10(2)(b)). In deciding whether such a title has been shown the registrar may disregard the fact that the title is open to objection if he is of the opinion that the defect will not cause the holding under the title to be disturbed (ss.9(3) and 10(4)).

Qualified title may be approved if the registrar is of the opinion that the applicant's title (or in the case of leasehold title the lessor's title to the reversion) has been established only for a limited period or subject to certain reservations which cannot be disregarded (ss.9(4) and 10(5)).

Possessory title may be approved if the registrar is of the opinion that:

(a) the applicant is in actual possession of the land, or in receipt of the rents and profits of the land, by virtue of the estate which is being registered; and

(b) there is no other class of title with which he may be registered (ss.9(5) and 10(6)).

The effect of registration with a particular class of title is set out below.

Public authorities: certificates of title

The registrar has made arrangements with a number of local **4–010** and other public authorities whereby when the authority sells land it gives the buyer a certificate as to the title in an agreed form instead of deducing title in the ordinary way. The certificate is effective at the date of the completion of the sale and it contains a statement of the incumbrances that affect the land on that day. The Registry accepts this statement, and accordingly, when the buyer applies for the first registration of his title, he need not produce the normal conveyancing evidence of the authority's title; nor is a search in the Land Charges Department against the name of the authority required.

Public sector housing/Right to buy

Under s.154(2) of the Housing Act 1985 a landlord is obliged to **4–011** give to a tenant who exercises his right to buy under that Act a certificate of title in a form approved by the registrar. Three such forms of certificate of title, PSD1 (where the landlord conveys a freehold dwelling house), PSD2 (where the landlord owns the freehold and grants a lease) and PSD3 (where the landlord does not own the freehold and grants an underlease) have been so approved. Similarly Forms PSD13, PSD14 and PSD15 have been approved for use in preserved right to buy cases and Form PSD16 has been approved for use in extended right to buy cases. These forms of certificate of title are only for use in right to buy cases and they should not be used in any other circumstances. The certificate must be signed as provided and, in the case of a local authority, by the chief executive officer or by some other officer approved by the registrar.

The certificate of title procedure entirely replaces the need for a normal examination of title. Not only does it obviate the need for production of the title deeds but it also makes it unnecessary for a search to be made by the buyer against the name of the seller in the Land Charges Department. The landlord is responsible for the accuracy of the certificate and must refund to the Registry any indemnity paid because the certificate was incorrect.

A lease granted pursuant to the right to buy must be registered whether or not the lease is granted for a term of more than seven years (s.4(1)(e)).

When applying for first registration following the exercise of the right to buy an "X" should be placed in the box provided in Panel 14 in Form FR1 to show that title has not been examined and reliance has been placed on the certificate of title lodged with the application.

Where the title to a property acquired in exercise of the right to buy is already registered, the normal provisions as to registration of a disposition of registered land will apply. As such applications will not be accompanied by a certificate of title to identify them, it would assist the Registry if the application form, AP1, were clearly marked 'Housing Act 1985: Right to buy case' or as appropriate.

The fee payable under Scale 1 on any application following a sale at a discount under the right to buy provisions is assessed on the price actually paid and not on the full market value.

Similarly on first registration of a shared ownership lease granted under the 1985 Act, a fee under Scale 1 will be payable on an amount equal to the sum of the premium actually paid plus the rent reserved at the time of granting the lease.

Housing defects (Housing Act 1985, Part XVI)

4–012 Paragraph 17 of Sch.20 to the Housing Act 1985 extends the provisions for compulsory registration of title to defective dwellings repurchased under that Act. It is provided that the acquiring authority must supply a certificate of title in a form approved by the registrar. Two such forms have been approved, PSD11 (freeholds) and PSD12 (leaseholds).

No application for the first registration of a leasehold interest is necessary where the acquiring authority is the owner of the reversion. If the title to the reversion is registered, an application should be made for cancellation of notice of the lease acquired from the reversionary title. If the reversion is not registered, the leasehold deeds should merely be placed with the title deeds to the reversion.

If the title to a repurchased dwelling is already registered, application for registration should be made in the normal way.

The effect of first registration (ss.11 and 12)
When registration is of a *freehold estate* with *absolute title* it is **4–013** vested in the proprietor with all interests subsisting for the benefit of the estate subject only to the following interests affecting the estate at the time of registration:

(1) interests which are the subject of an entry in the register;

(2) unregistered interests that override first registration (see below); and

(3) interests acquired under the Limitation Act 1980 of which the proprietor has notice.

If the proprietor is not entitled to the estate for his own benefit, or not solely for his own benefit, then, as between himself and the persons beneficially entitled, the estate is vested in him subject to such of their interests as he has notice of.

When registration is of a *leasehold estate* with *absolute title* it is vested in the proprietor with the same effect as registration of a freehold estate but subject also to implied and express covenants, obligations and liabilities incident to the estate. Registration with *good leasehold title* has the same effect as registration with absolute title, except that it does not affect the enforcement of any estate, right or interest affecting, or in derogation of, the title of the lessor to grant the lease.

Registration with *qualified title* has the same effect as registration with absolute title except that it does not affect the enforcement of any estate, right or interest which appears from the register to be excepted from the effect of registration.

Registration with *possessory title* has the same effect as registration with absolute title, except that it does not affect the enforcement of any estate, right or interest adverse to, or in derogation of, the proprietor's title subsisting at the time of registration or then capable of arising.

Unregistered interests that override first registration (ss.11 and 12 and Sch.1 to the Act)
On first registration the proprietor is subject to any of the **4–014** following interests which affect the registered estate even though they are not noted on the register:

(1) A leasehold estate in land granted for a term not exceeding seven years from the date of the grant, except for a lease which the lessee is under a duty to register (see para.4–001 above).

(2) An interest belonging to a person in actual occupation (including for a period of three years from October 13,

2003), a right acquired under the Limitation Act 1980 (para.7 of Sch.12 to the Act) relating to land of which he is in actual occupation, except for an interest under a settlement under the Settled Land Act 1925.

(3) A legal easement or profit à prendre.

(4) A customary or a public right.

(5) A local land charge.

(6) An interest in any coal or coal mine, the rights attached to any such interest and the rights of any person under ss.38, 49 or 51 of the Coal Industry Act 1994.

(7) In the case of land to which title was registered before 1898, rights to mines and minerals (and incidental rights) created before 1898.

(8) In the case of land to which title was registered between 1898 and 1925 inclusive, rights to mines and minerals (and incidental rights) created before the date of registration of the title.

(9) A franchise.

(10) A manorial right.

(11) A right to rent which was reserved to the Crown on the granting of any freehold estate (whether or not the right is still vested in the Crown).

(12) A non-statutory right in respect of an embankment or sea or river wall.

(13) A right to payment in lieu of tithe.

(14) A right in respect of the repair of a church chancel (added by the Land Registration Act 2002 (Transitional Provisions) (No.2) Order 2003).

At the end of a period of 10 years beginning on October 13, 2003, (9) to (14) above will cease to be interests that override first registration (s.117). It is important that an application to enter a notice to protect such interests on the registers of all titles affected is made before that 10-year period expires.

4–015 The following judicial decisions under s.70 of the Land Registration Act 1925 illustrate the importance of the overriding interests of persons "in actual occupation".

(a) *Bridges v Mees* **[1957] 2 All E.R. 577, Harman J.** Purchaser of registered land under an oral contract went into possession but neither took a transfer of the land nor protected his rights by a caution on the register of the vendor's title. He had an overriding interest under s.70(1)(j) and (g) of the 1925 Act which prevailed against a later purchaser of the same land who took a transfer and was registered as proprietor. Rectification of the register was ordered.

(b) *London and Cheshire Insurance Co. Ltd v Laplagrene Property Co. Ltd* **[1971] 1 All E.R. 766, Brightman J.** Lessee, in occupation as lessee, had a lien on the land as an unpaid vendor. Lessee found to have an overriding interest under s.70(1)(g) of the 1925 Act in respect of the lien which prevailed against a chargee of reversion. Lessee subsequently went out of occupation, but overriding interest not lost.

(c) *Hodgson v Marks* **[1971] 2 All E.R. 684, CA.** Beneficial owner who was not the registered proprietor was held to have an overriding interest under s.70(1)(g) of the 1925 Act by virtue of her actual occupation as one of the persons living in the house. (The registered proprietor also was living there.) The overriding interest prevailed against a purchaser from the registered proprietor and against the purchaser's mortgagee.

(d) *Williams & Glyns Bank Limited v Boland; Same v Brown* **[1980] 2 All E.R. 408; HL.** Two appeals on similar facts. In each case the wife had contributed substantially to the purchase of a house and she and her husband were living in it as their matrimonial home. The husband was the sole registered proprietor. The wife had registered no caution, restriction or notice and the husband without her knowledge charged the land to the bank, which made no inquiry of the wife. The husband defaulted on the mortgage and the bank sought to enforce its security. Held that the wife was in actual occupation; therefore, her equitable interest, as tenant in common, was protected as an overriding interest under s.70(1)(g) of the 1925 Act and prevailed against the bank.

(e) *City of London Building Society v Flegg* **[1987] 3 All E.R. 435, HL.** "Bleak House" was purchased in the joint names of Mr and Mrs Flegg. More than half the purchase money was provided by the wife's parents and the balance from a building society mortgage. Unknown to the wife's parents, who were in occupation, the Fleggs first created two further charges and then borrowed sufficient funds from the plaintiffs to pay off the original building society and two further loans. The plaintiffs sought an order for possession against the wife's parents. Held that the wife's parents' interest, as equitable tenants in common, was not an overriding interest under s.70(1)(g) of the 1925 Act and it was overreached under Part I of the Law of Property Act 1925 because the charge had been executed by two trustees for sale.

(f) *Lloyds Bank plc v Rosset* **[1990] 1 All E.R. 1111, HL.** Property was being bought in the husband's sole name but it was agreed that the wife would have an interest. The purchasers were allowed into possession before completion to carry out renovation work and the wife spent almost every day at the property helping the builders. Without his wife's knowledge the husband borrowed money from the plaintiff. Completion of the purchase and of a charge to the plaintiff took place on the same day. The husband subsequently defaulted and the plaintiff took proceedings for possession. Held that although discussions had taken place between the husband and wife no decision had been taken that she was to have an interest in the property. The wife's actual contribution was "de minimis". The wife did not have a beneficial interest and the question of whether she had an overriding interest under s.70(1)(g) of the 1925 Act did not arise.

Duty to disclose unregistered interests that override first registration (r.28)

4–016 Information about any of the interests that override first registration which are:

(1) within the actual knowledge of the applicant; and

(2) affect the estate to which the application relates,

must be provided in the application for first registration on Form DI.

But it should be noted that there is no requirement to provide information about interests apparent from the documents lodged with the application nor is it necessary to disclose:

(a) interests that cannot be protected by notice (see Chapter 15);

(b) public rights;

(c) leases granted for a term not exceeding seven years from the date of the grant, not being a lease which the lessee is under a duty to register, when at the time of the application, the term granted by the lease has one year or less to run; and

(d) local land charges.

Form FR1 requires the applicant or his conveyancer to certify either that Form DI accompanies the application or that no disclosable interests affect.

Where the applicant provides information about such an interest the registrar may enter a notice in the register in respect of that interest and once noted it will cease to be an interest that overrides.

Chapter 5

Lost or Destroyed Deeds

When the title deeds of unregistered land have been lost or **5–001** destroyed, an application for the first registration of the title may be made. Such an application must be supported by evidence:

(1) to satisfy the registrar that the applicant is entitled to apply under s.3(2), *i.e.* the unregistered legal estate sought to be registered is vested in him or he is entitled to require the estate to be vested in him, or required to apply under s.6(1), *i.e.* on the occurrence of the events listed in s.4 (see Chapter 4), and

(2) to account for the absence of documentary evidence of title.

This evidence will normally be provided in a statutory declaration. The evidence lodged will need to cover:

(a) the circumstances of the loss or destruction;

(b) the reconstruction of the title; and

(c) possession of the land.

In some circumstances evidence of identity of the applicant will also be required (see below).

Generally

An application for first registration in these circumstances must **5–002** be lodged using Form FR1 accompanied by Form DL (see Chapter 4).

A fee calculated in accordance with the current Fee Order will need to accompany the application.

The applicant's conveyancer should also enclose with the application an undertaking to produce the title deeds to the Registry if they are subsequently discovered. Any favourable or unfavourable evidence of title which comes to light after first registration should be produced to the Registry.

The loss or destruction

5–003 This is usually proved by a statutory declaration or declarations by a person or persons with first hand knowledge of the facts. What must be shown is:

(1) where and by whom the deeds were held immediately before their loss or destruction;

(2) whether they were held as security for money or merely for safe custody without any lien, charge or incumbrance;

(3) the full circumstances of their loss or destruction; and

(4) the efforts made to recover them or their remains if recovery was possible.

If the deeds were lost or destroyed whilst in the custody (or in the post from) a conveyancer, building society, bank or other well-known institution, this information should normally be supplied by a member of that firm or organisation.

Reconstruction of the title

5–004 The best available secondary evidence of how title has devolved to the applicant must be produced. The nature and quality of this will vary depending on the circumstances of the particular case. What follows are suggestions that may sometimes be useful. A certified copy or a completed draft of the conveyance or assignment to the applicant (and of any subsisting mortgage) should be lodged if possible, together with completed drafts or examined abstracts of as much of the earlier title as it is possible to reconstruct. These documents can be exhibited to a statutory declaration by the conveyancer who acted when the applicant bought, declaring that the title was investigated in the usual way, indicating from where the copy documents lodged with the application came, and confirming the due execution and stamping of the conveyance or assignment (and mortgage).

If all original deeds, copies, abstracts and drafts held by the applicant or conveyancer have been lost or destroyed, it is sometimes possible to obtain copies, abstracts or drafts from the conveyancer who acted for the applicant's seller. A receipted schedule of deeds, if its source and origin are satisfactorily proved, may provide some evidence of custody and title. Copies of particulars delivered pursuant to s.28 of the Finance Act 1931 (obtained from the appropriate District Valuer), copies of documents relating to capital gains tax or inheritance tax, fire insurance policies, and receipts for rates, other taxes and insurance premiums, may be useful as confirmation of ownership.

If the deeds were held by a mortgagee when they were lost or destroyed, it is useful to have a declaration by the conveyancer who acted for the mortgagee as to investigation of the title prior to the making of the loan. If in a position to do so, the conveyancer should also declare that the mortgage is still subsisting or give an account of its repayment.

If the property was not in mortgage when the deeds were lost or destroyed, the application should include an explicit statement that at the time of the loss or destruction the owner had not created any mortgage, charge or lien on the property and had not deposited any of the title deeds with any person, firm or body as security for money.

If the property is leasehold and the lease has been lost or destroyed, a certified copy of the counterpart can usually be obtained; and the lessor may be able to provide information relating to licences to assign and production of documents by lessees for registration. In any event, the lessor will know who has paid the rent.

As regards land in an area formerly covered by the Middlesex or one of the Yorkshire Deeds Registries, a conveyancer who has examined memorials of deeds may be able to establish or help to establish a chain of title. The records of the former deeds registries can be inspected.

N.B. The City of York did not fall within the areas formerly covered by the Yorkshire Deeds Registries.

County of Middlesex
The registers of the Middlesex Deeds Registry, being copy **5–005** memorials 1709 to 1938 with covering indexes, may be inspected at the London Metropolitan Archives, 40 Northampton Road, London EC1R 0HB. (Telephone: 020 7332 3820).

East Riding of Yorkshire
The records of the former East Riding Registry of Deeds, **5–006** including memorials and indexes and covering the period 1708 to 1974, are now in the custody of the East Riding of Yorkshire Archives and Record Service, County Hall, Champney Road,

Beverley, East Yorkshire HU17 9BA. (Telephone: 01482 392790).

North Riding of Yorkshire

5–007 The North Riding Register of Deeds, which contains copies and memorials of deeds made between 1736 and 1970 is now in the custody of the North Yorkshire County Record Office held by the County Archivist, whose address for correspondence is County Hall, Northallerton, North Yorkshire DL7 8AF. (Telephone: 01609 777585).

West Riding of Yorkshire

5–008 The records of the former West Riding Registry of Deeds, including copies and memorials of documents of title (freehold) for the period 1704 to 1970 are now in the custody of the West Yorkshire Archive Service, Registry of Deeds Building, Newstead Road, Wakefield WF1 2DE. (Telephone: 01924 305982).

Land Charges Searches against all known estate owners must also be lodged. If there is any risk of the non-disclosure of restrictive covenants, an entry will be made on the register to the effect that the land is subject to such restrictive covenants as may have been imposed on it before the date of first registration so far as they still subsist and are capable of being enforced. This protective entry will extend to rentcharges in areas where they are common. Where unverified copies of restrictive covenants are supplied, the Registry may note the absence of verified particulars on the register, in some circumstances.

An entry will also be made in respect of any easements adversely affecting the title which are revealed in the reconstructed title or disclosed as overriding interests in the application. In view of the changes to the provisions regarding overriding interests effected by the Act, since October 13, 2003; if there is a risk that the land may be subject to easements which are not apparent from the application, a protective entry will be made.

Possession of the land

5–009 The applicant is usually expected to provide satisfactory evidence that since the date of acquisition the applicant has been in actual occupation of the whole of the land or in receipt of its rents and profits (particulars of which should be given) without any adverse claim. Any other relevant facts should be provided.

Evidence of identity

Where title deeds have been lost or destroyed, the Registry may **5–010** require evidence of identity. Such evidence is not required when the application is lodged by:

(1) a conveyancer who is applying for registration because the title deeds were lost or destroyed in their custody; or

(2) a major mortgage lender, where the deeds were being held as security for the lender's mortgage and were lost whilst in their custody; or

(3) a duly authorised official of a local authority, government department or nationally well known body, where the deeds relating to their land, or land on which they hold a mortgage, were lost whilst in their custody; or

(4) an applicant who is a receiver or liquidator of a company, where evidence of the appointment is supplied with a certified copy of the mortgage or charge where the applicant is a receiver appointed under such a deed.

Where the applicant is an individual, evidence of identity on Form ID1 must be completed (for each applicant where there are more than one). The exact requirements depend upon whether the applicant has been known to the conveyancer for at least two years. If he has the Registry will accept a certificate to that effect as set out on Form ID1 and the conveyancer will not have to check documentary evidence of identity.

Where that certificate cannot be given, items of documentary evidence of identity as set out on Form ID1 must be inspected and a different certificate given.

In all cases the Registry requires a recent passport sized photograph of each applicant which must be affixed to Form ID1 where indicated. The conveyancer must personally certify (not in the name of the firm) that the photograph is a true likeness of the applicant.

For corporate applicants, or those applicants which are some other kind of institution, evidence of identity in Form ID2 must be provided.

Forms ID1 and ID2 are available from law stationers in the usual way and from the Registry's website at *www.landregistry.gov.uk*.

Class of title

Where the available evidence of title is incomplete an applicant **5–011** will not necessarily fail to obtain a registered title. If the Registry's other requirements have been satisfactorily dealt with a possessory title may be granted. Each application is considered on its merits, but normally absolute or good leasehold title will not be granted where the loss or destruction of the deeds cannot be adequately explained.

Lost or destroyed land or charge certificates

5–012 Since October 13, 2003, no new land or charge certificates have been issued. It is no longer possible to apply for a replacement certificate where a certificate issued prior to that date has been lost or destroyed.

Chapter 6

Adverse Possession

What is adverse possession?

In the leading case of *JA Pye (Oxford) Ltd v Graham* [2002] 3 **6–001**
All E.R. 865 at p.885 Lord Hope of Craighead dismisses a
popular misconception about what is required for adverse
possession:

> "At first sight, it might be thought that the word 'adverse'
> describes the nature of the possession that the squatter needs
> to demonstrate. It suggests that an element of aggression,
> hostility or subterfuge is required. But an examination of the
> context makes it clear that this is not so. It is used as a
> convenient label only, in recognition simply of the fact that
> the possession is adverse to the interests of the paper owner
> or, in the case of registered land, of the registered
> proprietor."

Adverse possession is having *"factual possession"* with an
"intention to possess" without the consent of the owner. Possession is not enough and there can be no adverse possession
without the necessary intention.

The *Pye* case strongly endorses the decision in *Powell v
McFarlane* (1977) 38 P & CR 452 where at pp.470–471 Slade J.
says:

> "Factual possession signifies an appropriate degree of physi-
> cal control. It must be a single and [exclusive] possession,
> though there can be a single possession exercised by or on
> behalf of several persons jointly. Thus an owner of land and a
> person intruding on that land without his consent cannot
> both be in possession of the land at the same time. The
> question what acts constitute a sufficient degree of exclusive
> physical control must depend on the circumstances, in par-
> ticular the nature of the land and the manner in which land

of that nature is commonly used or enjoyed . . . Everything must depend on the particular circumstances, but broadly, I think what must be shown as constituting factual possession is that the alleged possessor has been dealing with the land in question as an occupying owner might have been expected to deal with it and that no-one else has done so."

And at pp.471–472 Slade J. defines the "intention to possess" stating that it is the:

"intention, in one's own name and on one's own behalf, to exclude the world at large, including the owner with the paper title if he be not himself the possessor, so far as is reasonably practicable and so far as the processes of the law will allow."

In *Pye* at p.887 Lord Hutton in endorsing Slade J.'s judgment states:

"Where the evidence establishes that the person claiming title under the Limitation Act 1980 has occupied the land and made full use of it in the way in which an owner would, I consider that in the normal case he will not have to adduce additional evidence to establish that he had the intention to possess. It is in cases where the acts in relation to the land of a person claiming title by adverse possession are equivocal and are open to more than one interpretation, that those acts will be insufficient to establish the intention to possess."

In the *Pye* case at p.879 Lord Browne-Wilkinson distinguishes an intention to possess to the exclusion of all others including the owner from an intention to own and confirms that a willingness to pay the proprietor if asked is no bar:

"Once it is accepted that the necessary intent is an intent to possess not to own, and an intention to exclude the paper owner only so far as is reasonably possible, there is no inconsistency between a squatter being willing to pay the paper owner if asked and his being in the meantime in possession."

There is no requirement that the possession must be inconsistent with the proprietor's intentions. Again in the *Pye* case at p.878 Lord Browne-Wilkinson said:

". . . if the squatter is aware of a special purpose for which the paper owner uses or intends to use the land and the use made by the squatter does not conflict with that use, that may provide some support for a finding as a question of fact that the squatter had no intention to possess the land in the ordinary sense but only an intention to occupy it until needed by the paper owner. For myself I think there will be few occasions in which such inference could be properly drawn in cases where the true owner has been physically excluded from the land. But it remains a possible, if improbable, inference in some cases."

The decision in *Pye v Graham* has been appealed to the European Court of Human Rights and the result of that appeal is currently awaited.

Adverse possession of registered land

The law
Under the Limitation Act 1980 if a person is in adverse **6–002** possession of unregistered land the owner's title will be extinguished after the appropriate period of limitation has elapsed.

The periods of limitation under the 1980 Act do not now apply to registered land so that time cannot run against a registered proprietor so as to extinguish his registered title.

Title to registered land can be acquired as a result of adverse possession but only under the provisions of the Act. If a person in adverse possession makes a successful application under Sch.6 to the Act he will be registered as proprietor in place of the existing registered proprietor.

Transitional provisions
Where title to registered land was acquired by adverse posses- **6–003** sion before the Act came into force the registered proprietor of the land affected held title to that land in trust for the adverse possessor under the provisions of s.75 of the Land Registration Act 1925.

In the case of *Beaulane Properties Ltd v Palmer* [2005] All E.R. (D) 413 Nicholas Strauss QC, sitting as a deputy judge of the High Court, held that the law on adverse possession in relation to registered land under s.75 of the Land Registration Act 1925 was incompatible with Art.1 to the European Convention on Human Rights, so that the court is obliged, by s.3 of the Human Rights Act 1998, to give effect to the statutory provisions in such a way as to render them compatible with the Convention if it is possible to do so. In the case the squatter contended that he had enclosed the land and allowed cattle and horses to graze on it for 12 years. On the evidence, 12 years' adverse possession had been completed at the end of June 2003, by which date the 1998 Act had come into force. As a result of a reinterpretation of the relevant legislation in accordance with s.3 of the 1998 Act, the defendant's claim to have acquired the disputed land failed and the claimant remained the owner of it.

As a result Land Registry has issued the following additional note to Practice Guide 5, which deals with cases where a squatter claims the right to be registered as owner by reason of adverse possession prior to October 13, 2003:

"Note that in light of *Beaulane Properties v Palmer* [2005] All E.R. (D) 413, where an application is made under paragraph 18 of Schedule 12 to the Land Registration Act 2002, and the necessary period of adverse possession started after October 2, 1988, the applicant must show an arguable case for the possession being inconsistent with the use or intended use of the land by the registered proprietor, and not merely that the possession was without the registered proprietor's consent."

If the adverse possession started on or before 2 October 1988, the 12 years will have expired before the coming into force of the Human Rights Act 1998 on October 2, 2000, in which case s.3 of that Act does not apply.

However, if immediately before October 13, 2003, a registered title to land is held in trust by virtue of s.75 of the 1925 Act the adverse possessor is entitled to be registered as proprietor of that land (para.18(1) of Sch.12 to the Act).

Such an adverse possessor has a defence to any action for the possession of the land affected and if a court decides that a person is entitled to such a defence it must order the registrar to register the adverse possessor as the proprietor of the title to that land (para.18(2) and (3) of Sch.12 to the Act).

For a period of three years from October 13, 2003, where a person is entitled to be registered as proprietor of a registered estate because of his adverse possession under s.75 of the 1925 Act, that right will be an interest which overrides registered dispositions notwithstanding that he is not in actual occupation at the time the disposition is registered (para.11 of Sch.12 to the Act). If such an adverse possessor is in occupation at the relevant time then, even after the three year period, his interest will override the disposition in certain circumstances as to which see Chapter 9.

Who can apply for registration based on adverse possession of registered land?

6–004 A person who has been in adverse possession for the ten years prior to the application may apply for registration in place of the registered proprietor. The land need not have been registered for the whole period of adverse possession. At any time when a property is held in trust and the beneficiaries' interests are not in possession no-one can be regarded as in adverse possession. Successive periods of adverse possession count as one period (see para.11 of Sch.6 to the Act).

He may apply even if in the period of six months ending on the date of the application he was evicted by the registered proprietor, or a person claiming under him, and:

(1) on the day before his eviction he was entitled to make an application for registration; and

(2) the eviction was not pursuant to a judgment for possession (para.1(2) of Sch.6 to the Act).

He cannot apply:

(a) when there are possession proceedings against him or judgment for possession was given against him in the last two years (para.1(3) of Sch.6 to the Act); or

(b) when the registered proprietor in wartime is an enemy or a prisoner of war or, in certain circumstances, he is under a mental disability or is suffering from a physical impairment (para.8 of Sch.6 to the Act).

In the case of foreshore the period of adverse possession required is 60 years not 10.

How is such an application made? (r.188)
Application is made on Form ADV1, accompanied by: **6–005**

(1) a plan to identify the land;

(2) a statutory declaration made by the applicant not more than one month before the application, with:

    (a) any supporting statutory declarations; and
    (b) any additional evidence which the applicant considers necessary to support the claim,

providing evidence of adverse possession for the relevant period and evidence that the applicant is a person entitled to apply;

(3) a fee (at the time of writing £100 for each registered title affected) under the current Fee Order is payable. Further fees may be payable to meet the cost of surveys or other special enquiries; and

(4) the facts which would enable the applicant to rely on one or more of the conditions set out in para.5 of Sch.6 to the Act, if required (see below).

Service of notice of the application

6–006 If satisfied with the evidence provided (normally a site inspection will be carried out) the registrar will serve notice of the application on:

(1) the registered proprietor of the land;

(2) the registered proprietor of any charge;

(3) the registered proprietor of any superior registered estate;

(4) any person who the register states is to receive notice of an adverse possession application (see para.6–009, below); and

(5) any other person the registrar considers appropriate.

The period for lodging an objection in response to the notice is 65 business days.

Response to the notice

6–007 If all recipients of notice do not respond to the notice or consent the applicant will be registered as proprietor in place of the existing proprietor free of any registered charge.

If a recipient of the notice objects (on Form NAP or otherwise in writing) on the basis that the applicant is not in adverse possession or the applicant is not entitled to apply then the matter will have to be resolved by agreement or referred to the Adjudicator (see Chapter 22).

If a recipient of a notice serves a counter notice in Form NAP during the notice period, requiring the application to be dealt with under para.5 of Sch.6 to the Act the application will be rejected unless the applicant can establish that one of the following three conditions is met:

(1) it would be unconscionable by virtue of equitable estoppel for the proprietor to seek to dispossess the applicant and in all the circumstances the applicant ought to be registered. An example might be where the applicant has built on registered land believing it was his land and the registered proprietor has knowingly acquiesced in the mistake; or

(2) the applicant has an independent right to be registered. An example would be if he had contracted to buy and paid the purchase price but never taken a conveyance or transfer; or

(3) it is a "boundary dispute" case. There are four requirements:

(i) the land concerned must adjoin land owned by the applicant;

(ii) the exact line of the boundary must not have already been determined (see Chapter 2);

(iii) the applicant must have reasonably believed the land was his for at least 10 years of the period of adverse possession; and

(iv) the land must have been registered for more than one year.

If an applicant intends to rely on one of these conditions he must set out the relevant facts in his supporting statutory declaration and tick the appropriate box on Form ADV1.

If the applicant successfully establishes that he meets one of the three conditions he will be registered in place of the proprietor subject to any registered charge. If that charge also affects other land the new proprietor of the land acquired by adverse possession may require the charge to be apportioned on the basis of the respective values of the two areas of land charged. Once the charge has been apportioned the land can be discharged from the charge by payment of the amount apportioned to it and the costs of apportionment (para.10 of Sch.6 to the Act).

Right to make a further application for registration
If the original application is rejected because the applicant fails **6–008** to establish that he meets one of the three conditions in para.5 of Sch.6 to the Act (see above) and if:

(1) he has remained in adverse possession;

(2) no possession proceedings are pending against him;

(3) no judgment for possession has been given against him in the last two years; and

(4) he has not been evicted,

the applicant may reapply two years after the date of rejection of his original application.

The application must be in Form ADV1 accompanied by:

(a) the documents, evidence and fee as set out at para.6–005 above;

(b) full details of the previous rejected application; and

(c) evidence that he is still in adverse possession and that none of the restrictions on applications in paras.6 and 8 of Sch.6 to the Act apply (r.188).

Fifteen business days notice of the application will be served on the person referred to at para.6–006 above.

If the applicant is still in adverse possession and the registered proprietor is not under a mental disability or suffering from a physical impairment or in wartime is not an enemy or a prisoner of war, he will be registered in place of the registered proprietor. Registration will be subject to the entries on the register excluding any registered charge.

Registration as a person entitled to be notified of an application for adverse possession (r.194)

6–009 If a person can satisfy the registrar that he has an interest in a registered title which would be prejudiced by the registration of any other person as proprietor of that estate by adverse possession under Sch.6 to the Act he may apply, in Form ADV2, to be registered as a person to be notified of such an application (see para.6–006 above). An example of such a person might be a beneficiary under a trust not in possession.

The name of such a person who successfully applies will be entered in the proprietorship register as a person entitled to be notified under para.2 of Sch.6 to the Act.

Adverse possession of unregistered land

6–010 If a person has acquired title to unregistered land under the Limitation Act 1980 he may apply to be registered as the proprietor of that land.

The application will be an application for first registration (see Chapter 4). It must be supported by evidence of adverse possession (see above) which will consist of statements in statutory declarations by the applicant or his seller and others setting out in full the facts relied on to support the claim to title by adverse possession. Any other available evidence, *e.g.* photographs or evidence of the paper title should also be lodged.

The Registry will normally inspect the site and will serve notice as it considers appropriate. Notice will not normally be served before the applicant has been informed and has been given the opportunity to withdraw his application.

6–011 A fee calculated under the current Fee Order will be payable. The applicant may be called upon to pay an additional fee to meet the cost of surveys or other special enquiries. The applicant may also be asked to pay for the publication of advertisements but this would be very unusual.

Chapter 7

Covenants, Easements and Profits à prendre

Covenants

Burden of restrictive covenants: first registration

When the deeds and documents accompanying an application **7–001** for first registration show that the land is subject to restrictive covenants (other than covenants between lessor and lessee affecting the land in the lease (s.33(c)) notice of the covenants will be entered in the register. An entry in the charges register will refer to the deed containing the covenants. Also, if the deed or a certified copy or examined abstract of it accompanies the application, the text of the covenants and stipulations (or of the abstract) will be made available. This may be done by setting out the covenants and stipulations, or the abstract, verbatim in the register or by referring to a filed document. The filed document will be the deed or a copy or abstract of it according to the circumstances of the particular registration.

Sometimes neither the original deed nor a certified copy nor examined abstract will accompany the application. The action taken by the Registry will then depend on the circumstances. If an unverified copy or an unverified abstract of the covenants and stipulations accompanies the application, and the Registry considers the risk of its being inaccurate to be so small that it can properly be treated as though it were verified, it will be so treated and an entry will be made in the register accordingly, as explained above.

If an unverified copy or an unverified abstract of the covenants and stipulations accompanies the application but cannot properly be treated as though it were verified, and if a conveyancer so requests, an entry will be made in the charges register on the following lines:

"A [Conveyance] of the land in this title [and other land] dated . . . . made between . . . . contains restrictive covenants but no verified particulars were produced on first registration. The details set out . . . . of what purport to be the said covenants were provided by (*Conveyancers*) acting for a vendor in [*2005*]."

No indemnity (see Chapter 22) will be payable if such extracts set out on the register using such qualified entries are not complete or correct.

If an unverified copy or an unverified abstract of the covenants and stipulations accompanies the application, but cannot be treated as verified and is not the subject of a request by conveyancers as indicated in the preceding paragraph, the entry in the register will refer to the deed containing the covenants and stipulations and will state that it contains restrictive covenants but that:

". . . neither the original deed nor a certified copy nor an examined abstract thereof was produced on first registration."

Such an entry will also be made when no particulars, verified or unverified, of the covenants or stipulations accompany the application.

A full verified copy, or a full examined abstract, of the words of covenant and of the stipulations should be provided whenever possible but when only particulars of the restrictive stipulations, without the words of covenant, accompany an application, a modified form of entry, indicating that the words of covenant were not available, will be used.

The documents lodged with some applications for first registration do not contain adequate information as to whether or not restrictive covenants affect the land. These applications arise in the following types of situation:

(1) unregistered land acquired by adverse possession;

(2) lost deeds;

(3) short titles; and

(4) a good statutory root of title behind which there may be restrictive covenants protected by registration in the Land Charges Department but not discoverable by the buyer.

It is the Registry's practice where applications are based on (1) and (2) to make an entry in the register to the effect that the land is subject to such restrictive covenants as may have been imposed thereon before a specified date (normally the date of the application) so far as they are subsisting and capable of being enforced. The same entry is also likely to be made for applications based on (3) but not those based on (4).

Restrictive covenants imposed on land already registered
Restrictive covenants (other than those between lessor and **7–002** lessee affecting the land in the lease (s.33(c)) imposed on land already registered must be protected by notice on the register of the burdened title (see Chapter 15). This may be done by setting out the covenants verbatim on the register, or by filing the document imposing them (or a copy of it).

If a transfer of part imposes restrictive covenants on the transferee's title or on the title out of which it is created, notice of these covenants is entered automatically on the register of the burdened title. However, if the transfer imposes restrictive covenants on any other title, a specific application for the entry of notice of the covenants on that title is necessary. If in a transfer of the whole of the land in a title, restrictive covenants are imposed on land in another title, a separate application to enter notice of the covenants on the register of that other title is necessary. Similarly, if restrictive covenants are imposed otherwise than in a transfer, *e.g.* by a deed of covenant, or a deed of grant, an application must be made for notice of the instrument imposing them to be entered on the register of title to the burdened land. It is important to identify the burdened land clearly (by plan if necessary); and, of course, the identity of the land intended to be benefited should not be left in doubt.

Benefit of restrictive covenants
The Act does not provide for the entry of the benefit of **7–003** equitable rights on the register. It follows that no entry can be made on the register of the benefit of restrictive covenants as such a benefit is an equitable not a legal right.

Release, waiver or modification of restrictive covenants
It is usually difficult, if not impossible, to prove that a deed **7–004** purporting to release, waive, discharge or modify covenants is fully effective; and it is the Registry's practice to enter notice of such deeds in the register and leave the original notice of the covenants uncancelled.

When the Land Tribunal has made an order under s.84 of the Law of Property Act 1925, in relation to restrictive covenants, the entry to be made in the register will depend on the terms of the order.

Indemnity and other positive covenants

7–005 Under rr.64 and 65 the registrar may make an appropriate entry in the proprietorship register of any positive covenant given by the proprietor or any previous proprietor or any indemnity covenant given by the proprietor. Such an entry must, where practicable, refer to the deed containing the covenant and must be deleted if it appears to the registrar that it does not bind the current proprietor.

Where a deed contains positive covenants which are intermixed with restrictive covenants they will not normally be edited out and entered separately but will be entered on the register using whatever method is used to give notice of the restrictive covenants. If they are not so intermixed they will be referred to in a note on the proprietorship register referring to a schedule where they will be set out or to a filed deed or copy.

Where a transfer contains indemnity covenants in respect of restrictive or positive covenants already set out on the register or contained in a filed deed a note will be entered in the proprietorship register stating that the transfer to the proprietor contains a covenant to observe and perform the covenants in the particular deed referred to in the charges register and of indemnity in respect thereof. If the transferee has not covenanted to observe and perform the original covenants the note will merely state that the transfer to the proprietor contains a covenant of indemnity in respect thereof.

Implied covenants

7–006 A registrable disposition may be expressed to be made either with full title guarantee or with limited title guarantee (r.67(1)).

In the case of a disposition to which s.76 of the Law of Property Act 1925 applies by virtue of s.11(1) of the Law of Property (Miscellaneous Provisions) Act 1994:

(1) a person may be expressed to execute, transfer or charge as beneficial owner, settlor, trustee, mortgagee, or personal representative of a deceased person or under an order of the court, and the document effecting the disposition may be framed accordingly; and

(2) any covenant implied by virtue of s.76 of the Law of Property Act 1925 in such a disposition will take effect as though the disposition was expressly made subject to:

(a) all charges and other interests that are registered at the time of the execution of the disposition and affect the title of the covenantor; and

(b) any unregistered interests which override the disposition (see Chapter 9) (r.67(2)).

The benefit of any covenant implied under ss.76 and 77 of the Law of Property Act 1925 will, when the disposition in which it is implied is registered, be annexed and incident to and will go with the title for the benefit of which it is given and will be capable of being enforced by the proprietor for the time being of that title (r.67(3)).

Where a disposition of leasehold land limits or extends the covenant implied under s.4 of the 1994 Act a reference to that fact may be made in the register (r.67(6)).

But no other reference to any covenant implied by virtue of Pt 1 of the 1994 Act, or by s.76 of the Law of Property Act 1925 as applied by s.11(1) of the 1994 Act, can be made in the register (r.67(5)).

A disposition which contains a provision limiting or extending any covenant implied by virtue of Pt 1 of the 1994 Act must include a statement in one of the following forms (r.68):

(1) "The covenant set out in section (*number*) of the Law of Property (Miscellaneous Provisions) Act 1994 shall [not] extend to   "; or

(2) "The [transferor *or* lessor] shall not be liable under any of the covenants set out in section (*number*) of the Law of Property (Miscellaneous Provisions) Act 1994".

Paragraph 20 of Sch.12 to the Act sets out the indemnity covenants which are implied on the transfer of a pre-1996 lease — an old tenancy under the Landlord and Tenant (Covenants) Act 1995. Where a transfer of a registered lease modifies or negatives any covenants so implied by para.20(2) and (3) of Sch.12 to the Act, an entry that the covenants have been so modified or negatived must be made in the register (r.66).

Easements

In certain circumstances legal easements will be overriding **7–007** interests and this is covered in Chapter 4 and Chapter 9.

The effect of first registration is to vest in the proprietor all interests subsisting for the benefit of the registered estate (ss.11(3) and 12(3)). If the land registered has the benefit of any appurtenant easements, such as rights of way, rights of drainage, etc. these will be included in the registration whether or not expressly mentioned on the register.

Under r.33 the registrar may enter an appurtenant right on the register on first registration if he is satisfied that it exists as a legal estate and benefits the land.

The registrar must enter a notice in the register of the burden of any easement which appears from his examination of the title on first registration to affect the registered estate. But this does not apply to an easement which appears to the registrar to be of a trivial or obvious character, or the entry of a notice in respect of which would be likely to cause confusion or inconvenience (r.35).

Transfers and deeds of grant

7–008 A registered proprietor has the power, subject to any restriction on the register, to grant or reserve any easement permitted by the general law (s.23). To be effective, a grant or reservation of an easement affecting registered land must be (para.7 of Sch.2 to the Act):

(1) entered as an appurtenant right in the register of the benefiting land if that land is registered; and

(2) noted in the register of the land which is subject to it.

Rule 72 provides that when a transfer of part of the land in a title grants an easement over land remaining in the transferor's title for the benefit of the land transferred, the Registry will make appropriate entries relating to the benefit and burden of the grant in the registers of the transferee's and the transferor's titles respectively when the transfer is registered. It further provides that if the transfer reserves an easement over the land transferred for the benefit of the land remaining in the title from which it is transferred, appropriate entries relating to the benefit and burden of the reservation will also be made in the registers of the transferor's and transferee's titles respectively when the transfer is registered.

No additional fee is payable in respect of such entries.

If, where a grant or reservation of an easement is made in a transfer of part, the benefiting or burdened land is registered but lies wholly or partly outside the land transferred and outside the remainder of the land in the title from which it is transferred, a specific application to enter the benefit or burden, as the case might be, of the grant or reservation in the register of the "outside title" should be lodged with the application to register the transfer.

In accordance with the current Fee Order no fee will usually be payable.

If a transfer of whole or of part grants to the transferee an easement over unregistered land, evidence of the transferor's title to make the grant should accompany the application to register the transfer so that the right granted may be registered as appurtenant to the land transferred. If the transfer reserves an easement over the land transferred for the benefit of unregistered land, an entry relating to the burden of the reservation will be made in the register of the title to the land transferred as a matter of course when the transfer is registered.

If a transfer of whole grants or reserves an easement over or for the benefit of land in another registered title, a specific application to enter the burden or benefit of the grant or reservation in the register of the other title should be lodged with the application to register the transfer.

In accordance with the current Fee Order no fee will usually be payable.

When an easement is granted by a deed of grant (independently of any other transaction) the grantee should apply for the right to be registered as appurtenant to the benefiting land, if registered, and for notice of the grant to be entered in the register of the land which is subject to it, if registered. When both titles are registered, care must be taken to refer to both title numbers on the application form.

A fee will be payable in accordance with the current Fee Order.

If the burdened land is unregistered, ordinary conveyancing evidence of the grantor's title to make the grant should accompany the application.

When a grant or reservation of an easement cannot be fully completed by registration (for example, where both the benefiting and burdened land are registered but the application is made in respect of the benefiting land only, or where the burdened land is unregistered and no evidence of the grantor's title to it is produced) the registrar may enter details of the right claimed with such qualification he considers appropriate (r.75). Normally no such entry will be made.

A buyer of registered land takes the title subject only to what appears in the register and to overriding interests (s.29). An easement granted over registered land on or after October 13, 2003 must be registered in accordance with para.7 of Sch.2 to the Act. If it is not, the easement will not be an overriding interest affecting the burdened land because it will not be a legal easement for the purpose of para.3 of Sch.3 to the Act as it has not been completed by registration.

To meet these registration requirements, application must be made to register the easement using Form AP1 (r.90). You must use Form AP1 to register the easement on the burdened title even if the benefiting title is not registered. If you apply on Form AN1 or UN1 the registration requirements will not be met and the easement will be noted as an equitable easement only with the following note to the entry:

"NOTE: The grant or reservation of the rights . . . . . . has not been completed by registration in accordance with section 27 of the Land Registration Act 2002 and so does not operate at law."

Freehold flats

7–009 When houses on registered land are converted into flats the Registry tries to ensure that complete particulars of the rights and easements granted and reserved on the sale of each freehold flat are referred to on the register of both the seller's and buyer's titles. These particulars are entered in one of two ways according to circumstances. Either (1) they are set out verbatim on the register, or (2) reference is made to the documents creating them. In complicated cases the Registry may consult the conveyancers concerned in an endeavour to frame the entries in the register to meet their requirements.

Prescriptive easements

7–010 Prescription is the acquisition of a right through long use or enjoyment. The use must be for at least 20 years and must also be without force, without secrecy and without permission, by or on behalf of a freehold owner against another freehold owner, continuous and not illegal.

An application to register the benefit or claim to the benefit of or burden of a prescriptive easement should be made on Form FR1, when the application accompanies a first registration application, or AP1 accompanied by a Statutory Declaration which must be completed with evidence of the basis of the claim as explained in the Registry's Practice Guide 52. An inspection may be carried out. If the application is to register the benefit rather than a claim to the benefit, notice will be served on the owner of the burdened land, unless the consent of that owner is lodged with the application.

A fee is payable calculated in accordance with the current Fee Order. An inspection fee may also be payable and if so, the Registry will ask for it.

If both the benefiting land and the freehold in the burdened land are registered, once the application is approved an entry is made in the property register of the benefiting land that the land has the benefit of the easement and an entry is made in the charges register of the burdened land that that land is subject to the easement.

If only the freehold in the burdened land is registered, once the application is approved the Registry will enter notice of the easement claimed in the charges register of the title to the burdened land.

If only the benefiting land is registered and the claimant deduces title to the burdened land with the address of the freehold owner and no objection is received following the service of appropriate notices an entry will be made in the property register of the benefiting land that the land has the benefit of the easement.

If the title to the burdened land is not deduced or the claimant does not supply the address of the freehold owner of that land an entry will be made in the property register of the benefiting land in the following terms:

> "The registered proprietor claims that the land has the benefit of a right [terms of right as claimed by claimant]. The right claimed is not included in this registration. The claim is supported by statutory declaration/s [details of date(s) and deponent(s) of the statutory declaration (s)].
> NOTE: Copy statutory declaration/s filed."

Copies of the statutory declarations lodged in support of the claim may be inspected and official copies obtained in the same way as other documents (see Chapter 8). Where a claim to an easement was noted in the property register of the benefiting land before March 25, 2002, the entry does not refer to the statutory declarations lodged in support of the claim. Chapter 8 deals with the circumstances in which it may be possible to obtain a copy of any such declaration which the Registry has retained in its files.

The use of a right of way for vehicles cannot be relied on to establish a prescriptive easement if such use is illegal. This point has recently been considered by the House of Lords in *Bakewell Management Limited v Brandwood* [2004] UKHL 14. Regulations made under s.68 of the Countryside and Rights of Way Act 2000 enable a right of way for vehicles to be claimed in cases where the use would have given rise to a prescriptive easement had it not constituted an offence. A prescribed form of notice accompanied by prescribed information must be served and there is provision for objections. The easement is actually created when compensation is paid, either to the owner of the burdened land or into court.

Profits à prendre

Before October 13, 2003, the benefit of a profit à prendre **7–011** attached to land could be registered as appurtenant to a registered title to land but a profit in gross (*i.e.* not attached to any land) could not be registered.

Since the Act came in to force profits à prendre which exist in gross are capable of substantive registration in their own right (s.2 and see Chapter 4).

The property register of a profit à prendre in gross must, contain a description of the profit (r.5) and sufficient particulars of any instrument which created it to enable it to be identified (r.7).

Notice of the burden of a profit à prendre is entered in the same way as notice of the burden of an easement.

As to the overriding status of legal profits à prendre see Chapter 4 and Chapter 9.

Chapter 8

Inspection, Official Copies and Searches

Inspection of the register

Any person may, subject to formalities and fee, inspect and **8–001** make copies of the register, any document kept by the registrar which is referred to in the register, any other document kept by the registrar which relates to an application to him and the register of cautions against first registrations (s.66). There is no exception, as there was under the 1925 legislation, for leases and charges and the right to inspect is now much wider. This is in line with the Freedom of Information Act 2000. Although that Act only came into force on January 1, 2005 the Land Registration Act 2002 and the Land Registration Rules 2003 were drafted to take account of its provisions. However the general right of inspection is subject to rules which provide for exceptions to this right.

This general right to inspect does not extend to the index of proprietors' names (see below).

Inspection of the index of proprietors' names

The index of proprietors' names (see Chapter 1) is not open to **8–002** general inspection. However, in addition to the special right to a search discussed below, any person may apply in Form PN1 for a search to be made of the index in respect of either his own name or the name of some other person in whose property he is able to satisfy the registrar that he is interested generally, *e.g.* as his trustee in bankruptcy or his personal representative. Separate applications should be made in respect of any former or alternative names, and every address which may have been used as an address for service for entry on the register should be stated. Because of the effect of the Freedom of Information Act 2000, anyone can search against a non-private individual, such as a company.

The reply to the application will state whether or not the person named in the search appears in the index. If the person named does so appear, the reply will also give the relevant title number(s). The reply constitutes an official search the accuracy of which is guaranteed.

A fee is payable, calculated in accordance with the current Fee Order.

Personal inspection

8–003   Land Registry offices are open to the public between the hours of 8.30am and 6pm Mondays to Fridays, excluding public holidays. During those hours anyone may apply on Form PIC to make a personal inspection of the register and the documents referred to in s.66(1) subject to the exceptions referred to below. Form PIC is available at offices when the visit is made or from HMSO or law stationers. It can also be downloaded from the Registry's website at *www.landregistry.gov.uk*. Fees are payable for inspection of the register, each title plan and any or all of the documents kept by the registrar and referred to on the register or relating to an application to him. If the title number is not known an additional fee may be payable. Enquiries as to fees currently payable may be made at any office.

Rule 133 is relevant to such an application and sets out the exceptions to the right to inspect. They are:

(1) any exempt information document;

(2) any edited information document which has been replaced by another edited information document;

(3) any Form EX1A;

(4) any Form CIT;

(5) any Form to which Form CIT has been attached;

(6) any document or copy of any document prepared by the registrar in connection with an application in a Form to which Form CIT has been attached; and

(7) during the transitional period, any transitional period document.

These exceptions apply also to applications for official copies and are dealt with in more detail below, as are the meanings of the terms used and the forms referred to above.

Access by remote terminal (Land Registry Direct) and Land Register Online

These are covered in Chapter 1.   **8–004**

Official copies

What can be supplied?

(1) *An official copy of the entries in the register (r.134(1)(a)).* This **8–005** will include any schedule to the register. The copy will carry two dates; the date on which it was issued and the time and date on which the entries shown were subsisting (the significance of these dates is discussed below).

(2) *An official copy of the title plan (r.134(1)(b)).* The delay usually involved in obtaining an official copy of a large plan can normally be avoided by means of a certificate of official inspection of the title plan (see below).

(3) *An official copy of an individual cautions register and any caution plan referred to in it (r.134(1)(c)).*

(4) *An official copy of a document kept by the registrar which is referred to in the register (r.135(1)).* unless the document falls within one of the exceptions set out in r.135(2) which are the same as the exceptions set out in r.133 relating to the right to inspect (see above). These exceptions are dealt with in more detail below.

(5) *An official copy of any other document kept by the registrar which relates to an application to him (r.135(1)(b)).* unless the document falls within one of the exceptions set out in r.135(2) which are the same as the exceptions set out in r.133 relating to the right to inspect (see above). These exceptions are dealt with in more detail below.

What cannot be supplied?

(1) *Copies of certain documents during the transitional* **8–006** *period.* During the transitional period (two years from October 13, 2003) leases and charges kept by the registrar since before

that date, where an entry referring to the lease or charge was made in the register before that date and any other document (other than one referred to on the register) kept by the registrar which relates to an application to him and was received by the registrar before that date will not be available to inspect as of right. These documents are defined in r.131 as transitional period documents. Inspection and the provision of official copies of transitional period documents is at the registrar's discretion. However, there is also now a right to inspect under the Freedom of Information Act 2000. It seems therefore that the registrar is unlikely to exercise his discretion to refuse inspection or the provision of an official copy in cases where the document could be inspected under the Freedom of Information Act 2000 in any event (see below). Where a transitional period document is an exempt information document, the question of the exercise of the registrar's discretion as such does not apply, but see below for comments regarding the effect of the Freedom of Information Act 2000.

(2) *A copy of a document designated as an exempt information document unless certain conditions are satisfied (see below).* The edited information document, a version of the exempt information document from which all the prejudicial information (see below) has been removed, can be supplied.

(3) *A copy of an edited information document which has been replaced by another edited information document (see below).*

(4) *A copy of Form EX1A.* Form EX1A sets out the reasons for exemption in support of an application to designate a document as an exempt information document and accompanies Form EX1 (see below).

(5) *A copy of Form CIT.* Form CIT is the application form for use where inspection or copies are sought in connection with court proceedings, insolvency and tax liability (see below).

(6) *A copy of a form to which Form CIT has been attached or a copy of a document prepared by the registrar in connection with such an application (see below).*

Exempt information documents

8–007   Under r.136 a person who claims a "relevant document" contains "prejudicial information" can apply to the registrar to designate it as an exempt information document. A "relevant document" is defined in r.136(7) as a document which is referred to in the register of title, or which relates to an application to the registrar, where the original or a copy has been kept by the registrar, or which will be so referred to as a result of an accompanying application or which relates to that application and the original or a copy will be or is for the time being kept by the registrar. If so designated it is subject to special provisions that except it from the general right of inspection under s.66(1) and regulate the circumstances in which the registrar may allow inspection or provide official copies. Application for designation should be made on Forms EX1 and EX1A. Form EX1A must state the grounds upon which the applicant claims that the document contains prejudicial information. Form EX1A cannot be inspected but Form EX1 can be, as can accompanying letters. Prejudicial information is defined in r.131 as:

(1) information that relates to an individual who is the applicant for designation and if disclosed to other persons (whether to the public generally or specific persons) would, or would be likely to, cause substantial unwarranted damage or substantial unwarranted distress to the applicant or another; or

(2) information that if disclosed to other persons (whether to the public generally or specific persons) would, or would be likely to, prejudice the commercial interests of the applicant for designation.

The application must be accompanied by a certified copy of the document with the prejudicial information edited out, the "edited information document". Provided the application is in order and the registrar is satisfied that the applicant's claim is not groundless he must designate the relevant document as an exempt information document. If the registrar considers that designating the document as an exempt information document would prejudice the keeping of the register, he can cancel the application. Where a document is an exempt information document, the registrar can make an appropriate entry in the register of any affected registered title. Where a subsequent application is made for exemption in respect of further information in the document, the registrar must prepare another edited information document which excludes the information excluded from the existing edited information document and any further information excluded from the edited information document lodged by the subsequent applicant.

Subject to what is said below about the effect of the Freedom of Information Act 2000, a person can only obtain an official copy of the complete original exempt information document if he applies under r.137 on Form EX2, stating why an official copy of the relevant edited information document is not sufficient for his purposes and (if such be the case) why he considers that the information claimed to be prejudicial information is not such information or, if he accepts that all or some of the information is prejudicial information, why he considers that the public interest in providing an official copy of the exempt information document outweighs the public interest in not doing so. Application for an official copy of an exempt information document may also be made under r.140 in connection with court proceedings, insolvency or tax liability (see below).

Where application is made under r.137 the registrar must serve notice on the applicant for exempt information document designation unless he is satisfied that such notice is unnecessary or impracticable. He may consider any information the recipient provides in response to the notice in reaching his decision.

If the registrar decides that none of the information claimed to be prejudicial information is prejudicial information or although the information is prejudicial information in whole or in part, the public interest in providing an official copy of the exempt information document to the applicant outweighs the public interest in not doing so, he will provide an official copy of the exempt information document to the applicant.

Under r.138, the person who applied for designation of a document as an exempt information document may apply for the designation to be removed. The application should be on Form EX3. The registrar must remove the designation and any entry which relates to that designation, if he is satisfied that the application is in order. Where a document has been made an exempt document as a result of more than one application by different persons, the registrar must replace the existing edited information document with one that reflects only the current exemptions.

Freedom of Information Act 2000

8–008   The Freedom of Information Act 2000 now generally allows inspection of all documents held by the Registry. A request for information covered by the Freedom of Information Act may only be refused in the following circumstances:

- where the Registry reasonably requires further information to identify and locate the information requested but the applicant has failed to supply it; or
- where the request is "vexatious", for example where the Registry has previously complied with an identical or

similar request from the same applicant and a reasonable time has not elapsed between compliance with the previous request and the making of the current request; or

- where the Registry estimates that the cost of complying with the request would exceed the "appropriate limit", currently £600; or

- where an exemption applies and applying the public interest test (if applicable) leads to the decision that it is not in the public interest to disclose.

Exemptions from the obligation to disclose information can be absolute or non-absolute. If an absolute exemption applies, the information requested need not be disclosed and, in many cases, the Registry is not obliged to comply with the duty to confirm or deny whether it holds the requested information. Absolute exemption applies to requests for information reasonably accessible by other means. This means that the Freedom of Information Act does not apply, for example, to requests for official copies of registers, title plans, and documents relating to applications received on or after October 13, 2003 or to requests for historical copies of registers. Information covered by the Registry's Publication Scheme is also absolutely exempt. The Freedom of Information Act requires the Registry to adopt and maintain a publication scheme setting out classes of information which it intends to make available to the public as a matter of course, the manner in which the information is to be made available and whether the information will be provided free or for a charge. The Registry's Publication Scheme is available on its website. Other examples of information covered by absolute exemption are information supplied by or relating to court records.

In the case of non-absolute exemptions the Freedom of Information Act requires the Registry to consider first whether or not the exemption applies and, if it does, then the Registry must consider the "public interest test" before withholding or disclosing information. Examples of information covered by the non-absolute exemptions are personal information about third parties and information that constitutes a trade secret or the disclosure of which would, or would be likely to, prejudice the commercial interests of any person. Under the public interest test there is likely to be a public interest in disclosing information where it:

- facilitates the accountability and transparency in the spending of public money; or

- allows individuals to understand decisions affecting their lives and, in some cases, assists individuals in challenging those decisions; or

- brings to light information affecting public safety.

Since January 1, 2005, if the Registry is not intending to allow inspection under an EX2 application (see below), before refusing disclosure it must consider whether that information should be disclosed under the Freedom of Information Act.

As indicated above, the Act and Rules were drafted to take account of the provisions of the Freedom of Information Act so it seems unlikely that inspection of exempt information would be allowed under that Act where it would not be allowed under the Rules. However it remains a possibility and that possibility should be taken into account by practitioners when they are drafting documents relating to registered land and advising their clients.

The application

8–009 There are three forms of application for official copies. Form OC1 is for requests for official copies of the register, title plan, caution register and plan and certificate of inspection of the title plan (see below). Form OC2 is for requests for official copies of documents referred to in the register and kept by the registrar and any other documents kept by the registrar that relate to an application to him. With regard to Form OC2 it is essential that those documents referred to in the register which are required are listed specifically with their nature and dates being given. The title number(s) under which the documents are kept must be given and the number of copies required stated. Generalised requests will not be accepted. Where documents which are not referred to in the register are required, as much detail as possible should be supplied. Form EX2 is for requests for official copies of exempt information documents.

The application should be lodged at the appropriate office. If the title number is not known the words **"Please supply the title number"** should be written boldly at the head of Form OC1 (an additional fee may then be payable — see below). Separate Form OC1 applications should be made in respect of each registered title or individual caution register.

Delivery of the application

8–010 The application can be delivered by post, personally or by document exchange. Credit account holders can also make application by fax or by telephone. Telephone applications may only be made between 8.30am and 6pm Monday to Friday and

8.30am to 1pm on Saturday, excluding public holidays, to the Registry's Telephone Services on 0845 308 4545. Land Registry Direct and National Land Information Service applicants are able to order official copies from their own computer direct to the Registry's computer.

Fees for official copies

Fees are payable in accordance with the current Fee Order (see **8–011** Appendix IV).

A credit account (see Chapter 1) can be used for payment of fees for official copies.

Certificate of official inspection of the title plan

Instead of an official copy of the title plan a certificate of official **8–012** inspection of the title plan may be obtained.

The application is generally made by reference to an estate layout plan approved by the Registry (see Chapter 20). In the case of postal applications only, application may be made by reference to a plan annexed to the application; the plan should be prepared on the same basis as a plan for use with a search of part discussed below.

The application form is Form OC1. A fee is payable, calculated in accordance with the current Fee Order.

The certificate will be in Form CI. It will state that the land to which it relates is in the title concerned and what, if any, colour or other references shown on the title plan and mentioned in the entries on the register affect it. The accuracy of the certificate will be guaranteed, but it will not confer on the applicant priority for the registration of any dealing.

When a transaction relates to only a part of the land in a large registered title and a certificate in Form CI would give the applicant all the information about the title plan that he needs, the use of such a certificate can save the additional expense and (usually) delay entailed in obtaining an official copy of the title plan. The main use of certificates in Form CI is in connection with developing registered building estates (see Chapter 20) but the procedure may be used in relation to any title plan.

Historical information

The register of title only provides details of the title at a **8–013** particular point in time. It does not show how the title has changed historically. Section 69 and r.144 now provide a mechanism for a person to obtain such information. This will only apply where the registrar holds previous editions of a registered title, or a registered title which has been closed, in electronic form. He is not under an obligation to keep such records.

Application can be made on Form HC1 for a copy of either the last edition, or every edition for a specified day, of a specified registered title, or registered title which has been closed, kept by the registrar in electronic form. If the application is in order, the registrar will issue the requested copies if they are kept in electronic form.

In addition to providing historical information under r.144 in appropriate cases, historical information may be provided in response to a letter or a written request under the Freedom of Information Act 2000. It is likely that this will be provided by letter or by supplying copies of documents. When applying a person should state why they want the information requested so that the registrar can decide whether and what to provide.

Inspection in connection with court proceedings, insolvency and tax liability

8–014   Under r.140 certain specified officials responsible for investigating crime and recovering the proceeds of crime, acting as receiver in special circumstances, administering the affairs of insolvent individuals or corporations or assessing tax liability may apply:

> (1) to inspect, make copies of, or obtain official copies of:
>> (a) any exempt information document;
>> (b) any edited information document which has been replaced by another edited information document;
>> (c) any Form EX1A;
>> (d) any Form CIT;
>> (e) any Form to which Form CIT has been attached;
>> (f) any document or copy of any document prepared by the registrar in connection with an application in a Form to which Form CIT has been attached; and
>> (g) during the transitional period, any transitional period document;
>
> (2) for a search in the index of proprietors' names in respect of the name of a person specified in the application.

Schedule 5 to the Rules sets out who can apply and the appropriate certificate which must be given.

Such an application should be made on the relevant Form PIC, OC2 or PN1, with Form CIT attached. Form CIT is the application form for use in connection with court proceedings, insolvency and tax liability and sets out the nature of the application and the appropriate certificate. This form can also be attached to Forms PIC, OC1, OC2, HC1, SIM and SIF used for applying for documents to which the general right to inspection applies, for historical editions of registered titles and for official searches of the index map and index of relating franchises and manors (see Chapter 2). Form CIT cannot be inspected, nor can any form to which it has been attached as indicated above or any document or copy of a document prepared by the registrar in connection with an application in a form to which Form CIT has been attached.

Official searches of the register

To obtain up-to-date information as to all subsisting entries on **8–015** the register of a title, it is not enough to read what appears in a land or charge certificate, a Title Information Document or in an official copy; the current state of the register must be ascertained. Entries may have been made in the register since the date (shown on the inside cover of the certificate) on which a land or charge certificate was last officially made to correspond with the register or since the date when the Title Information Document or official copy was issued. For example, the registration of a transfer of the land subject to a registered charge would not necessarily be recorded in a charge certificate, and the registration of a second charge may not appear in a first charge certificate. Cautions and entries relating to bankruptcy commonly do not appear in any certificate. Also, land and charge certificates have not been issued since October 13, 2003, so any in existence at that time may be out of date. All these matters, however, would be the subject of entries in the register and would be revealed by an inspection of the register.

At any time an up-to-date official copy of the register may be obtained. However recent the date on which the Title Information Document or official copy was issued, it is never safe to assume that no new entry, not appearing in the certificate, Title Information Document or official copy, has been made in the register since that date. It is clearly of great importance to persons dealing with registered land that they are not caught by entries of which they were unaware; to protect against this a system of official searches of the register is operated under the provisions of the Rules.

Official searches of the register with priority

Purpose

8–016 The purpose of these searches is to enable a "purchaser", defined in r.131 as "a person who has entered into or who intends to enter into a 'protectable disposition' as disponee", to obtain an official certificate as to the entries on the register of the disponor's title immediately before completion and to ensure that (if he complies with the procedure laid down) he will be unaffected by any entry made between the date of this certificate and the registration of his "protectable disposition". "Protectable disposition" is defined in r.131 as "a registrable disposition (including one by virtue of r.38) of a registered estate or registered charge made for valuable consideration". Reference should be made to Chapters 4 and 9 for more information about what constitutes a registrable disposition.

Who may apply?

8–017 Official searches with priority are available only to a "purchaser" as defined by r.131 (see above). Therefore, they are not available to a mortgagee who intends to protect the mortgage on the register by a notice under s.32. Other persons may, however, apply for an official search without priority using Form OS3 (see below).

The application

8–018 Application for an official search with priority may be made in documentary form ("a paper search"), by fax, by telephone, orally or through Land Registry Direct or the National Land Information Service (see below). As explained below the commencement of the priority period is governed by the method of application adopted.

(1) *Paper searches* — A paper search should be in Form OS1 where the protectable disposition is of all the land in the title or in Form OS2 where it is of part of the land only. The form must be signed because it contains a certificate that the applicant is a person who may apply for a search with priority.

Except as stated below, an application in Form OS2 must be accompanied by a plan, in duplicate, which should be drawn to a suitable scale (generally not less than 1/1250—urban areas or 1/2500 rural areas); and, when necessary, sufficient figured dimensions must be entered on the plan to define the part affected and to tie it to the existing physical features (such as road junctions, fences or walls) shown by firm black lines on the official plan of the disponor's registered title. The plan should be a copy of the plan intended to be bound up in the protectable disposition (see Chapters 10 and 20). No plan need accompany the Form OS2 if the part affected is a numbered plot on an estate layout plan of a registered building estate approved by the Registry as described in Chapter 20 for the purpose of official searches, provided that the plot number(s) and the date of the Registry's approval of the estate layout plan are stated on the Form OS2.

The application must be delivered to the appropriate office. Official search certificates are always despatched from the Registry using first class mail or document exchange.

(2) *Fax searches* — A credit account holder (see Chapter 1) may apply for an official certificate of search with priority by fax. The application is in Form OS1 (search of whole) or Form OS2 (search of part). Searches of part can only be made in respect of plot number(s) on an approved estate plan (see Chapter 20) and the relevant information is provided in panel 10 of Form OS2 and no plan accompanies the application or where the extent of the land to be searched can be adequately depicted on a single A4 sized plan. Such a plan must accompany Form OS2, be referred to in panel 10, show clearly and unambiguously the extent of the land to be searched, be drawn to a stated scale of not less than 1/1250, be sufficiently detailed to allow accurate plotting to be undertaken, include a north point and not be referred to as being supplied for the "purpose of identification only".

The search forms must be completed in black print or black ink.

The application must be faxed to the fax number specified for that purpose at the appropriate office.

(3) *Telephone searches* — An application for an official certificate of search of whole with priority may be made by telephone by a credit account holder (see Chapter 1). The Registry will ask for the following information:

(a) the credit account key number and name and address of the account holder;

(b) the name and address to which the result is to be despatched if different from (a);

(c) the title number;

(d) the name of the registered proprietor;

(e) the district or London Borough and address (only if there is doubt that the correct title number has been given);

(f) the search from date (see below);

(g) the account holder's reference and, if different, the reference of the person to whom the result is to be despatched;

(h) the name of the applicant;

(i) whether a purchase, charge or lease is sought to be protected; and

(j) a name and telephone number to phone back in case of need.

The caller may request as many searches as he wishes in any one call.

Telephone requests may be made between 8.30am and 6.30pm Monday to Friday and between 8.30am and 1pm on Saturdays other than public holidays. The call must be made to 0845 308 4545 and not to the appropriate office.

(4) *Oral searches* — Anyone who is, or who acts for, a "purchaser" may apply for an official certificate of search with priority orally at the Customer Information Centre of any office. The search must be in respect of the whole of the land in any registered title; searches of part cannot be requested in this way.

The Registry will require the same information as set out at (3) above in respect of telephone searches. The applicant may request as many searches as he wishes in any one visit.

Oral requests for searches by personal attendance at one of the Registry's offices can only be made between 8.30am and 6pm Monday to Friday (other than public holidays).

(5) *Land Registry Direct and National Land Information Service searches* — Customers with Land Registry Direct or using the National Land Information Service (see Chapter 1) can use the facility to order some searches direct computer to computer.

The "search from date"

8–019 Application for an official search with priority must be from a date which is the date shown on an official copy as the date on which the entries on that official copy were subsisting. A time is also printed on the official copy but this time need not be quoted on an application for an official search. The search commences from 00.01 hours on the date given.

In the case of Land Registry Direct only the search can be made from the date stated at the time of an access by remote terminal to the register as the date on which the entries accessed were subsisting.

The more recent the "search from date" the less likelihood there is of the searcher becoming aware of adverse information for the first time immediately prior to completion of the transaction which the search is intended to protect.

The date on which a Land or Charge Certificate was last officially examined with the register cannot be used as a "search from date".

The result of search

If:

8–020

(1) a search is made by telephone, orally or through Land Registry Direct;

(2) there have been no entries made in the register since the search from date; and

(3) there are no pending applications or unexpired searches with priority on the day list,

a guaranteed result of search will be given immediately by the same means as the search was made.

Except where a Land Registry Direct or National Land Information Service applicant has been able to apply for an official search certificate to be issued in electronic form, in all cases (including those where an immediate result has been given) an official certificate of search will be issued by post or document exchange in paper form. The certificate will contain details of:

(a) any adverse entries made in the register on or after the search from date (see above). These will normally be shown by reference to an up to date official copy issued with the result of search which will have to be compared with the official copy by reference to which the search was made;

(b) any applications for registration pending but not completed by entry on the register; and

(c) any other official search with unexpired priority, including the date and time of deemed delivery of such a search.

In addition the certificate will state the date and time that the priority period began and the date when priority will end.

Accuracy is guaranteed (s.103 and para.1 of Sch.8 to the Act).

Where an oral or telephone search does not produce a "clear" result the Registry will usually give the applicant such details as it can of the adverse entries or pending applications or unexpired searches which the certificate will reveal. Such information is not guaranteed. In the case of a search by Land Registry Direct, the Registry will usually inform the applicant of the situation but not give details.

Search results are not issued by fax.

The priority period

8–021 The period of priority begins when the official search application is deemed to be delivered. It will be deemed to be delivered at the time and on the date notice of it is entered on the day list.

Notice of a search application delivered in documentary form or by fax to the appropriate office before noon on one business day will normally be entered on the day list on the same day. Where an application is received after noon, notice of it will normally be entered on the day list the same day or the following business day. Notice of a search application delivered by telephone, orally or by Land Registry Direct or the National Land Information Service will normally be entered on the day list immediately after it is delivered unless it is lodged through Land Registry Direct or the National Land Information Service on a day that is not a business day when it will be entered on the day list on the next business day.

The priority period ends at midnight marking the end of the thirtieth business day after the day on which the search was deemed to be delivered regardless of how the original application was made. "Business day" is defined in r.217 as "a day when the land registry is open to the public under rule 216". The 30 business day priority period will be extended to 36 business days under r.131 if the registrar gives notice under r.216(2) that the Registry will be open on Saturdays.

The effect of priority

8–022 Any entry made in the register during the priority period will be postponed to a subsequent application to register the instrument effecting the protectable disposition to which the search relates, and, if that disposition is dependent on a prior dealing, to a subsequent application to register the instrument effecting that dealing, provided that each such subsequent application:

(1) is deemed to have been delivered at the appropriate office within the priority period (see Chapter 1) — to ensure that this is the case, the application must be delivered by noon on the date when priority expires;

(2) affects the same land or charge as the postponed entry; and

(3) is in due course completed by registration.

It follows that where there is a transfer on sale, and the purchase money or part of it is being raised by a legal charge, a search on behalf of the chargee will protect both him and the transferee.

Points on the operation of priority periods

Two or more official certificates of search relating to the same **8–023** land or charge may be in operation at the same time. Rule 153 provides for the determination of priorities in situations where priority is not clear, and in case of doubt reference should be made to that rule.

Rule 154 provides that where an official search has been made in respect of a particular title and an application relating to that title is deemed to have been delivered at the same time as the expiry of the priority period relating to that search, the time of delivery of the application shall be deemed to be within that priority period.

Sub sales and re-sales

A registered proprietor (S) may sell part of the land in his title **8–024** to a buyer (B1), who agrees to sell that land to a sub-buyer (B2) before the registration of the transfer by S to B1 has been completed. In these circumstances B1 will be unable to prove his title to B2 by producing an official copy of the register of B1's title because that register will not exist. However, if Bl can supply to B2 an official copy of the register of S's title, the following procedure can be followed.

B2 can apply in Form OS3 for a "non-priority" official search of the register of S's title based on the official copy of that title (see below). The official certificate of the result of the search will: (1) disclose any adverse entry made in S's register since the beginning of the day that the official copy is dated; (2) reveal the presence in the Registry of the pending application to register the transfer to B1, stating whether or not it has been approved for entry in the register; and (3) reveal any other pending application for registration or for an official search affecting the land transferred to B1. Also B2 should obtain from B1 a copy of the transfer to B1.

Just before completion of the sub-sale to him, B2 will wish to apply for a purchaser's official search of the register, principally to obtain the statutory priority period within which to deliver his transfer for registration. If the registration of the transfer by S to B1 has by that time been completed, B1 will be able to provide B2 with an official copy of the register of B1's title. B2 can apply in Form OS1 for an official search in respect of the whole of the land in B1's title based on the official copy. If the registration of the transfer by S to B1 has not been completed, B2 can apply in Form OS2 for an official search in respect of the relevant part of the land in S's title based as before on the official copy of the register of S's title supplied to him by B1.

This procedure can be adapted for a chargee who proposes to lend to a sub-buyer whose transfer has not yet been registered or where either of the two transactions is by way of lease.

Official search with priority in respect of land the subject of a pending first registration application

Purpose

8–025 The purpose of these searches is to enable a "purchaser" of land the subject of a pending first registration application to confirm that the property is, in fact, the subject of such an application lodged by a named applicant and received on a stated date, and to ascertain whether or not any applications affecting the property have been received since that date. Provided the pending first registration application is subsequently completed, the "purchaser" is enabled to ensure (if he complies with the procedure laid down) that he will be unaffected by an entry made between the date of his certificate and the registration of his protectable disposition.

Who may apply?

8–026 These official searches are available only to a "purchaser" as defined in r.131 (see above) of a "protectable disposition" which relates to a pending first registration application. The same considerations apply as in the case of already registered titles (see above).

The application

The same methods of application are available as set out above **8–027** in relation to searches of subsisting registers. Searches of the whole of the land in a pending first registration application can be delivered as paper searches, by fax, by telephone, orally and through Land Registry Direct or the National Land Information Service. Searches of part of the land in a pending first registration can only be made as paper searches or through the National Land Information Service. In all cases the procedures set out above should be followed.

Official search certificates are always despatched from the Registry using first class mail or document exchange.

The same provisions apply in relation to the deemed time of delivery as are set out above. If the application is in order and is deemed to have been delivered to the appropriate office by noon on one day, the official certificate of search will usually be posted back to the applicant within two business days in the case of a search of whole or three business days in the case of a search of part. In some cases the respective periods may be longer as it will be necessary for the Registry to obtain the papers relating to the pending first registration application, which may be at any stage in the course of registration, in order to complete the official search certificate.

The result of search

The search will enable the purchaser to satisfy himself that the **8–028** property searched is the subject of a pending first registration application, and will state by whom the application was made and on what date the application was received. The certificate will state whether or not any applications have been received since that date which are pending, and which may affect the property, and will disclose particulars of any other official search with unexpired priority. Its accuracy is guaranteed (s.103 and para.1 of Sch.8 to the Act).

Priority conferred by the search

The priority period conferred by an official search with priority **8–029** of land the subject of a pending first registration application is the same as that given by an official search with priority of a subsisting register (see above).

If the application for first registration is subsequently completed by registration of all or any part of the land comprised in the protectable disposition, any entry which is made in the register during the priority period relating to the search will be postponed to a subsequent application to register the instrument affecting the protectable disposition and, if that disposition is dependent on a prior dealing, to a subsequent application to register the instrument effecting that dealing subject to the same provisos as are set out above.

It must be noted that until the pending first registration application has actually been completed, no guarantee is given that any registered title will be granted or, if granted, that it will be of the class sought. Also, no information will be provided as to the entries which may eventually be made on the register. It is for the purchaser to satisfy himself by enquiry of the applicant for first registration that the title lodged is in order, and to identify the entries which are likely to be made. Should it be necessary, the Registry will usually be prepared to return documents lodged with an application for first registration temporarily to the conveyancer or other person who originally lodged them, but the application for first registration will not proceed until they are relodged.

Withdrawal of official search with priority

8–030   Under r.150 a person who has made an application for an official search with priority of a registered title or in relation to a pending first registration application can withdraw that official search by application to the registrar. There is no prescribed form.

Official searches without priority

8–031   Any person may at any time apply in Form OS3 for an official search without priority of the register. This form of official search is available to persons who are not "purchasers", for example, to a mortgagee who intends to protect the mortgage on the register by a notice under s.32.

The application can be made as a paper search or by fax in the case of a search of whole or part. It can only be sent to the appropriate office. The position with regard to plans for a search of part is as stated above for official searches in Form OS2.

If the application is in order, a certificate of the result of the search will be issued. This will show, if they affect the land in respect of which the application was made:

(1) any adverse entries made in the register since the search from date (see above);

(2) any applications for registration pending but not completed by entry on the register; and

(3) any other applications for an official search.

The accuracy of the certificate is guaranteed; but the certificate will not confer on the applicant priority for the registration of any dealing.

Any credit account holder can apply for a search without priority by telephone to the appropriate office. The search may only be against the whole of a title. The search cannot be against a pending first registration application. The result will be given by telephone and will consist of the information available to the Registry's staff at the time. The result is not guaranteed against error and confers no priority.

Official search by mortgagee in Form MH3

The procedure whereby the proprietor of a registered charge or **8–032** a mortgagee of registered land may search the register to enable him to comply with the provisions of s.56(3) of the Family Law Act 1996 is outlined in Chapter 16.

Fees on searches

Fees on searches are payable in accordance with the current Fee **8–033** Order (see Appendix IV).

Outline applications

Outline applications can be lodged under r.54 to reserve periods **8–034** of priority for interests that cannot be protected by official searches. This is covered in Chapter 9.

Searches in the Land Charges Department

Section 86 of the Act provides that where a debtor has been **8–035** adjudged bankrupt, a disponee to whom a registrable disposition is made is not subject to the title of the debtor's trustee in bankruptcy if the disposition is made for valuable consideration, the disponee acts in good faith, at the time of the disposition no notice or restriction was entered in relation to the registered estate or charge and the disponee had no notice of the bankruptcy petition or the adjudication. Nothing in s.86 requires a disponee to make a search under the Land Charges Act 1972 (s.86(7)). Section 87 of the Act provides that pending land actions, writs or orders of the kind mentioned in s.6(1)(a) of the Land Charges Act 1972, orders appointing a receiver or sequestrator and deeds of arrangement are interests affecting an estate or charge for the purposes of the Act. None of those matters are capable of falling within para.2 of Sch.1 or Sch.3 to the Act (unregistered interests which override registration). This means that if their priority is not protected by means of an entry on the register (either a notice or a restriction) a disponee would take free from them under ss.29 and 30. Therefore, a disponee need not search the Land Charges Department.

Where land is registered with a title less than absolute, the need for searches in the Land Charges Department falls to be considered in relation to the pre-registration title or, in the case of a qualified title, in relation to the specified qualification, as though the title were unregistered.

Although it is considered that as a matter of strict law the position is as stated, some conveyancers apply for official searches in the Land Charges Department in relation to registered land because, whereas the register of title cannot provide information about the financial position of a proposing borrower who is not yet registered as proprietor, a search in the Land Charges Department will reveal any bankruptcy proceedings pending against him. Correct use of the official search machinery at the Land Registry will ensure the registration of both borrower and lender with priority over any last minute bankruptcy proceedings, but no one wants to lend money to a potential bankrupt. For the convenience of those whose sole purpose in applying for an official search in the Land Charges Department is to discover whether any proceedings in bankruptcy or deed of arrangement has been registered, that Department operates a system of limited official searches.

Local land charge searches

8–036 Searches in the registers of local land charges maintained by local authorities must be made in relation to registered land exactly as though it were unregistered.

Chapter 9

Dealings Generally

Dealings expressly authorised by the Act

A registered proprietor has power to deal with both registered **9–001**
land and registered charges in any way permitted by the general
law, except that a registered proprietor of land may not create a
mortgage by demise or sub-demise and a registered proprietor
of a registered charge may not create a legal sub-mortgage. A
registered proprietor of the land may also charge the title at law
with the payment of money (s.23). A registered chargee has
power to charge at law with the payment of money indebtedness
secured by the registered charge. These powers can be exercised
by the registered proprietor or someone entitled to be the
registered proprietor. Thus a transferee may immediately charge
or re-transfer the land.

The register is conclusive as to the registered proprietor's
powers of disposition (s.26). A disponee can therefore rely upon
the register to say whether there are any limitations on the
powers of the registered proprietor. Even if the registered
proprietor's powers are restricted by statute (other than the Act)
third parties can assume that there are no limitations on the
registered proprietor's powers unless there is an entry on the
register recording the limitation. The title of a disponee cannot
therefore be questioned due to an absence of power on the part
of the registered proprietor. However, although title will pass, a
transferor can still be liable if a transaction is unlawful, *e.g.*
where a transfer has been made by a trustee in breach of trust.

Transfers, leases, charges and other transactions relating to
registered land are discussed under their respective headings;
and an attempt has been made, in Chapter 1 and in the chapters
on specific topics, to deal with more important matters affecting
registration as a whole. Some remarks on general aspects of the
registration of dealings may, however, be helpful.

Dealings which are required to be registered

9–002 Section 27 sets out the dispositions which are required to be registered. In the case of a registered estate these are:

(1) a transfer;

(2) where the registered estate is an estate in land, the grant of a term of years absolute—

    (a) for a term of more than seven years from the date of the grant; or

    (b) to take effect in possession after the end of the period of three months beginning with the date of the grant; or

    (c) under which the right to possession is discontinuous; or

    (d) in pursuance of Pt 5 of the Housing Act 1985 (right to buy); or

    (e) in circumstances where s.171A of the Housing Act 1985 applies (disposal of land which leads to a person no longer being a secure tenant);

(3) where the registered estate is a franchise or manor, the grant of a lease;

(4) the express grant or reservation of an interest of a kind falling within s.1(2)(a) of the Law of Property Act 1925 (easements and profits à prendre, in gross or appurtenant to an estate), other than one capable of being registered under the Commons Registration Act 1965 or a grant as a result of the operation of s.62 of the Law of Property Act 1925;

(5) the express grant or reservation of an interest of a kind falling within s.1(2)(b) (a rent charge in possession issuing out of or charged on land being either perpetual or for a term of years absolute) or (e) (a right of entry exercisable over or in respect of a legal term of years absolute, or annexed, for any purpose to a legal rent charge) of the Law of Property Act 1925; and

(6) the grant of a legal charge other than the creation of a legal charge which is a local land charge.

In the case of a registered charge, the dispositions which are required to be registered are:

(a) a transfer; and

(b) the grant of a sub-charge.

Section 27 applies to dispositions by operation of law as it applies to other dispositions but with the exception of a transfer on the death or bankruptcy of an individual proprietor and a transfer on the dissolution of a corporate proprietor.

If a disposition of a registered estate or charge is required to be completed by registration it does not operate at law until the relevant registration requirements are met. Schedule 2 to the Act sets out the relevant registration requirements. There are different registration requirements for different types of interest. The registration requirements for specific transactions are dealt with under the relevant chapters.

If the relevant registration requirements have not been met due to an error by the Registry, the disposition still does not operate at law, but there may be grounds for an indemnity claim against the Registry.

Effect of registration

Subject to ss.29 and 30, the basic rule is that the priority of an **9–003** interest affecting a registered estate or charge is not affected by a disposition of the estate or charge. Sections 29 and 30 provide that where a registrable disposition, made for valuable consideration, is completed by registration, any interest affecting the estate immediately before the disposition whose priority is not protected at the time of registration is postponed to the interest under the disposition. Sections 29(2) and 30(2) define in what circumstances the priority of an interest is protected. The priority of an interest is protected in any case if the interest:

- is a registered charge or the subject of a notice in the register; or

- falls within any of the paragraphs of Sch.3 to the Act (see below); or

- appears from the register to be excepted from the effect of registration.

In the case of a disposition of a leasehold estate, the priority of an interest is protected if its burden is incident to the estate.

"Valuable consideration" no longer includes a transfer in consideration of marriage. "Valuable consideration" does not include a nominal consideration in money, where the general rule of priority applies.

Production of certificates

9–004 As stated in Chapter 1 the Act makes no provision for land certificates and charge certificates. There is no longer any requirement to lodge such a certificate when applying for registration of a disposition or the making of an entry on the register. Any land or charge certificate lodged will be destroyed. There is no requirement to lodge the Title Information Document which is issued as a matter of practice on a first registration and on the registration of a registrable disposition resulting in a change of ownership (see Chapter 1).

The application forms

9–005 Under r.13 Form AP1 (Application to change the register) is used as a "default" form. It must be used for any application for which no other application form is prescribed. Form AP1 is set out in Sch.1 to the Rules. It need not be used for applications to remove from the register the name of a deceased joint proprietor, or applications made under r.14 (electronic applications) and outline applications (see below).

In particular Form AP1 should be used for dealings with the whole of the land in a title or titles and dealings with part of the land comprised in a title.

In panel 5 there must be set out in their correct priority the dealings to be registered. So the discharge of a charge by a seller should appear before the transfer and any fresh charge. Details of the appropriate fees payable and method of payment should also be entered in panel 5.

If special expedition is desired, a written request should be made. If the request for expedition is made by way of an endorsement on the application form, it should be made prominently; and if the request is made by letter it is advisable also to endorse the application form boldly, "**PLEASE EXPEDITE**".

A list of the documents lodged should be set out in panel 6 in the same order as the applications to which they relate, originals and copies being treated as separate items. If the original and a copy of a document are supplied the Registry will assume that the applicant wants the original returned. If a certified copy of a document is not supplied, the Registry may retain (and ultimately destroy) the original. Therefore, if the applicant wants the original to be returned, a certified copy should be supplied.

The information which should be supplied as indicated in the numbered panels on Form AP1 includes the following:

Panel 4 — whether the application affects the whole or part of the land in the title(s).

Panel 7 — the full name(s) of the applicant and the key number (if any), name, address, reference, e-mail address and telephone and fax numbers of the conveyancer who has lodged the application and to whom any requisitions by the Registry, including requests for unpaid fees, are to be sent.

Panel 8 — instructions (if any) for the raising of any requisitions with, or issue of any document or confirmation of registration to, some person or firm other than that mentioned in panel 7.

Panel 9 — the address(es) for service (**including post-code**) for entry in the register of any new proprietor(s) of the land or instructions to take this information from the transfer, assent or lease. Particular care should be exercised in completing this panel. If this address becomes out of date, but is nevertheless entered in the register, there is a risk that official notices sent by the Registry might not reach the registered proprietor. In the case of an ordinary householder who on completion of the purchase moves to the property being registered, the address to be entered on the register will usually be the full postal address of that property. Any person may have up to three addresses, including the address of his conveyancers, entered in the register (r.198). One address for service must be a postal address but it can be inside or outside the United Kingdom. Where the registrar gives notice, the time period for responding to the notice is determined by reference to the date of issue of the notice, not the date it is deemed to have been received. A person providing an overseas address should bear in mind that notice periods are not extended for overseas addresses and there is a risk that they may not receive the notice in time to respond properly. Up to two additional addresses for service may be provided which can be a document exchange address and/or an electronic address.

Panel 10 — s.71 and r.57 provide that subject to certain exceptions an applicant must provide information to the registrar about interests falling within Sch.3 to the Act which are within the actual knowledge of the applicant or his conveyancer and affect the estate to which the application relates (see below). Panel 10 should be completed accordingly and the application accompanied by Form DI (see below) if appropriate.

Panel 11 — the full name(s) and address(es) for service (including post-code) of any new proprietor(s) of any new charge unless an MD reference is printed on the charge. The remarks at panel 9 in relation to the address for service apply also to this panel.

Details of a company chargee's registered number should also be entered here.

Panel 12 — Form AP1 should be signed in the firm's name.

No covering letter is necessary. The fees payable should accompany the application.

Associated dealings

9–006 Where several associated dealings relating to a particular title are delivered for registration together, the application forms may be numbered consecutively (*e.g.* when there are five applications, 1/5, 2/5, 3/5, 4/5 and 5/5) so that the Registry's staff will see readily that they should be dealt with together and in the order indicated. The appropriate number should be endorsed prominently at the top of the first page of each form.

Forms of dispositions: approval of draft instruments

9–007 Schedule 1 to the Rules contains a list of prescribed, *i.e.* compulsory, forms. Schedule 3 contains forms which must be used in all matters to which they refer but which can be adapted with the registrar's consent.

Schedule 9 contains approved forms of execution of Sch.1 and Sch.3 forms.

Specific forms are referred to under the relevant headings elsewhere in the text. Further information is in Chapter 1 and Appendix III.

The Registry's approval of a draft instrument may be sought:

(1) when it is desired to adapt a Sch.3 prescribed form to a particular transaction (r.206(2)); or

(2) when it is desired to effect a disposition which is within the powers conferred by the Act but for which no form is prescribed (r.212); or

(3) when it is desired to make an application for which there is a prescribed form but the applicant wishes to rely on an alternative document to a Sch.1 or Sch.3 form (r.209).

Care should be taken to see that the draft conforms generally to the Act and Rules and that it clearly identifies the land which is to be the subject of the disposition. The draft (with plan if any) and a copy (with a copy of any plan) should be sent to the appropriate office. No fee is payable.

Approval will be limited to matters of form; and the person lodging the instrument for registration will be responsible for ensuring that it carries out the intention of the parties, and for all matters of substance, due execution and matters of a like nature. Section 25 provides that a registrable disposition only has effect if it complies with requirements as to form and content as rules may provide and this should be borne in mind when instruments are drafted.

The special procedure for the approval of draft instruments in connection with registered building estates is discussed in Chapter 20.

Deeds and their execution

Section 1 of the Law of Property (Miscellaneous Provisions) Act **9–008** 1989 and s.36A of the Companies Act 1985 (as added by s.130(2) of the Companies Act 1989) which came into force on July 31, 1990, contain provisions relating to the form and execution of deeds. These provisions apply to deeds executed for land registration purposes. In addition Sch.9 to the Rules contains the forms of execution which must be used to execute Sch.1 and Sch.3 forms.

For an instrument to be a deed it must be in writing, it must make it clear on its face that it is intended to be a deed and it must be validly executed as a deed by the person making it or one or more of the parties to it. An instrument will be accepted by the Registry as intended to be a deed if it so describes itself; or if it is expressed to be executed as a deed; or if of its nature it is required by law to be a deed, *e.g.* "This Conveyance . . ." or "This Legal Mortgage . . .", or it is in an appropriate form prescribed in the Rules.

Section 1 of the 1989 Act contains minimum requirements for execution by individuals. In the normal way, the individual must sign (signature includes making one's mark) and the deed and his signature must be witnessed. A seal is unnecessary. There is provision for an individual to arrange for someone else to sign on his behalf. In this case the deed must be signed in the presence of the individual whose deed it is and of two other witnesses. The attestation clause should be amended accordingly.

Following the bringing into force of s.36A of the 1985 Act, there are two methods of execution by companies registered under the 1985 Act. First, a company may execute under its common seal in the presence of such witness(es) as are authorised by its articles of association. Alternatively, under s.36A, it may execute by the signature of a director and its secretary or of two directors. Where the first method is adopted and the witnesses are a director and the secretary in accordance with s.74(1) of the Law of Property Act 1925, no question will arise. If attestation is not in accordance with s.74(1) the Registry may call for evidence that the persons attesting the sealing are authorised by or under the company's articles of association. If the s.36A method of execution is adopted, a purchaser is entitled to assume due execution and the Registry will accept without question a deed executed in this manner and lodged by a purchaser.

Execution by an unregistered company in one of the two alternative registered company forms will normally be accepted by the Registry. Execution by foreign companies which complies with s.74(1) will be accepted without further evidence, but if any other method of execution is adopted, evidence that it is authorised will be required.

In the normal way, any deed presented for registration will be presumed to have been delivered from the fact that it has been so presented unless there is evidence to the contrary.

Schedule 9 to the Rules provides forms of execution by an individual, a person signing by direction of an individual, a company under seal, a company not under seal, a limited liability partnership or an overseas company without using a common seal. These forms must be used to execute dispositions in Sch.1 or Sch.3 forms. If circumstances require that the prescribed wording is not followed, *e.g.* execution by a blind or illiterate person, then the prescribed form should be followed as closely as possible and advance approval may be sought.

The Registry's Practice Guide 8 provides guidance on the execution of deeds.

Execution by attorney

9–009 The method of execution by an attorney will vary according to whether the attorney is an individual or a company. If the attorney is an individual he may sign with his own signature or in the name of the donor either way in the presence of a witness. If the donor is a company the individual as attorney may sign in the company's name in the presence of a witness. If the attorney is a company it may either execute in one of the two ways outlined above or through one of its officers duly authorised by resolution to execute in the name of the donor, in the presence of a witness.

Rule 61 provides that if any instrument executed by an attorney is delivered to the Registry, there must be produced also:

(1) the instrument creating the power of attorney; or

(2) a copy of the power by means of which its contents may be proved under s.3 of the Powers of Attorney Act 1971; or

(3) a document which under s.4 of the Evidence and Powers of Attorney Act 1940 or s.7(3) of the Enduring Powers of Attorney Act 1985 is sufficient evidence of the contents of the power (a complete copy of the power of attorney (including any explanatory notes) certified on each page as a true and complete copy by a solicitor is acceptable); or

(4) a conveyancer's certificate in Form 1 (see Sch.3 to the Rules). This must state:

- that the power is in existence;
- the statutory provision under which the power is made;
- the date of the power;
- that the conveyancer is satisfied the power is validly executed as a deed and authorises the attorney to execute that document on behalf of the donor of the power; and
- he is holding one of the other forms of evidence mentioned in r.61.

If an order has been made pursuant to s.8 of the Enduring Powers of Attorney Act 1985 with respect to a power or the donor thereof or the attorney thereunder, the order must be produced to the Registrar.

Rule 62 provides that if any transaction between the donee of a power of attorney and the person dealing with him is not completed within twelve months of the date on which the power came into operation, the registrar may require the production of sufficient evidence to satisfy him that the power had not been revoked at the time of the transaction. The evidence the registrar may require may consist of or include a statutory declaration by the person who dealt with the attorney or a certificate given by that person's conveyancer, if he knows the full facts, in Form 2 (see Sch.3 to the Rules).

A declaration or certificate in Form 2 states that the person dealing with the attorney did not know of:

- a revocation of the power; or
- the death or bankruptcy of the donor or, in the case of a corporate body donor, its winding up or dissolution; or
- any incapacity of the donor where the power is not a valid enduring power.

Where the power is in the form prescribed for an enduring power the statutory declaration or certificate must confirm an absence of knowledge:

- that the power was not in fact a valid enduring power; or
- of an order or direction of the Court of Protection which revoked the power; or
- of the bankruptcy of the attorney.

Where the power was given under s.9 of the Trusts of Land and Appointment of Trustees Act 1996 (see below) the statutory declaration or certificate must confirm an absence of knowledge:

- of an appointment of another trustee of the land in question; or
- of any other event which would have the effect of revoking the power; or
- of any lack of good faith on the part of the person(s) who dealt with the attorney; or
- that the attorney was not a person to whom the functions of the trustees could be delegated under s.9 of the 1996 Act.

Where the power is expressed to be given by way of security the statutory declaration or certificate must confirm an absence of knowledge:

- that the power was not in fact given by way of security; or
- of any revocation of the power with the consent of the attorney; or
- of any other event which would have had the effect of revoking the power.

Powers of attorney given by joint proprietors

9–010 General powers under s.10 of the Powers of Attorney Act 1971 dated before March 1, 2000, cannot be used for dealing with land of which the donor is a joint proprietor. A general or enduring power dated after February 29, 2000, can be used in those circumstances but only if the donor has a beneficial interest in the property and there is no indication in the power that the donor did not intend the attorney to exercise trustee functions. A written statement by the attorney given within three months of the date of the document confirming that the donor had a beneficial interest in the property is, in favour of a purchaser, conclusive evidence that the power could be used (s.2(2) of the Trustee Delegation Act 1999).

From March 1, 2001, an enduring power dated before March 1, 2000, can only be used by a donor who is a joint proprietor if the donor has a beneficial interest in the property and there is no indication in the power that the donor did not intend the attorney to exercise trustee functions, or the power is registered with the Court of Protection following an application to the Court before March 1, 2001, or an application made to the Court before March 1, 2001, for registration of the power has not been finally refused.

A "trustee" power may also be used by a trustee to delegate the trustee's functions as trustee to the attorney (see s.25 of the Trustee Act 1925 as substituted by the Trustee Delegation Act 1999). A "trustee' " power can only have effect for a maximum period of 12 months. The s.25 trustee power is only for use where a single donor delegates trustee functions under a single trust to a single donee. It is not necessary for the donor to have a beneficial interest in the property. Prior to March 1, 2000, the only other co-trustee of the donor could not be the attorney. The Trustee Delegation Act 1999 removed that limitation but because a trustee also acting as attorney for the only other co-trustee cannot give a valid receipt for capital money and therefore overreach beneficial interests it is best to appoint a third party.

Under s.9 of the Trusts of Land and Appointment of Trustees Act 1996, all the trustees of a trust of land can together appoint a beneficiary or the beneficiaries to exercise their functions in relation to the land. However, as the beneficiary attorneys are not treated as trustees for the purpose of receiving capital money the trustees themselves must join in any disposition under which capital money arises if beneficial interests are to be overreached. As a result, this power will be rarely used. An example of where it may be appropriate is when no capital money is passing, *e.g.* on the grant of a lease without payment of a premium.

Rule 63 provides that if any document executed by an attorney to whom functions have been delegated under s.9 of the 1996 Act is delivered to the registrar, the registrar may require the production of sufficient evidence to satisfy him that the person who dealt with the registrar did so in good faith and had no knowledge at the time of completion of the transaction that the attorney was not a person to whom the trustee functions in relation to the land could be delegated under that section. This evidence may consist of or include a statutory declaration or certificate in Form 3 (see Sch.3 to the Rules) or, if evidence of non-revocation is also required pursuant to r.62, in Form 2.

Powers of attorney given to receivers

9–011 The subject of powers of attorney given to receivers in debentures is discussed in Chapter 19.

Correction of mistakes in an application or accompanying document

9–012 Rule 130 allows for an alteration to be made by the registrar for the purpose of correcting a mistake in any application or accompanying document. The alteration has effect as if made by the applicant or other interested party or parties in all circumstances if it is a case of a mistake of a clerical or like nature. In the case of any other mistake it only has this effect if the applicant and any other interested party has requested or consented to the alteration.

Electronic lodgement of applications to change the register

9–013 Some applications to change the register can be lodged electronically. This includes change of name of a registered proprietor or other person referred to on the register by marriage or deed poll, change of address for service of the registered proprietor, change of property description and entry of a restriction in Form A following the severance of an equitable joint tenancy by notice. Only certain categories of customer can lodge electronic applications — only conveyancers, as defined by r.217 (as amended by the Land Registration (Amendment) Rules 2005), can use this service. Instead of supplying some form of documentary proof for such alterations of the register, where application is lodged electronically a conveyancer must certify that he has seen the appropriate evidence. Electronic lodgement of applications is only open to users of Land Registry Direct. Once the e-application is delivered, Registry staff make the necessary changes to the register. Once completed, the conveyancer receives an acknowledgment through the post or document exchange as usual. Other users must lodge a paper application, in the usual way, accompanied by suitable documentary evidence of the change.

Plans containing a statement of disclaimer

9–014 Reference should be made to Chapter 2.

Unregistered interests which override registered dispositions

Schedule 3 to the Act lists those interests which override **9–015** registered dispositions notwithstanding the fact that they are not mentioned on the register. They are as follows:

(1) A leasehold estate in land granted for a term not exceeding seven years from the date of the grant, except for a lease which the lessee is under a duty to register.

(2) An interest belonging at the time of the disposition to a person in actual occupation except for:

- an interest under a settlement under the Settled Land Act 1925;
- an interest of a person of whom enquiry was made before the disposition and who failed to disclose the right when he could reasonably have been expected to do so;
- an interest of a person whose occupation would not have been obvious on a reasonably careful inspection of the land at the time of the disposition and which the person acquiring the interest did not know about at that time; and
- a leasehold estate granted to take effect in possession more than three months from the date of the grant but which has not taken effect in possession at the time of the disposition.

Judicial decisions under s.70 of the Land Registration Act 1925 illustrate the importance of the overriding interests of persons "in actual occupation". These are highlighted in Chapter 4.

(3) A legal easement or profit à prendre except for one which is not registered under the Commons Registration Act 1965, which at the time of the disposition is not within the actual knowledge of the person to whom the disposition is made and would not have been obvious on a reasonably careful inspection of the land over which the easement or profit is exercisable (unless the person entitled to the easement or profit proves that it has been exercised in the period of one year ending with the day of the disposition).

(4) A customary right.

(5) A public right.

(6) A local land charge.

(7) An interest in any coal or coal mine, the rights attached to any such interest and the rights of any person under ss.38, 49 or 51 of the Coal Industry Act 1994.

(8) In the case of land to which title was registered before 1898, rights to mines and minerals (and incidental rights) created before 1898.

(9) In the case of land to which title was registered between 1898 and 1925 inclusive, rights to mines and minerals (and incidental rights) created before the date of registration of the title.

(10) A franchise.

(11) A manorial right.

(12) A right to rent which was reserved to the Crown on the granting of any freehold estate (whether or not the right is still vested in the Crown).

(13) A non-statutory right in respect of an embankment or sea or river wall.

(14) A right to payment in lieu of tithe.

At the end of a period of 10 years beginning on October 13, 2003, (10) to (14) above will cease to be interests that override registered dispositions (s.117). Paragraph 8 of Sch.12 to the Act inserts a further paragraph into Sch.3. It provides that those who are in receipt of rents and profits from the land upon the coming into force of Sch.3 are granted overriding status whilst they continue to be in receipt of those rents and profits. The overriding status is lost once they are no longer in receipt. Furthermore, there will be no overriding status where the recipient was asked prior to the disposition but failed to disclose the right when he could reasonably have been expected to do so.

Article 2(2) of the Land Registration Act 2002 (Transitional Provisions) (No.2) Order 2003 inserts a further paragraph into Sch.3 for the period of 10 years beginning on October 13, 2003. For that period a right in respect of the repair of a church chancel has overriding status.

The effect of para. 9 of Sch.12 to the Act is that easements which had overriding status by virtue of the 1925 Act, but which would not under Sch.3, will retain that status indefinitely.

Paragraph 10 of Sch.12 to the Act provides that for a period of three years from October 13, 2003, any legal easement or profit that is not registered will override a registered disposition and that the exception mentioned at (3) above will not have effect.

For a period of three years from October 13, 2003, where an adverse possessor is entitled to be registered as proprietor of a registered estate because of his adverse possession under s.75 of the 1925 Act, that right will be overriding (para.11 of Sch.12 to the Act).

Paragraph 12 of Sch.12 to the Act ensures that leases granted prior to October 13, 2003, for less than 21 years retain the overriding status they enjoyed by virtue of s.70(1)(k) of the 1925 Act.

Duty to disclose unregistered interests which override registered dispositions

Section 71 and r.57 impose a new duty on the applicant for **9–016** registration of a registrable disposition of a registered estate to provide information to the registrar about any of the interests that override first registration which are:

(1) within the actual knowledge of the applicant, and

(2) affect the estate to which the application relates.

Such information must be provided in the application for registration on Form DI. There is no requirement to provide information about:

(a) interests that cannot be protected by notice (see Chapter 15);

(b) public rights;

(c) leases granted for a term not exceeding seven years from the date of the grant, not being a lease which the lessee is under a duty to register, when at the time of the application, the term granted by the lease has one year or less to run; and

(d) local land charges.

Form AP1 requires the applicant or his conveyancer to certify either that Form DI accompanies the application or that the application is not one to register a registrable disposition or that it is but no disclosable interests affect.

Once an interest has been disclosed the registrar will make any appropriate entry on the register and the interest will then cease to be overriding.

Outline applications

9–017 Outline applications can be lodged under r.54 to reserve periods of priority for interests that cannot be protected by official searches (see Chapter 8). The interest protected by the outline application must exist at the time that it is lodged. It cannot be used in respect of first registration applications and can only be used to protect an interest in the whole of the land in a title. If the outline application is to work, the papers supporting the application must be lodged at the appropriate office by noon on the fourth business day (as defined in r.217) following the day the outline application was taken as made. The supporting application must quote the official reference number of the outline application that was provided when it was lodged.

If the supporting papers are lodged in the time specified, registration will be effected from the date and time the outline application was received. The outline application will be subject to any other outline applications or pending applications or searches that existed when it was made.

Application can be made by telephone by credit account holders, through LR Direct by subscribers and orally by personal attendance at a Customer Information Centre.

The details which are required when an outline application is lodged are:

(1) credit account key number;

(2) the title number affected;

(3) the name of the registered proprietor or applicant for first registration;

(4) the nature of the application;

(5) the name of the applicant;

(6) the name and address of the person or firm lodging the application.

A fee calculated in accordance with the current Fee Order, is payable.

Requisitions from the Registry

9–018 Requisitions from the Registry should be dealt with as expeditiously as possible and in accordance with the time limits for reply specified. Delay may result in the cancellation of the application. For more details see Chapter 1.

Chapter 10

Transfers

Sale of registered land

Contract

When a formal contract is desired, one of the usual printed **10–001** forms may be used. The contract may be protected on the register by a notice under s.32. A plan will usually be necessary on a sale of part of the land in a title (see below).

Deduction of title

How title is deduced by a seller to a buyer is a matter of **10–002** negotiation and contract but on a sale of registered land the seller will normally provide the buyer's conveyancer with:

(1) a copy of the subsisting entries on the register;

(2) copies or abstracts of any documents referred to on the register which affect the land except those relating to incumbrances to be discharged on or before completion; and

(3) a copy of the plan of the title (see Chapter 8 "Certificate of official inspection of the title plan" as to the provision of an official certificate of inspection of the title plan instead of an official copy of that plan where the disposition affects part of the land in a title — rr.134(1)(d) and 143).

The preferred method of providing these copies is to obtain from the Registry an official copy of the register and of any document or plan required. These can be requested on Forms OC1, OC2 and EX2 (see Chapter 8). They may also be requested or inspected via LR Direct. Official copies do not require verification, since s.67(1) provides that such copies shall be admissible in evidence to the same extent as the originals would be admissible.

The seller will also normally provide the buyer with such copies, abstracts and evidence (if any) as the buyer would have been entitled to if the land had been unregistered in respect of:

(a) any subsisting rights and interests as to which the register is not conclusive; and

(b) any matters excepted from the effect of registration.

An example of (a) would be a right of way as to which the register recorded merely that the proprietor claimed it. Examples of (b) would be weekly tenancies and local land charges.

Investigation of title

10–003 If official copies have been supplied no verification of them is necessary. However, if copies or a Title Information Document or land or charge certificate only are supplied, it is necessary to examine these against the register, title plan and documents kept by the registrar at the Registry.

Requisitions on title may be made but, apart from the usual common form requisitions, it is likely that very little will need to be the subject of any inquiry. The buyer's conveyancer must, of course, consider all subsisting entries on the register. He must ensure that any restriction limiting the seller's powers of disposition will be complied with, and that such action (if any) as may be appropriate will be taken in regard to other entries, for example that a registered charge will be discharged, or that a caution will be withdrawn, at or before completion.

Conveyancers must use the prescribed forms of transfer (see below). When the prescribed form of transfer is used without addition or alteration, the submission of a draft is unnecessary.

Except as discussed in Chapter 8 there is no need to search the registers maintained by the Land Charges Department when investigating an absolute registered title, but the usual searches in local land charges registers and other local inquiries must be made.

Where land is registered with absolute title, a buyer from a limited company acting in good faith and having the backing of an official search need not search in the Companies Registry. However, in any case of doubt it might well be prudent for an intending chargee of a company's registered land to make a prior search in the Companies Registry because, for example, the fact of the chargor company's dissolution would be discovered.

The possibility of interests which are binding on persons who acquire an interest in registered land notwithstanding that there is no entry in the register (s.29, r.57 and Sch.3 to the Act) must be considered; and in this context judicial decisions relating to the rights of persons in actual occupation should be kept in mind (see Chapter 4).

Official search of the register
Immediately before completion the conveyancer must find out **10–004** whether any adverse entry has been made in the register since the date of an official copy of the register or the date given as the subsisting entries date at the time of access by remote terminal using Land Registry Direct.

This information is obtained by making an application for an official search of the register in Form OS1 or OS2 as explained in Chapter 8.

In addition to disclosing the state of the register, the official certificate of search enables the purchase to be safely completed at a distance from the appropriate office without personal attendance there to make a last-minute search of the register. This is so because the official certificate of search gives priority to the application to register the transfer if that application is deemed to have been delivered to the appropriate office within the priority period conferred by the official certificate of search. The official search procedure is also available to chargees and lessees; and if the transferee is to charge the land, a search on behalf of the chargee will give priority to both the application to register the transfer and an application to register the charge. These matters are more fully discussed in Chapter 8.

Completion
On completion of a purchase the buyer's conveyancer must **10–005** obtain the executed transfer from the seller's conveyancer. If the whole of the land in a registered title has been purchased and there is a subsisting registered charge, which is to be paid off at completion, the seller's conveyancer will hand over a discharge in Form DS1 or, as is more likely, an undertaking that as soon as he receives the Form DS1 it will be forwarded to the buyer's conveyancer (see below). Some lenders use the Electronic Notification of Discharge system (ENDs) to discharge registered charges (see Chapter 13). In those circumstances the buyer's conveyancer will need to obtain a different form of undertaking from the seller's conveyancer, namely one to send the moneys required to discharge the charge and the Form END1 to the lender. Otherwise the arrangements for completion are no different. Where Form DS1 has been handed over at completion the application to register the discharge and the application to register the transfer can be made together (see Chapter 9 as to the form of the application, and Chapter 13 as to discharges generally).

Where Form DS1 cannot be handed over at completion or the discharge is to be via an END, and the buyer's conveyancer receives a suitable form of undertaking from the seller's conveyancer, it is unnecessary to defer lodging the application for registration until the Form DS1 is received or confirmation is received from the lender that an END has been sent to the Registry. If the priority secured by obtaining the official certificate of search of the register mentioned above might be lost the application may be lodged at once with Form AP1 being endorsed to the effect that a Form DS1 is awaited or the END system is being used. In due course if the Form DS1 or END has not been received the Registry will requisition for it.

If the land is being transferred subject to the charge, the transfer alone will need to be handed over, the chargee being a party to the transfer.

If the transfer is of part of the land in the title and the part being transferred is being released from the registered charge, rather than the whole registered charge being discharged, the buyer's conveyancer must obtain from the seller's conveyancer a release in Form DS3 or a suitable undertaking. An END cannot currently be used to discharge part of the land in a title from a charge.

After completion: registration of the transfer

10–006 The land transaction effected by the transfer must be notified to the Inland Revenue by the completion and submission of a Land Transaction Return, unless the transaction is one not requiring notification to the Inland Revenue but one requiring a self-certificate form signed by the buyer (or one which is exempt from Stamp Duty Land Tax or outside its scope and not requiring notification or a self-certificate). The Land Transaction Return Certificate or self-certificate (or letter of explanation if neither of these two documents is appropriate) must be submitted to the Registry when registering the transfer (see Chapter 1).

The transfer must be delivered to the appropriate office for registration within the priority period conferred by the official search of the register in Form OS1 or OS2 (see Chapter 8).

The application to register the transfer, which will, of course, commonly be delivered together with applications to register a discharge of a registered charge and a new charge by the transferee, should be made on a Form AP1. (For points arising on this form, see Chapter 9).

Section 27 and Sch.2 to the Act provide that for a transfer to operate at law, the transferee or his successor in title must be entered in the register as proprietor. In the case of a transfer of part, such details of the transfer as rules may provide must also be entered in the register in relation to the registered estate out of which the transfer is made (see r.72).

Transfers attract a fee which should be calculated in accordance with the current Fee Order. A statement in writing, signed by the applicant or his conveyancer, of the full open market value, free from any charge of the land, must be supplied in the case of a transfer otherwise than for monetary consideration.

Forms of transfers

The Rules prescribe various forms of transfers for use according to the circumstances (Sch.1 and Sch.3 to the Rules — see Chapter 9). Rule 58 states that a transfer must be in Form TP1, TP2, TP3, TR1, TR2, TR5, AS1 or AS3, as appropriate. Rule 59 prescribes the forms of transfer which must be used to effect a transfer by way of exchange and deals with the need for a receipt for equality money and suitable additional wording for the transfer. Rule 60 covers transfers of leasehold land where the rent is being apportioned or the land is being exonerated. Schedule 1 and Sch.3 forms are listed in Appendix III. **10–007**

Covenants, implied covenants and easements

These are covered in Chapter 7. **10–008**

Transfer of part: plan

Rule 213 provides that a transfer of part of the land in a registered title must have attached to it a plan clearly identifying the land dealt with. The only exception to this is when the land dealt with is clearly identified on the title plan of the registered title when it may be described by reference to that title plan rather than attaching a new plan. Where a plan is attached the transferor must sign the plan. Ideally a plan should be based on the title plan of the transferor's title or be capable, in the case of new developments, of being associated with it. If the land transferred is not physically defined other than by surveyors' pegs, the boundaries shown on the plan should be tied to permanent features by accurate measurements (see Chapter 20 as to transfers of plots on registered building estates). **10–009**

Transfers to two or more transferees

10–010 A transfer to two or more persons is not required to include any special form of words on this account. However, the prescribed forms of transfer contain a panel entitled "Declaration of trust" for completion where there is more than one transferee. The appropriate box should be completed depending upon whether the transferees are holding the property on trust for themselves as joint tenants beneficially, or as tenants in common in equal shares, or as the case may be.

Completion of the declaration and execution by the transferees should not be overlooked.

If the registrar enters two or more persons in the register as the proprietor of a registered estate in land, he is obliged, under s.44, to enter the following restriction (Form A of Sch.4 to the Rules — see r.95) to ensure that interests which are capable of being overreached on a disposition of the estate are overreached:

> "No disposition by a sole proprietor of the registered estate (except a trust corporation) under which capital money arises is to be registered unless authorised by an order of the court."

Fees on transfers to give effect to dealings with undivided shares

10–011 The current Fee Order contains express provisions as to the fee payable on the registration of a transfer for the purpose of giving effect to a disposition of a share in registered land or a registered charge.

Subject to some exceptions, if the disposition of a share is for monetary consideration (as defined in the Fee Order) the fee is payable on the amount of the consideration.

If the disposition of a share is otherwise than for monetary consideration the fee is payable on the value of that share.

The value of the land is the open market value free of any charge at the date of the application and a statement of such value, signed by the applicant or his conveyancer, should accompany the application.

Particular parties to transfers

Corporations

10–012 Rules 181 to 183 cover the registration of companies, limited liability partnerships, trustees of charitable, ecclesiastical or public trusts and other corporations. Those rules set out the

Registry's requirements when application is made for registration of one of those bodies as registered proprietor of a registered estate or registered charge. It should be noted in particular that where a company registered in England and Wales or Scotland under the Companies Acts applies to be registered, the application must state the company's registered number. Where a corporation or body of trustees holding on charitable, ecclesiastical or public trusts applies to be registered, the application must be accompanied by the document creating the trust. Where some other corporation aggregate applies to be registered, the application must be accompanied by evidence of the extent of its powers to hold and sell, mortgage, lease and otherwise deal with land and, in the case of a charge, to lend money on mortgage.

These provisions enable any appropriate restrictions to be entered in the register. In the absence of any relevant restriction in the register, no evidence of a corporation's power to transfer land of which it is the registered proprietor is required. The question as to whether a purchaser of registered land from a company should search in the Companies Registry to guard against the possibility that the company may have been dissolved is considered above.

Insolvency is considered in Chapter 19.

Overseas companies
Where an application is made to register an overseas company **10–013** as proprietor of land or of a charge it should be accompanied by a certified copy of the equivalent of the memorandum and articles with a certified translation if not in English. The Registry will be particularly anxious to ensure that the applicant is a legal entity with power to purchase and charge or to accept a charge on English and/or Welsh land and to ascertain the formalities applicable to execution of documents by the applicant. The registrar will enter any appropriate restriction to reflect any limitations on the power of the company to deal with land, revealed by the documentation lodged.

Personal representatives
Transfers by personal representatives are discussed in Chapter **10–014** 18.

Trustees and Charities
These topics are considered in Chapter 17.   **10–015**

Chapter 11

Leases

Leases of registered land

The lessor's title to grant and lease

Paragraph 2 of Sch.10 to the Act allows for rules to be made as **11–001** to the evidence of title which must be provided on a lease of registered land but no such rules have been made. An intending lessee of registered land is, therefore, entitled to such evidence of his intending lessor's title as the agreement for lease provides. However, an intending lessee can obtain an official copy of the register and title plan of the lessor's title and of any superior title and use the official search procedure. Inspection of the register, official copies and official searches are discussed in Chapter 8.

A proprietor of registered land has full power to lease his land (or to sub-lease if it is leasehold) subject to any entry to the contrary in the register. For example a restriction may have to be complied with, or a registered chargee's consent obtained. Where a lease is registered with good leasehold title that title is only guaranteed so far as the lessor had power to grant it (s.12). A lessee who takes his title from a registered freeholder or a registered leaseholder takes subject to any restrictive covenants on the lessor's register even though the covenants do not appear on the register of his own title (s.12).

Form of lease

No form of lease was prescribed by the Rules as originally made **11–002** so that the lease could be in any form provided that it referred to the lessor's title number and, if it was a lease of part of the land in a title, it referred to a plan enabling the demised premises to be identified on the title plan of the lessor's title. The route of any easements and like rights must similarly be clearly identified. See Chapter 9 as to the execution of the lease and Chapter 10 as to the signature of any plan. Usually, in the case of a lease, the lessor will sign the plan to the lease and the lessee will sign the plan to the counterpart.

Prescribed clauses lease

11–003 The Land Registration (Amendment) (No.2) Rules 2005, the relevant provisions of which come into force on January 9, 2006, introduce prescribed clauses lease. Starting on June 19, 2006 use of a prescribed clauses lease will be compulsory (with certain limited exceptions) for registrable leases granted out of a registered title. For a six month voluntary period beginning in January 2006, conveyancers will be encouraged to use the prescribed clauses. During the voluntary period, the Registry will provide advice on how to improve applications so that by June conveyancers should have no problems in using the new forms.

A prescribed clauses lease must begin with the required wording (*see below*) or that wording must appear immediately after any front sheet. "Front sheet" means a front cover sheet, or a contents or index sheet at the beginning of the lease, or a front cover sheet and contents or index sheet where the contents or index sheet is immediately after the front cover sheet.

"Required wording" means the wording in Sch.1A to the Rules as inserted by the Land Registration (Amendment) (No 2) Rules 2005 completed in accordance with the instructions in that schedule as appropriate for the particular lease, The Schedule sets out in table form prescribed clauses numbered LR1 to LR14.

A "prescribed clauses lease" is a lease of registered land granted on or after June 19, 2006 which is required to be registered under s.27(2)(b) of the Act and which is not granted in a form, expressly required by:

(i) an agreement entered into before June 19, 2006;

(ii) an order of the court;

(iii) or under an enactment;

(iv) a necessary consent or licence for the grant of a lease given before June 19, 2006.

A lease created by a variation of a lease which is a deemed surrender and re-grant is not a prescribed clauses lease.

A new r.72A, inserted by the Land Registration (Amendment) (No.2) Rules 2005, specifies certain entries which the registrar is obliged to make based on the required wording on registration of a lease of registered land granted on or after June 19, 2006 which is required to be registered under s.27(2)(b) of the Act. Rule 72A also specifies situations where the registrar is required to take no action.

Under r.72A, on completion of such a lease by registration the registrar must (where appropriate) make entries in the relevant registers in respect of interests contained in the lease referred to in clauses LR9 (rights of acquisition), LR10 (restrictive covenants), LR11 (easements) and LR 12 (estate rentcharge). The requirement to make an entry in respect of an interest referred to in clause LR12 is satisfied by entry (where appropriate) of notice of the interest created.

Where the lease is a prescribed clauses lease and it contains clause LR8 (prohibitions or restrictions on disposing of the lease) or it contains interests of the nature referred to in clauses LR9, LR10, LR11 and LR12, but the prohibition or restriction or interests are not specified or referred to in those clauses, then the registrar need take no action in respect of them unless a separate application is made. Rule 6(2) which requires the registrar to make an entry on registration in respect of a prohibition or restriction on disposing of a lease is amended accordingly.

The registrar is not required to make entries in respect of interests of the nature referred to in clauses LR9, LR10 or LR11 or clause LR13 (standard form of restriction) where:

(a) in the case of a prescribed clauses lease, the title numbers of the individual registers have not been given in clause LR2.2, or

(b) in any other case, the title numbers of the individual registers required by clause LR2.2 have not been given in panel 2 of the Form AP1 lodged for the purpose of completing the lease by registration,

unless a separate application is made in respect of the interests or restriction.

Where a separate application is made in Form AP1 in respect of either a prohibition or restriction on disposal or an easement, the AP1 must specify the particular clause, or paragraph of a schedule, where the prohibition or restriction or easement is contained in the lease.

Rule 92 is altered so as to relax the requirement for a Form RX1 to be lodged where application for the entry of a standard form of restriction is made in clause LR13 of a relevant lease. "Relevant lease" is defined as:

(a) a prescribed clauses lease or

(b) any other lease which complies with the requirements as to form and content of a prescribed clauses lease and which either is required to be completed by registration under s.27(2)(b) of the Act or is the subject of an application for first registration of the title to it.

If it appears to the registrar that a lease is not a prescribed clauses lease, then these requirements shall not apply to that lease even though the lease would otherwise be a prescribed clauses lease.

Searches

11–004 The usual local searches and inquiries are necessary. An official search, see Chapter 8, of the register of the lessor's title should be obtained. No search in the Land Charges Department or at the Companies Registry against a lessor registered with absolute or good leasehold title is necessary.

Completion

11–005 In addition to obtaining the lease the lessee's conveyancer should obtain any consents, *e.g.* by a chargee, that the register of the lessor's title shows to be necessary.

Registration (s.27)

11–006 A lease of land for a term of years absolute granted by the proprietor of a registered title must be completed by registration and by the entry of notice of the lease in the register of the lessor's title (para.3 of Pt 1 of Sch.2 to the Act) where:

(1) it is granted for a term of more than seven years from the date of the lease;

(2) whatever the length of the term, it will take effect in possession after the end of a period of more than three months beginning with the date of the lease;

(3) the right to possession is discontinuous, *e.g.* a timeshare lease; or

(4) the lease is a right to buy lease granted pursuant to Pt 5 of the Housing Act 1985 or a lease where the right to buy is preserved under s.171A of the Housing Act 1985.

This is the position whether the registered land out of which the lease is granted is freehold or leasehold.

A lease must be lodged with appropriate evidence complying with the provisions as to Stamp Duty Land Tax or stamp duty as explained in Chapter 1.

An application for substantive registration of the title to the lease must be made on Form AP1. The form and its completion are discussed in Chapter 9. Notice of the lease is entered on the lessor's title by the Registry as a matter of course whenever substantive registration of the title to a lease of registered land takes place.

Leasehold interests incapable of substantive registration
There are two cases in which leasehold interests created out of **11–007** registered land are incapable of substantive registration. These are:

(1) a lease granted for a term of seven years or less except for those mentioned at para.11–006 above; and

(2) an agreement for a lease.

As regards (1), the lease will be an overriding interest not requiring protection on the register (see Chapter 9) unless it contains an option (see below).

As regards (2), the agreement may be protected as an estate contract (see Chapter 15).

Easements and restrictive covenants in registered leases

The following note appears at the head of registers of leasehold **11–008** titles:

> "The register describes the land and estate comprised in the title. Except as mentioned below, the title includes any legal easements granted by the registered lease but is subject to any right that it reserves, so far as those easements and rights exist and benefit or affect the registered land."

The appurtenant easements referred to are included in the registration with the same class of title as the land.

If the purported grant of a particular easement by a lease registered with absolute leasehold title is not effective, an entry stating that it is not included in the title will be made in the register.

If a lease of registered land grants to the lessee an easement over land of the lessor lying in a registered title other than that out of which the lease was granted, notice of the grant must be entered in the register of the latter title if the grant is to be effective at law (para.7 of Pt 1 of Sch.2 to the Act).

A restrictive covenant made between a lessor and lessee so far as relating to the demised premises is entered neither on the lessor's nor the lessee's title to the demised premises (s.33(c)) but it should be noted on any other title affected.

Options and rights of pre-emption in leases of registered land

11–009 Where a lease of registered land contains an option or a right of pre-emption granted by the lessor, that option or right should be protected by the entry of notice on the register of the lessor's title. The Registry will make such an entry automatically when notice of the lease is entered on the lessor's title, but if the lease is an overriding interest (see Chapters 4 and 9) a separate application to protect the option or right on the register of the lessor's title, by means of a notice or restriction, is necessary (see Chapter 15).

Official copies of registered leases

11–010 Official copies of registered leases may be obtained from the Registry as explained in Chapter 8.

Apportionment of or exoneration from rent

1–1011 Under r.60 a transfer of a registered leasehold title containing a legal apportionment of or exoneration from the rent reserved by the lease must include the following statement in the additional provisions panel, with any necessary alterations and additions:

> "Liability for the payment of [*if applicable* the previously apportioned rent of £(*amount*) being part of] the rent reserved by the registered lease is apportioned between the Transferor and the Transferee as follows—
> £(*amount*) shall be payable out of the Property and the balance shall be payable out of the land remaining in title number (*title number of retained land*) or
> the whole of that rent shall be payable out of the Property and none of it shall be payable out of the land remaining in title number (*title number of retained land*) or
> the whole of that rent shall be payable out of the land remaining in title number (*title number of retained land*) and none of it shall be payable out of the Property".

A proprietor's title to registered land may be affected by a ministerial order apportioning a rent either unconditionally or conditionally upon the redemption of the apportioned rent. An application should then be made to the appropriate office for effect to be given to the order on the register of the title; but where the apportionment is made conditional on the redemption of the apportioned rent the application should not be made until after the redemption has taken place. If it is not known whether the title of the land affected is registered, an application for a Search of the Index Map — see Chapter 2 — should be made.

The application should be made on Form AP1. It should be supported by:

(1) an official copy of the order and, in the case of a conditional order, an official copy of the certificate of redemption; and

(2) the fee assessed as below.

If the proprietor making the application is a lessee and he applies for the order to be registered not only on his own title but on his lessor's, there must also be lodged the lessor's consent to the application; and this requirement applies, equally, where a lessor proprietor making the application applies against his own and his lessee's title.

A fee calculated under the current Fee Order is payable.

Variation of leases

An application to register notice of a deed of variation of a **11–012** registered lease or of a lease that is merely noted against the lessor's title should be made against the registered title (or, if both lease and reversion are registered, against both titles). The application should be made on Form AP1 and should be accompanied by the deed of variation and evidence that the variation has effect at law (r.78).

A fee calculated under the current Fee Order is payable.

Where the title to the lease is registered, if all persons appearing from the register to be interested in the lease are parties to the deed or have concurred in the application the entry in the register will state that the deed has varied the lease. In any other circumstances the entry will give notice of the deed but will not guarantee its validity.

Deed of variation varying the term — If a lessee takes a new lease of the same property before the existing lease has expired then the original lease is treated as surrendered immediately before the new lease. As the term of a lease cannot be altered by deed of variation, the Registry will treat any deed purporting to vary the term of a registered lease as a new lease which will, therefore, have the effect of surrendering the original lease. The proper application in such a case will be for closure of the title to the original lease and registration of the new lease (if as varied, it is for a registrable term). The deed of variation, in such a case, will have to be accompanied by a Land Transaction Return certificate or self certificate or by a letter explaining why neither certificate is required.

Determination of leases

Registered lease

11–013 Where a registered lease has determined the registered title will be closed by application made on Form AP1 accompanied by the appropriate evidence of determination including the lease if available. If the lease cannot be produced an explanation should be given. If there is a registered charge of the lease, the charge must be discharged. Any caution on the register of the title to the lease must be withdrawn. If the title to the lease is possessory, evidence sufficient for its conversion to good leasehold must be lodged, and any incumbrance that would prevent merger revealed by such evidence must be discharged before merger of the lease can be registered. If the merger or surrender requires the consent of any incumbrancer of the superior estate, that consent must also be lodged. If the surrender is by deed for value the application should be accompanied by a Land Transaction Return certificate or self certificate or by a letter explaining why neither certificate is required.

If the lease is to be surrendered by deed, it may take the form of a transfer in Form TR1 suitably adapted. For example, it may be appropriate to insert before the words of transfer: "For the purpose of surrendering the term comprised in the registered title and in consideration of   ".

If the lease has been surrendered not in writing but by operation of law, evidence must be given of the acts from which surrender is to be implied. Surrender may be implied, for example, from the grant of a new lease to the same lessee. If the surrender is to be implied from the acts of the parties in giving up and accepting possession, evidence of the facts should be given in a statutory declaration. The statutory declaration must be made by a reliable person with full knowledge of the facts. It must:

(1) specify the amount of any consideration paid for the surrender;

(2) confirm that there was no deed of surrender;

(3) if the tenant was occupying the property describe when and how the premises were vacated and the keys returned to the landlord; and

(4) if an underlessee is occupying the property, contain evidence that the landlord is receiving the rent directly from that underlessee. He may do this by exhibiting to a statutory declaration the counterpart of the underlease and a copy of the authority requiring the underlessee to pay the rent directly to him.

If possible, the registered proprietor of the surrendered lease should be persuaded to join in the application to close his registered title. In such a case a statutory declaration will not be required but a letter from either party's conveyancer will be required confirming that there has been no deed of surrender.

A fee calculated under the current Fee Order is payable.

Unregistered lease noted on a registered title
Application must be made on Form CN1 accompanied by all the **11–014** title documents to the determined lease which should be listed on Form DL.

If the lease has determined on merger, surrender or disclaimer the applicant or his conveyancer must certify either that:

(1) all rights, interests and claims affecting the property known to the applicant are disclosed in the title documents and there is no-one in adverse possession of the property or any part of it; or

(2) in addition to the rights, interests and claims affecting the property disclosed in the title documents, the applicant only knows of those set out on the Form CN1.

If the lease has determined on forfeiture a statutory declaration or other supporting evidence of the facts relied on must be lodged (see Land Registry Practice Guide 26).

If the lease has determined by effluxion of time the applicant or his conveyancer must certify that the provisions of the Landlord and Tenant Act 1954 and the Local Government and Housing Act 1989 do not apply.

If the lease has determined as a result of notice under the Landlord and Tenant Act 1954 or the Local Government and Housing Act 1989 and the provisions of that Act have been complied with the applicant or his conveyancer must so certify.

Merger of an unregistered lease on the first registration of the superior estate

11–015 The lease and all the deeds and documents of title relating to it should be lodged with the application for first registration with the documents of title of the superior estate. The question of merger will be considered by the Registry, in conjunction with the examination of the title to the superior estate, according to the ordinary principles of land law.

A fee calculated under the current Fee Order is payable.

Assignment or surrender of an unregistered lease to the owner of the immediate reversion where the term is to merge in that reversion

11–016 If as a result of an assignment or surrender there is an immediate merger of the leasehold estate in the immediate reversion the provisions requiring compulsory registration do not apply (s.4(4)(b)).

Agreement for lease

11–017 An agreement for a lease of registered land may be protected as an estate contract on the register of the title to the land by a notice or a restriction (see Chapter 15).

Leasehold Reform Act 1967 ("the 1967 Act")

Preliminary investigations

11–018 A tenant who wishes to enfranchise or to have an extended lease may wish to find out whether his landlord's or any superior landlord's title is registered. He can do so by a search of the index map (see Chapter 2).

If superior titles are registered, the tenant may apply for official copies of the registers and of documents referred to on the registers including leases and charges as described in Chapter 8.

Protecting the tenant's claim (s.5(5) of the 1967 Act)

11–019 The rights of a tenant arising from a notice under the 1967 Act do not take effect as overriding interests (see Chapters 4 and 9). When a tenant has given his landlord notice of his wish to enfranchise or to take an extended lease, he can protect his claim by the entry of a notice on the register(s) of the reversionary title(s) affected (see Chapter 15).

Assignment of the rights under the 1967 Act of a tenant who has served notice of his wish to enfranchise or to have an extended lease

The assignment of such rights should not be included in a **11–020** transfer of a registered leasehold estate but should be carried out by a separate instrument off the register.

No entry of such an assignment will be made on the register of the tenant's title but if the rights are protected by unilateral notice, the assignee should apply to be registered as beneficiary of the notice on Form UN3 (see Chapter 15).

Enfranchisement

Rights and burdens under s.10 of the 1967 Act — If the Registry is **11–021** aware that a conveyance or transfer has been made under the 1967 Act, appropriate entries will be made in the register as to the benefit and burden of rights passing under s.10(2) of that Act when the conveyance or transfer is registered. If the conveyance or transfer includes new easements or restrictive covenants under s.10(3) or (4), entries will be made in the register in the ordinary way.

In some instances rights originally granted or reserved affecting the leasehold interest will, by virtue of s.10 of the 1967 Act, now affect the freehold estate. If reference to the deed which granted or reserved those rights is required to be made on the register, this should be expressly requested and the original deed, or, where appropriate, a certified copy or examined abstract of it, should be lodged.

Discharge of charges on the landlord's registered or unregistered title — The chargee may have expressly discharged the charge or released the land from it in the appropriate way according to whether the landlord's title is registered or unregistered. If not, and if the tenant claims that he has paid to the chargee enough money to discharge the land from the charge, a verified copy of the chargee's (appropriately worded) receipt must be lodged. If, however, there has been no express discharge or release, but sufficient money to discharge or release the land has been paid into court by the tenant under s.13 of the 1967 Act, there must be lodged a verified copy of the affidavit the tenant will have made for that purpose, and a verified copy of the court's official receipt.

If there has been an express discharge or release, or if, on the receipt of the appropriate evidence of payment to the chargee or into court, the Registry is satisfied that the tenant may be registered as the freeholder free from the charge, no entry of the charge will appear on the register of the tenant's freehold title. In appropriate cases notice will be served on the registered chargee explaining the nature of the transaction and inviting him to consent. If in response to the notice the chargee gives prima facie grounds for objection, the application cannot proceed until the objection is disposed of either by agreement or following reference to the Adjudicator.

In the case of a floating charge by a landlord company, a certificate by the solicitor, secretary or other responsible officer of the company or of the debenture holder that the charge had not crystallised at the date of the conveyance or transfer on enfranchisement will be accepted as sufficient evidence for the registration of the tenant's freehold free from the charge.

Rentcharge on the landlord's title — Where the land has been discharged from a rentcharge and money has been paid into court under s.11(4) of the 1967 Act, the evidence of payment to be lodged at the Registry should be a verified copy of the tenant's or landlord's affidavit and a verified copy of the court's receipt (*cf. discharge of registered charges on the landlord's registered or unregistered title,* above).

Extended lease

11–022 An application to register the title to an extended lease should take the form of a normal application for first registration, associated, when appropriate, with an application to give effect on the register to the surrender of the tenant's existing lease, which must be taken to have been surrendered by operation of law.

When a tenant's title to his existing lease is neither registered nor noted on a landlord's registered title, the application for first registration of the title to the extended lease should be accompanied by ordinary conveyancing evidence of the tenant's title to his existing lease. This is necessary, whether absolute or good leasehold title is sought, so that appropriate entries can be made on the register of the tenant's title to the extended lease as to any rights of a mortgagee of the existing lease.

If the extended lease incorporates the terms of the existing lease, a certified copy or examined abstract of the existing lease is required for filing in the Registry.

If the title to the existing lease is registered, an application to close the title, and to cancel the notice of the lease on the register of the landlord's title if that title is registered, should be made and should be accompanied by the lease.

If a charge of the existing lease is registered and is being discharged, the discharge should be lodged.

Where there is charge noted or registered against the existing registered lease the Registry will serve on the chargee a notice explaining the nature of the application. If no objection is received in reply to the notice, the registered title to the existing lease will be closed.

If the landlord's title is unregistered, prima facie evidence (*e.g.* an examined abstract) of it will be needed. The extended lease or its counterpart (or where appropriate the lodgment of an application to register the tenant's title to the extended lease) will be sufficient evidence of the surrender.

See under para.11–013 above for details of fees payable.

If the title to the existing lease is unregistered, but notice of it is entered on the landlord's registered title, an application to cancel the notice should be made on Form CN1 (see above).

A fee assessed under the current Fee Order will be payable.

The ordinary considerations governing the grant of absolute or good leasehold title (see Chapter 1) apply, except that for the grant of absolute title express consent to the grant of the extended lease by a landlord's chargee or mortgagee is only necessary where the existing lease was:

(1) granted after January 1, 1968; and

(2) granted after the date of the charge or mortgage; and

(3) outside the landlord's leasing powers under the charge or mortgage (see s.14(4) of the 1967 Act).

When a subsisting charge of the existing lease is not discharged, an entry will be made in the charges register of the title to the extended lease to the effect that the extended lease is subject to such rights as may be subsisting in favour of the persons interested in the charge of the original lease. The original charge, if lodged, will be marked "Notice registered against title number the (*number of the title to the extended lease*)" and issued to the person who lodged it. If it was a registered charge, the registration markings will be cancelled. The entry will not be a registration of the charge under s.27. Where, however, a charge of the existing lease is discharged and a new legal charge of the extended lease is executed, the latter can be registered under s.27 if the title to the extended lease is registered.

If the Registry does not know whether an undischarged charge affects the existing lease or not, a suitable entry to protect any rights of any chargee of that lease will be made in the register of the title to the extended lease.

Disclosure to the Registry
When an application to register a transfer of registered land or **11–023** an application for first registration is made to give effect on the register to an enfranchisement or the grant of an extended lease under the 1967 Act, it is essential that the Registry be made aware of this fact.

In the case of an application to register a transfer of registered land, it is best that the fact be disclosed by a suitable addition, *e.g.* "in pursuance of the provisions of the 1967 Act", to the transfer in Form TR1. If not it should be disclosed by a letter accompanying the application. In the case of an application for first registration, it is best that there should be an appropriate recital in the conveyance or lease inducing the application. If not the rights and interests, or potential rights and interests, affecting the applicant's title should be disclosed in the form of application for first registration.

The Landlord and Tenant Act 1987 ("the 1987 Act")

11–024 Where the court has appointed a manager under s.24 of the 1987 Act, because of the landlord's failure to manage his flats properly, if the building is registered the order may be protected by entering a notice or restriction (see Chapter 15).

An application for an acquisition order in respect of registered land under the 1987 Act and an acquisition order made under the 1987 Act may also be protected by a notice or restriction.

The Leasehold Reform, Housing and Urban Development Act 1993 ("the 1993 Act")

Exercise of the tenant's right to collective enfranchisement of flat premises

11–025 Under the 1993 Act certain tenants have the right to have the premises in which they are tenants of a flat acquired by a person or persons whom they appoint. The following special considerations arise when such a right is exercised:

(1) The initial notice served by the tenants on the landlord is not an overriding interest but may be protected on the register of the landlord's title by the entry of a notice (s.97(1) of the 1993 Act and see Chapter 15).

(2) If the tenants make an application to the court for a vesting order because the landlord cannot be found or identified (s.26(1) of the 1993 Act), that application and the order itself when made may be protected by the entry of a notice or a restriction (s.97(2)(b) of the 1993 Act and see Chapter 15).

(3) The conveyance or transfer to the nominee purchaser must contain a statement in the following terms (s.34(10) of the 1993 Act and r.196):

> "This conveyance (or transfer) is executed for the purposes of Chapter I of Part I of the Leasehold Reform, Housing and Urban Development Act 1993."

(4) Unless the landlord and the nominee purchaser agree otherwise the conveyance or transfer to the nominee purchaser discharges the land from any mortgage or charge and it is the duty of the nominee purchaser to apply the consideration payable, in the first instance, in or towards the redemption of any such mortgage or charge and, if there are more than one, then according to their priorities (s.35 and Sch.8(2) to the 1993 Act). Where the land is to be discharged from a mortgage or charge and for any reason difficulty arises in ascertaining how much is payable or difficulty arises in making a payment, *e.g.* because the person entitled cannot be found or refuses to accept payment, the nominee purchaser may pay into court an amount calculated in accordance with the provisions of Sch.8(4) to the 1993 Act. Any application for registration must be accompanied by normal evidence of discharge or by a statutory declaration establishing that the nominee purchaser has applied sufficient part of the purchase money in discharge of the mortgages or charges or into court (para. 2(1) of Sch.8 to the 1993 Act). If such evidence is not lodged the Registry will assume that the mortgage or charge is subsisting.

Grant of a new lease

Qualifying tenants of flats are entitled, on payment of a **11–026** premium, to take a new lease for a term expiring 90 years after the end of the existing lease at a peppercorn rent. If the immediate landlord does not have sufficient interest to grant such a lease the new lease must be granted by the nearest landlord whose lease is sufficient. The following specific points arise:

(1) A notice served by a tenant exercising his rights is not an overriding interest but it may be protected by a notice (s.97(1) of the 1993 Act and see Chapter 15). The benefit of service of notice is assignable. If assigned and protected by agreed notice no further action by the assignee

is necessary to protect his position. If the benefit assigned is of a notice protected by unilateral notice, the assignee should apply to be registered as beneficiary of the notice on Form UN3 (see Chapter 15).

(2) A new lease granted under these provisions must contain the following statement (s.57(11) of the 1993 Act and r.196):

> "This lease is granted under section 56 of the Leasehold Reform, Housing and Urban Development Act 1993."

If the reversion is not registered an application for compulsory first registration of the lease must be lodged (see Chapter 4); if the reversion is registered the lease is registrable as a disposition of registered land (see above).

(3) If the existing lease is subject to a mortgage or charge immediately before surrender, on the grant of a new lease, the mortgage or charge will attach to the new lease (s.58(4) of the 1993 Act). Entries in respect of the subsisting mortgage or charge will be made on the title to the new lease. The Registry will serve notice on the chargee before closing the old title.

Estate Management Scheme under the 1967 and 1993 Acts

11–027 Notice of such a scheme will not be entered on a registered title. To be effective, a scheme must be registered as a local land charge, and if it has been so registered, the entry of notice on a registered title will be unnecessary. Any statutory charge imposed by the scheme will have to be registered before it can be realised (s.55)). Rights under local land charges, unless and until registered or protected on the register of title in the prescribed manner, are overriding interests (see Chapters 4 and 9).

Chapter 12

Commonhold

What is commonhold?

Commonhold is a form of freehold ownership of properties **12–001** which share common parts. It was introduced by Pt 1 of the Commonhold and Leasehold Reform Act 2002 which came into force on September 27, 2004. Until it was introduced such properties were normally held as leasehold because positive covenants to maintain common parts were enforceable under a lease but not where the land was owned freehold.

Commonhold must be registered at Land Registry in accordance with the Commonhold (Land Registration) Rules 2004 and can only be created out of a freehold registered with absolute title. It must consist of a minimum of two residential, commercial or industrial units which share common parts. It cannot be

(1) a flying freehold;

(2) agricultural land; or

(3) a title which could in certain circumstances revert to someone other than the registered proprietor.

Unit-holders in a commonhold development own the freehold of their own unit and are members of a commonhold association, which owns and manages the common parts.

A commonhold unit is each property in the commonhold as defined in the commonhold community statement (see below). It may be a flat and a garage or a flat may be defined as one unit and a garage as another. Common parts are all parts of the commonhold which are not a unit.

A commonhold can be created either where there are no unit-holders and a new development is planned or where freeholders or leaseholders agree to convert an existing development into a commonhold.

An application to register commonhold land can be made by two or more persons who are the registered proprietors of different registered titles if all the land is included in a single commonhold community statement and an individual unit does not straddle more than one title.

If the title is not yet registered an application for first registration can be accompanied by an application to register the commonhold.

The commonhold association

12–002 A commonhold association is a private company limited by guarantee incorporated under the Companies Act 1985. The members of the company are the unit holders with each unit being represented by one member.

The two documents which govern a commonhold are the memorandum and articles of association of the commonhold association and the commonhold community statement. The form and contents of those two documents is prescribed by the Commonhold Regulations 2004.

The memorandum and articles define the powers of the association and contain the rules, *e.g.* voting rights and meetings, under which it operates.

Neither document can be designated as an exempt information document (r.3(3)(c) of the Commonhold (Land Registration) Rules 2004).

The commonhold community statement

12–003 The commonhold community statement:

(1) defines the extent of the commonhold and the extent of the units;

(2) sets out the framework for the commonhold including the regulations for the use and maintenance of the units and the rights and duties of the association and the unit holders; and

(3) describes how management decisions will be taken.

The plan to the commonhold community statement

12–004 The commonhold community statement will define the extent of the commonhold and the extent of each unit in the commonhold by reference to a plan.

To meet the technical requirements and specifications required by Land Registry the plan must:

- be on paper no larger than A0 size;
- clearly show the scale and orientation; and
- be drawn to the scale quoted.

The preferred scale is 1/500 although 1/1250 may be accepted if details of the layout including individual plot boundaries are clear.

Plans which bear a statement of disclaimer intended to comply with the Property Misdescriptions Act 1991 are not acceptable nor are plans marked "For identification only" or with a similar phrase.

The plan must show:

(1) the boundaries of the commonhold land in relation to the boundaries of the registered freeholder's title and the boundaries of the commonhold units in relation to the boundaries of the commonhold land;

(2) the extents of the commonhold units using a colour and number reference (if two or more floors of a block of units are co-extensive and the layout and extents of the units are identical on each floor, a plan of one floor showing the number and floor level for each unit will be acceptable);

(3) the extent of the commonhold land using a colour reference distinct from the colour used to define the commonhold units; and

(4) any access drives and pathways which form unit boundaries.

Where more than one plan is used it must be made clear which define the extents of the commonhold and units and which are for another purpose.

Land Registry will approve the plan in advance if requested to do so. The whole of the commonhold community statement must be lodged although only the plan will be approved. There is no fee for this service.

Applying to register a commonhold

An application to register a freehold estate in commonhold land **12–005** must be made in Form CM1. Application can either be for registration without unit-holders, when it will be a new development, or with unit-holders when an existing leasehold or freehold development is being converted to commonhold.

The applicant must lodge the following documents with the CM1:

(1) certified copies of the community association's current certificate of incorporation and memorandum and articles of association;

(2) two certified copies of the commonhold community statement;

(3) consent to registration in Form CON1 from interest holders listed under **Consents to registration** below or, in appropriate circumstances, a court order dispensing with consent. A consent relating to an unregistered interest or to an interest the subject only of a notice, caution or restriction, must be accompanied by evidence, which can be a conveyancer's certificate, that the person whose consent has been lodged is the person entitled to that interest at the time the consent was given;

(4) a certificate given by the directors of the community association confirming that the memorandum and articles comply with the Commonhold Regulations 2004, that the commonhold community statement satisfies the requirements of the Commonhold and Leasehold Reform Act 2002; that the land is not land which cannot become commonhold land (see above); and that the community association has not traded and has not incurred any liability which has not been discharged;

(5) a statutory declaration given by the applicant listing all necessary consents that have been obtained or the court orders dispensing with consent; and confirming that a restriction in the register does not protect an interest in respect of which the consent of the holder is required, or if it does protect such an interest, that the appropriate consent has been obtained; that there are no other consents required by s.3 of the Commonhold and Leasehold Reform Act 2002 and the Commonhold Regulations 2004; that no consent has lapsed or been withdrawn; and that if a consent is subject to conditions, all conditions have been fully satisfied;

(6) when the application is for a registration with unit-holders:

(a) a statement in Form COV. This statement contains the request by the applicant that s.9 of the Commonhold and Leasehold Reform Act 2002 ("Registration with unit holders") should apply to the application; and a list of the commonhold units, giving the name and address of the proposed initial unit-holder or joint unit-holders for each unit;

(b) evidence of the discharge of all charges registered on the leasehold titles (which will be closed). If the appropriate lender is taking a charge on the new commonhold unit, a new charge, or a deed of substituted security must also be lodged;

(c) where the application involves the extinguishment of a charge of part of a unit, that is the subject of an entry in the register of title, the statutory declaration must:

- identify the charge to be extinguished;
- identify the registered title of the owner of the charge;
- give the name and address of the owner of the charge;
- and confirm that the consent of the owner of the charge has been obtained.

Fees are payable calculated in accordance with the current Fee Order. Note that the current Fee Order has been amended to cover commonhold applications by the Land Registration Fee (Amendment) Order 2004.

Consents to registration

Registration of land as commonhold land requires consent on **12–006** Form CON1 from the following:

(1) the registered proprietor of the freehold estate in the whole or part of the land;

(2) the registered proprietor of a leasehold estate in the whole or part of the land granted for a term of more than 21 years;

(3) the estate owner of any unregistered freehold estate in the whole or part of the land;

(4) the estate owner of any unregistered leasehold estate in the whole or part of the land granted for a term of more than 21 years;

(5) the proprietor of a charge protected by an entry in the register over the whole or part of the land;

(6) the owner of any mortgage, charge or lien for securing money or money's worth over the whole or part of any unregistered land;

(7) the holder of a lease granted for a term of not more than 21 years which will be extinguished under ss.7(3)(d) or 9(3)(f) of the Commonhold and Leasehold Reform Act 2002. Such consent is not required if the leaseholder is entitled to the grant of a new lease of the same premises, on the same terms, at the same rent, for a term equivalent to the unexpired term of the extinguished lease, which does not contain any provision which would create a term of more than 21 years, and the lessee has protected his entitlement to the grant of a new lease by registering a notice in the register of the freehold title or in the land charges register in the name of the estate owner of the freehold title.

A court may dispense with the need for consent if, after all reasonable efforts have been made to ascertain his identity, the person required to give consent cannot be identified; or if, after all reasonable efforts have been made to trace him, that person cannot be traced; or if that person has been sent a request for consent but, after all reasonable efforts to obtain a response, he has not responded.

Consent is deemed to have been given by the applicant for registration and anyone deriving title from the applicant.

Consent is binding on the successor in title to the person who gave it but it will lapse if no application is made within twelve months of the date it was given, or such shorter period as is imposed by a condition. Consent cannot be withdrawn after the application has been submitted to Land Registry.

Registration

Registration without unit-holders

12–007 *The transitional period* — "Transitional period" relates only to applications without unit-holders and is the period between when the freehold is registered as a freehold in commonhold land and when a person other than the applicant becomes entitled to be registered as the proprietor of the freehold estate in one or more, but not all, of the commonhold units.

During the transitional period the common parts will be registered in one title and each individual unit will be registered in its own separate title. All titles (*i.e.* common parts and units) will be registered in the name of the applicant and will have the following entry in the Property Register:

"The freehold estate in the land is registered as a freehold estate in commonhold land under Part 1 of the Commonhold and Leasehold Reform Act 2002."

The following entry will also be made in the Property Register but it will be cancelled without application at the end of the transitional period:

"The rights and duties conferred and imposed by the commonhold community statement will not come into force until the end of the transitional period referred to in section 8(1) of the Commonhold and Leasehold Reform Act 2002."

The common parts title will also have the following entry:

"This title comprises the common parts of the commonhold defined by the commonhold community statement. The land in this title has the benefit of and is subject to the rights and duties conferred and imposed by the commonhold community statement.

NOTE 1: Version . . . of the commonhold community statement is dated . . .

NOTE 2: Version . . . of the memorandum and articles of association of the commonhold association is dated . . .

NOTE 3: Copies filed."

The unit titles will have a similar entry except that they will refer to the copies of the commonhold community statement and memorandum and articles of association being filed under the common parts title.

The common parts title also has either of the following entries:

"The commonhold units described in the commonhold community statement referred to below have been removed from this title." or

"The commonhold units within the parts tinted green on the title plan and described in the commonhold community statement referred to below have been removed from this title."

The following restriction in Form CA is entered on the common parts title:

"No charge by the proprietor of the registered estate is to be registered other than a legal mortgage which is accompanied by a certificate by a conveyancer or a director or secretary of the commonhold association that the creation of the mortgage was approved by a resolution complying with section 29(2) of the Commonhold and Leasehold Reform Act 2002."

The following restriction in Form CB is entered on the unit titles:

"No disposition by the proprietor of the registered estate (other than a transfer or charge of the whole of the land in the title) is to be registered without a certificate by a conveyancer or a director or secretary of the commonhold association that the disposition is authorised by and made in accordance with the provisions of the Commonhold and Leasehold Reform Act 2002 or the regulations made under that Act."

All entries on the pre-commonhold title, *e.g.* charges, cautions, notices etc. are carried forward to both the common parts and unit titles unless evidence of their discharge, cancellation or withdrawal accompanies the application.

Commonhold land ceasing to be registered as commonhold during the transitional period — A registered proprietor may decide, after registering land as commonhold without unit-holders, that he no longer wants to create a commonhold development. During the transitional period, he may apply for the land to cease to be registered as commonhold. The application must be made in Form CM2. A fee under the current Fee Order, as amended by the Land Registration Fee (Amendment) Order 2004, is payable. The consent provisions apply to such an application in the same way that they apply to the original application. Consents, from all those people whose interest subsists at the time of the application, in Form CON2 must be lodged and the application must be accompanied by a statutory declaration (as above under **Applying to register a commonhold** and **Consents to registration**). When such an application is completed, the commonhold entries will be removed and the titles will revert to ordinary freehold but, unless the applicant requests amalgamation, the individual titles will be retained.

After the transitional period — The transitional period ends when a person other than the applicant becomes entitled to be registered as the proprietor of one or more, but not all, of the commonhold units. Land Registry then registers the unit/s which has/have been transferred in that person's name and registers the common parts in the name of the community association. Entries relating to charges on the common parts and notice of any leases, which have been extinguished under the statutory provisions, will be cancelled.

All other units will remain registered in the original applicant's name until they are sold.

Registration with unit-holders

This involves an existing freehold and/or leasehold development **12–008** where the owners/lessees wish to become a commonhold. When an application is lodged, the Land Registry will register the common parts in the name of the community association and the units in the names of the unit-holders listed on the Form COV. Entries will be made on common parts and unit titles as set out under *"The transitional period"* above, although the entry relating to the transitional period will not be made. Entries relating to charges and noted leases on the common parts title will be cancelled as they will have been extinguished under the statutory provisions.

If it was a leasehold development the leasehold titles under which the units were formerly registered will be closed. Evidence of the discharge of all charges on the leasehold titles must be lodged and if the lender is taking a charge on the new commonhold unit, a new charge, or a deed of substituted security, must be lodged.

Changes to the commonhold community statement and memorandum and articles of the community association

A commonhold community statement may be altered to change **12–009** the wording or to change the extent of the commonhold. The amendment or alteration has no effect until the amended commonhold community statement or altered memorandum and articles is registered.

An application must be made in Form CM3 accompanied by:

(1) a certified copy of the new version of the memorandum and articles or two certified copies of the new version of the commonhold community statement;

(2) the consent of the unit-holder and his chargee (if any) if the extent of a unit has been changed or a court order dispensing with consent;

(3) the consent of the chargee of any unit title from which land has been added to the common parts title; and

(4) a certificate by the directors of the community association that the amended commonhold community statement satisfies the requirements of the Commonhold and Leasehold Reform Act 2002 or that the altered memorandum and articles complies with the Commonhold Regulations 2004.

When an application is made to amend the commonhold community statement the amendments must be summarised in panel 10 of Form CM3. Where the extent of the units and/or the common parts is amended, the amendments must be reflected on a new plan attached to the commonhold community statement which complies with the requirements set out under "**The plan to the commonhold community statement**" above. Even where the extent of the units and/or the common parts remain unchanged, a plan must be attached to the commonhold community statement because an amended commonhold community statement cannot refer to an earlier commonhold community statement.

If the amendment of the commonhold community statement removes land from a unit over which there is a charge, the charge will be extinguished in respect of the land which has been removed. If it adds land to a unit, the charge will be extended so as to relate to the land which is added. The Commonhold Regulations 2004 prescribes that notice must be served on Land Registry when this happens. This notice must be in Form COE and must be included with the application to register the amended commonhold community statement.

If land is added to a commonhold development application must be made in Form CM4 accompanied by:

(a) consent in Form CON1 from those interest holders listed under "**Consents to registration**" above; or a court order dispensing with such consent;

(b) a statutory declaration as under "**Applying to register a commonhold**" above.

(c) an application in Form CM3 to register the commonhold community statement which has been amended to include the added land; and

(d) a certificate by the directors of the community association confirming that the land is not land which cannot be commonhold land (see above) and that the application was approved by a unanimous resolution.

Fees on these applications are calculated in accordance with the current Fee Order.

The surrender of a development right

A commonhold community statement may confer rights, called **12–010** "development rights", on the developer of a commonhold which allow him to complete the work on the development; advertise the sale of the units; add land to or remove land from a development; and/or appoint and remove directors of the community association. These rights can be surrendered by the developer.

If the developer surrenders any such rights, he must notify Land Registry by sending in a notice in Form SR1 with an application in Form AP1 against the common parts title. Land Registry then files a copy of the SR1 with the common parts title and puts a note in the Property Register of that title referring to the filed notice and sends a notice to the community association informing it that rights have been surrendered.

A fee calculated in accordance with the current Fee Order is payable.

Transfers of part of unit and common parts titles

If the community association transfers part of the common parts **12–011** title or a unit-holder transfers part of a unit, two applications must be lodged together — a Form AP1 to register the transfer of the land transferred and a Form CM3 to register the commonhold community statement which will have been amended to reflect the change in extent of the common parts and/or units. The only exception is when land which forms part of a unit is added to the common parts. This can be effected solely by an amendment to the commonhold community statement but if it is done by transfer an amended commonhold community statement is always required.

Application to register a successor community association

Where a community association has been wound up by the court **12–012** and a succession order has been made under s.51 of the Commonhold and Leasehold Reform Act 2002 an application to register the successor community association must be made on Form CM6 accompanied by:

(1) the succession order — this may make provision as to the treatment of any charge over all or part of the common parts or require Land Registry to take action of a specified kind;

(2) the winding up order; and

(3) a certified copy of the memorandum and articles of association of the successor community association.

If any charge is to be discharged over the common parts, or any part of the common parts, the usual evidence of discharge must be lodged.

No fee is payable to give effect to the court order.

Winding up or dissolution of a community association

Voluntary winding up

12–013 When a commonhold is voluntarily wound up, under ss.43–49 of the Commonhold and Leasehold Reform Act 2002, a termination application in Form CM5 must be lodged accompanied by:

(1) a termination statement specifying the community association's proposals for the transfer of the land and how its assets will be distributed;

(2) evidence of the liquidator's appointment;

(3) notification that the liquidator is content with the termination statement, or a copy of the court order which determines the terms of the termination statement; and

(4) a fee calculated in accordance with the current Fee Order.

The community association will then be registered as the proprietor of all the commonhold units and the commonhold entries will be removed from all the titles. The liquidator will then dispose of all the titles in accordance with the terms of the termination statement.

Winding up by the court

If the court has made a winding up order and has not made a **12–014** succession order in respect of the community association, an application must be made to terminate the commonhold registration on Form CM5 accompanied by:

(1) notification by the liquidator that the court has made a winding up order and has not made a succession order;

(2) any directions giving the liquidator supplementary powers;

(3) any notice of the liquidator vacating his office after the final meeting of the commonhold association;

(4) any notice of completion of winding up;

(5) any application made to the Registrar of Companies that there are insufficient assets; or of an early dissolution or of completion of winding up;

(6) any other matter which in the liquidator's opinion is relevant to Land Registry; and

(7) a fee calculated in accordance with the current Fee Order.

Land Registry will remove the commonhold entries from the common parts and all the unit titles. The titles will then be ordinary freehold titles and unit-holders will not be able to rely on the rights contained in the commonhold community statement and will need to make arrangements with the liquidator, or whoever the common parts are transferred to, to ensure that new deeds are completed granting them any necessary rights etc.

If the court makes a winding up order and a succession order proceed as under "**Application to register a successor community association**" above.

Termination by court order

Where a commonhold is registered in error the court may make **12–015** an order under s.6(6)(c) of the Commonhold and Leasehold Reform Act 2002, or, where the commonhold community statement or the memorandum and articles of association are incorrect, under s.40(3)(d) of that Act. The order may be that the land in relation to which a commonhold association exercises functions will cease to be commonhold land. When such an order is made, the court has the powers under s.55 of the 2002 Act which it would have if it were making a winding up order in respect of the commonhold association. A person appointed as liquidator by virtue of such an order has the powers and duties of a liquidator following the making of a winding up order by the court in respect of a commonhold association. But the order of the court may require the liquidator to exercise his functions in a particular way; impose additional rights or duties on the liquidator; and/or modify or remove a right or duty of the liquidator.

Following such an order an application must be made in Form AP1 accompanied by the court order to which Land Registry will then give effect. There is no fee payable.

Chapter 13

Charges

Registered charges

Power to create

By virtue of s.23, a registered proprietor has power to deal with **13–001** both registered land and registered charges in any way permitted by the general law, save that a registered proprietor of land cannot create a mortgage by demise or sub-demise and a registered proprietor of a registered charge cannot create a legal sub-mortgage. Section 23(1)(b) provides that a registered proprietor of land may charge the title at law with the payment of money. Section 23(2)(b) provides that a registered chargee may charge at law with the payment of money indebtedness secured by the registered charge. These powers may be exercised by the registered proprietor or someone entitled to be registered as the proprietor.

A chargee can rely upon the register to say whether there are any limitations on the powers of the registered proprietor. Save for a limitation imposed by or under the Act, a chargee can assume that there are no limitations on the registered proprietor's powers unless there is an entry on the register reflecting a limitation.

Form

Section 25 provides that a registrable disposition of a registered **13–002** estate or charge only has effect if it complies with such requirements as to form and content as rules may provide. Schedule 1 to the Rules contains a prescribed form of charge of registered land, Form CH1. Agreed terms, *e.g.* as to express covenants for the payment of secured moneys and interest, further advances and default events can be inserted in the general provisions panel. By virtue of r.103, use of this form is not compulsory. Many lenders have their own standard form of charge. Where Form CH1 is not used care should be taken to ensure that the form used charges the land in accordance with the general law and s.23. It must also clearly describe the land being charged by reference to the title number (if the charge is of the whole of the land in a title) or, where part of the land in a title is to be charged, a suitable plan signed by the chargor enabling the part charged to be clearly identified on the title plan.

Incorporated documents/Approval of standard forms of charge

13–003 If the Registry needs to see an incorporated document in order to complete the registration, a copy will be requested. The Registry approves standard forms of charge and allocates "MD references" and major lenders are encouraged to apply for such approval. This avoids the need to lodge Form RX1 and/or Form CH2 where the form of charge or incorporated terms and conditions contains a standard restriction and/or an obligation to make further advances (see below). The Commercial Arrangements Section, Land Registry, 32 Lincoln's Inn Fields, London, WC2A 3PH, DX No. 1098 London/Chancery Lane WC2 can advise on how to obtain approval.

Completion by registration

13–004 The grant of a legal charge or sub-charge must be completed by registration in accordance with s.27. Until this is done it does not operate at law. Application for registration should be made to the appropriate office on Form AP1 together with:

(1) the charge and a certified copy;

(2) any certificate or consent necessary to comply with any restriction on the register of the borrower's title;

(3) From CH2 in respect of an application to note an obligation to make further advances, if appropriate (see below);

(4) Form RX1 in respect of an application for a restriction unless the form of charge or incorporated terms and conditions contain a standard restriction and the form of charge has been approved (see above);

(5) the fee payable (see below).

In addition, special evidence may be required in relation to particular kinds of chargors and chargees (*e.g.* charities, as to which see Chapter 17).

The need to deliver the application for the registration of the charge to the appropriate office within the priority period of the protecting official search (see Chapter 8) must be kept in mind.

If the charge is to secure further advances (see below), the register entries will show this; and if the lender is under an obligation to make further advances and application is made (see below) this will also be shown.

If a charge accompanies an application in Form FR1 for first registration, no separate application for its registration will be necessary.

If the application to register the charge is being made at the same time as another application affecting the title (*e.g.* to register a transfer), one Form AP1 will cover both dealings. The completion of forms of application for first registration is dealt with in Chapter 4, and general points on completing Form AP1 are considered in Chapter 9. Particular points relating to charges by and to companies are discussed below.

Registration fees

Reference should be made to the current Fee Order for details **13–005** of the fees payable on registration of a charge.

Charges by companies incorporated under the Companies Acts

Registration of the charge at the Companies Registry should **13–006** precede its delivery to the appropriate office for registration. If a charge so delivered should have been registered at the Companies Registry but there is no evidence that it has been so registered, a note will be made on the register that it is subject to s.395 of the Companies Act 1985. It is important to bear in mind that registration of a charge of registered land at the Companies Registry is not sufficient protection. It must also be completed by registration in accordance with s.27. A legal charge or mortgage of registered land in a debenture trust deed can be registered as a registered charge. If the original trust deed and a certified copy are lodged, the copy will be filed and the original deed will be returned.

Charges to companies incorporated under the Companies Acts

13–007 If a company registered in England, Wales or Scotland under the Companies Acts is to be registered as the proprietor of a charge, no evidence of its incorporation, objects and powers need generally be provided. Its company registration number should be provided.

Priorities

13–008 Section 48 provides that registered charges on the same registered estate, or on the same registered charge, rank as between themselves in the order shown in the register. Rule 101 states that except as shown by an entry in the individual register to the contrary, the order in which registered charges are entered in an individual register shows the order in which the registered charges rank as between themselves. This means that where the identifying entry in respect of a registered charge ("the prior charge") appears in the charges register before that of another registered charge, the prior charge ranks in priority before the other charge. This general rule does not apply where there is an entry to the contrary in the register, *e.g.* where:

(1) priority has been altered under r.102 (see below); or

(2) a statutory charge has overriding priority under r.105 (see below).

Rule 102 provides a mechanism whereby the priority of registered charges can be altered. Application must be by or with the consent of the proprietor or person entitled to be registered as proprietor of any registered charge whose priority is adversely affected by the alteration. No such consent is required from a person who has executed the instrument which alters the priority of the charges. The registrar may accept a conveyancer's certificate that he holds any necessary consents. If the application is in order the registrar must make an entry in the register in such terms as he considers appropriate to give effect to the application.

Further advances

13–009 Under s.49 there are four ways in which an existing chargee can make further advances and obtain priority for those further advances over later charges:

(1) if he makes a further advance when he has not received from a subsequent chargee notice of the creation of the subsequent charge — s.49(1). The onus is no longer on the Registry to notify an existing chargee of the creation of a further charge as it was under s.30 of the 1925 Act. There are no prescribed methods of giving such notice but notice is treated as received at the time it ought to have been received in accordance with r.107. It is advisable for a subsequent chargee to use one of the methods referred to in r.107 in view of the certainty which this gives.

(2) if he makes a further advance in pursuance of an obligation and at the time of creation of the subsequent charge the obligation was entered in the register — s.49(3) (see below).

(3) if he makes a further advance where the parties to the prior charge have agreed to a maximum amount for which the charge is security and at the time of creation of the subsequent charge the agreement was entered in the register — s. 49(4) (see below).

(4) if he reaches agreement with the subsequent chargee.

Obligations to make further advances

Rule 108 provides that the proprietor of a registered charge or a **13–010** person entitled to be registered as the proprietor of a registered charge who, under the terms of the charge, is under an obligation to make further advances, may apply to the registrar for such an obligation to be entered on the register. Application must be made in Form CH2 unless the application is contained in panel 7 of Form CH1, or in a charge received for registration where the form of that charge has been approved by the registrar. The registrar will make an appropriate entry in the register.

When the proprietor of a registered charge is under an obligation, noted on the register, to make a further advance, a subsequent registered charge takes effect subject to any further advance made in pursuance of the obligation (s.49(3)) (see above).

No fee will normally be payable but if, unusually, the application is lodged on its own a fee is payable, calculated in accordance with the current Fee Order.

Agreement of maximum amount of security

13–011 Rule 109 provides that where the parties to a legal charge which is a registered charge or a registrable disposition have agreed a maximum amount for which the charge is security, the proprietor of the charge or person applying to be the proprietor can apply to the registrar for such agreement to be entered in the register. Application must be made in Form CH3 (even if the maximum amount is stated in the charge itself and the charge has previously been approved by the Registry). The registrar will make an appropriate entry in the register.

When there is such an entry on the register, priority is given to further advances up to the sum agreed over any charge created after the agreement is noted (s.49(4)) (see above).

Overriding statutory charges

13–012 Section 50 provides that if the registrar enters a person in the register as the proprietor of a charge which is created by or under any enactment, and has effect to postpone a charge which at the time of registration of the statutory charge is entered on the register or is the basis of an entry in the register, the registrar must give notice of the creation of the statutory charge in accordance with rules. The relevant rules are 105 and 106. Rule 105 deals with applications to register statutory charges and r.106 deals with service of notice.

Application for registration must be made on Form SC. The applicant must state the statute under which priority is claimed and the registered charges over which the statutory charge has priority. If the registrar is satisfied that the statutory charge has the priority claimed, he will make an entry showing that priority in the charges register. If the registrar is not so satisfied but considers that the applicant has an arguable case the registrar may make an entry to the effect that the specified priority is claimed. In either case the registrar will give notice of the entry to the registered proprietor of the registered charge (and to any person who appears to the registrar to be entitled to a charge protected by notice if that person's name and address for service is set out in the register) entered in the charges register at the time of registration of the statutory charge. If the registrar has made an entry regarding a claim to such priority the proprietor of that charge or a charge which would, but for the entry of that claim, be shown on the register as ranking in priority or having equal priority to the statutory charge may apply for the entry to be removed or replaced by one showing that the charge has the priority claimed. Notice of such an application is served on the proprietors of the affected charges. If a dispute cannot be resolved it will be referred to the Adjudicator under s.73(7) (see Chapter 22).

Powers of the proprietor of the land

Subject to any express contrary intention, the proprietor of the **13–013** land whilst in possession has the powers of leasing and accepting surrenders of leases given by ss.99 and 100 of the Law of Property Act 1925 as extended by the charge or any instrument varying it. All other dispositions by the proprietor of the land made without the concurrence of the proprietor of the charge take effect subject to the charge. The proprietor of the land can transfer his equity of redemption without the consent of the registered chargee provided that there is no contrary entry (*e.g.* a restriction) on the register or in any registered charge.

Powers of the proprietor of the charge

The effect of s.51 is that, subject to any entry on the register to **13–014** the contrary, the proprietor of a registered charge has all the powers conferred by law on the owner of a legal mortgage. Section 52 provides protection for a disponee. If nothing appears to the contrary in the register, the chargee is taken to have all the powers of disposal of a legal mortgagee under the Law of Property Act 1925 so the title of the disponee cannot be questioned. However, it does not prevent a claim being brought by the chargor against the chargee.

A registered proprietor of a sub-charge has the same powers as the sub-chargor.

A transfer in the exercise of the chargee's power of sale should be in Form TR2 or TP2 which should be lodged for registration in the ordinary way together with a fee calculated in accordance with the current Fee Order.

A foreclosure order is obtained in the same way as if the land were unregistered. The order absolute should be lodged together with a fee calculated in accordance with the current Fee Order so that the proprietor of the charge can be registered as proprietor of the land (subject to prior charges) (r.112).

Transfer of charge

A transfer of the charge is required to be in Form TR3, TR4 or **13–015** AS2, as appropriate (r.116). It should be lodged for registration under cover of a Form AP1. A fee is payable, calculated in accordance with the current Fee Order.

Variation of the terms of registered charges

13–016 Rule 113 provides that an application to register an instrument varying the terms of a registered charge must be made by, or with the consent of, the proprietor of the registered charge and the proprietor of the estate charged, and with the consent of the proprietor, or a person entitled to be registered as proprietor, of every other registered charge of equal or inferior priority that is prejudicially affected by the variation. No such consent is required from a person who has executed the instrument. The registrar may accept a conveyancer's certificate that he holds any necessary consents. Application for registration of the variation should be made in Form AP1 accompanied by the original instrument and a copy of it. If the variation affects the priority of a registered charge of equal or inferior priority and there is no or insufficient evidence that the chargees of equal or inferior priority are bound then an entry will be made on the register to the effect that an instrument has been entered into which is expressed to vary the terms of the registered charge. If there is sufficient evidence, then a guaranteed entry to the effect that the charge has been varied will be made. A fee is payable, calculated in accordance with the current Fee Order.

Chargees' duty regarding proceeds of sale

13–017 Section 105 of the Law of Property Act 1925 provides that money received on a sale by a mortgagee is held by the mortgagee on trust after satisfying certain payments. The trust is for "the person entitled to the mortgaged property". Where there is a subsequent charge, this person is the later chargee, if the mortgagee has actual, constructive or imputed notice of the subsequent charge. The effect of s.54 of the Act is that a mortgagee in these circumstances is deemed to have notice of anything in the register immediately before the disposition on sale. This is a change to the 1925 legislation and means that such a mortgagee will need to consult the register when discharging his duty under s.105.

Discharges

13–018 Rule 114 provides that subject to r.115, which deals with electronic discharges and releases, a discharge of a registered charge must be in Form DS1 and a release of part of the registered title from a registered charge must be in Form DS3. Form DS1 or DS3 must be executed as a deed or authenticated in such other manner as the registrar may approve. However, in accordance with r.114(4), the registrar is entitled to accept and act upon any other proof of satisfaction of a charge which he may regard as sufficient.

Details of the appropriate methods of execution are referred to in Chapter 9.

Prior approval of the proposed method of execution of a significant number of discharges of registered charges may be obtained by approaching the Commercial Arrangements Section of the Registry at the address given above.

An application to register a discharge in Form DS1 must be made in Form AP1 or DS2. An application to register a release in Form DS3 must be made in Form AP1.

No fee is payable for the registration of a discharge of a registered charge.

If the discharged charge affects also an unregistered interest, *e.g.* a policy of insurance, or unregistered land, and the original deed will be required after registration of the discharge, a special request for its return should be made.

Rule 115 provides for discharges and releases of registered charges in electronic form. During the currency of a notice given by the registrar under Sch.2 to the Rules ("Notices publicising arrangements for electronic delivery of applications and other matters") and subject to and in accordance with the limitations contained in such notice, notification of the discharge of a registered charge may be delivered to the registrar in electronic form. The release of part in electronic form is not currently permitted. Such Electronic Notifications of Discharge ("ENDs") are also discussed in Chapter 10. Where this facility is available in relation to a particular lender, the ENDs are transmitted as electronic messages from the lender's computer system to that of the Registry. The Registry validates the message and it is then held on the computer system to await an application for the charge to be discharged. Once an application is received, it is matched up with the END and the entries relating to the charge are cancelled in the same way as if a Form DS1 had been lodged. If an application has already been received the entries will be cancelled immediately.

A new system of e-discharges is currently being developed.

Charges subsisting at the time of first registration

Where a charge or mortgage subsists at the time of first **13–019** registration, it must be disclosed in the documentation which accompanies the application for first registration. The charge will be registered under r.34. Commonly the purchase inducing the first registration has been made with money secured by a charge created under r.38 with a view to its completion by registration. In such a case, where the borrower and the lender are separately represented, it is usual for the borrower's conveyancer to prepare and sign the first registration application form, which is handed over to the lender's conveyancer at completion together with the deeds. The lender's conveyancer then lodges the application at the appropriate office, and in due course receives notification of completion of the registration and any returnable deeds from that office. In this situation it is important to make sure that the relevant address panels on the application form are correctly completed.

Public sector housing: discount charge

The discount charge

13–020 Sales under the right to buy provisions of the Housing Act 1985 (and earlier Acts) and voluntary sales under the 1985 Act and under the Housing Associations Act 1985 may allow or have allowed a discount. If so, the transfer, charge or lease must contain a covenant to repay the discount in the event of a further disposal within the statutory period. The statutory period is normally either three or five years. "Disposal" includes a conveyance of the freehold or the assignment of the lease or the grant of a lease for more than twenty-one years. It also includes the grant of an option to transfer or grant a lease of the property but not a mortgage. Certain disposals, including some inter-family transfers, vestings under a will or on intestacy, disposals on compulsory purchase and disposals of part of the garden or other land occupied with the dwellinghouse, are exempt from the repayment requirement.

The liability under the discount covenant is a charge on the property which takes effect as a charge by way of legal mortgage or a noted charge, depending on the type of discount covenant. The charge is protected by an entry in the charges register.

Priority

13–021 The discount charge has priority immediately after any legal charge in favour of the seller to secure an outstanding part of the purchase price or after any legal charge in favour of the Housing Corporation, building societies, friendly societies, the major banks, the Post Office and certain insurance and loan companies to secure an advance for the purposes of the purchase. The question of priority is disregarded when the entry is made. In practice the entry of the notice of the discount charge is made in the charges register before the entry of any legal charge. The discount charge is overreached on a sale by one of the corporations or companies specified above pursuant to the power of sale in a charge having priority to the discount charge.

Postponement

A discount charge may be postponed to an advance or further **13–022** advance made by one of the corporations or companies referred to above by means of a written notice signed on behalf of the seller or lessor to whom the covenant to repay the discount was given ("the discount chargee"). Any such postponement will be noted on the register on production of the signed notice of postponement.

Cancellation of a notice of a discount charge

Where a disposal takes place within the statutory discount **13–023** charge period and the discount is repaid application should be made to cancel the notice of a discount charge. There is no prescribed form of discharge but whatever evidence is lodged will need to satisfactorily show the discount chargee's concurrence with the application for the removal of the entry. The document should be executed by the discount chargee except in the case of a local authority, where it may be signed by the chief executive or some other authorised official.

On an application after the statutory discount charge period has expired the notice will be cancelled:

(1) only with the concurrence of the discount chargee as above, if there is evidence of a disposal within the statutory discount charge period which may have led to discount becoming repayable; or

(2) in certain other cases without the discount chargee's concurrence but in some cases only after service of notice by the Registry on the discount chargee.

No fee is payable for cancellation of the notice of a discount charge.

Equitable charges

13–024 Where a charge takes effect in equity only, consideration should be given to the need to apply for the interest to be protected on the register by a notice under s.32 or a restriction under s.40 as appropriate in the circumstances. Notices and restrictions are discussed in Chapter 15.

When a fixed equitable charge protected by notice has been paid off and cancellation of the notice is desired, any devolution of the title to the charge, and its discharge, must be proved according to unregistered conveyancing practice. A Form DS1 is not appropriate for the discharge. Notice of a floating charge created by a limited company will usually be cancelled on the production of an office copy of the memorandum of satisfaction filed at the Companies Registry.

Details of the appropriate application forms are set out in Chapter 15.

Debentures

13–025 A legal charge of registered land created by a debenture trust deed can be registered as a registered charge.

If a limited company or other corporation has created debentures or debenture stock constituting a fixed equitable or floating charge on its assets, the existence of the charge must be disclosed whenever the company or corporation makes an application for the first registration of its title to land. A certified copy of the debentures, or of one of them if all are certified to be in the same terms, and of any trust deed securing them, must be lodged with the application. Notice of the charge will be entered on the register, and the copies of the debenture(s) and trust deed (if any) will be filed.

Where a company that has created debentures acquires registered land or a registered charge, or where a company that is already the registered proprietor of land or a charge creates debentures, no entry will be made in the register to protect any charge created by the debentures (whether registered in the Companies Registry or not) in the absence of a specific application for an entry to be made. Such specific application, as regards any equitable charge created by the debentures, would usually be for the entry of notice of the charge or for a restriction.

A buyer taking a transfer of registered land from a limited company registered with absolute or good leasehold title is never concerned to search that company's file at the Companies Registry for debentures or debenture stock. If any had been created before the company became the first registered proprietor of the land, notice should appear on the register; and if the company had created debentures or debenture stock and then acquired land already registered, or had become proprietor of land already registered and then created debentures or debenture stock, a buyer of the registered land would not be concerned with any charge created by the debentures unless it was registered or protected on the register.

Where a company is the proprietor of registered land and notice of a fixed equitable charge by the company appears on the register, any application to register a lease by the company with absolute leasehold title must be accompanied by the consent of the chargee.

Where notice of a floating charge appears on the register, and a transfer on sale of the land by the chargor company is being registered, a certificate by the conveyancer or secretary of the chargor company that none of the events on the happening of which the charge would become fixed has occurred is usually accepted by the Registry as sufficient evidence for the cancellation of the notice. Alternatively a certificate to like effect from the chargee or his conveyancer would usually be accepted. Where a lease by the chargor company is being registered with absolute leasehold title the consent of the chargee will be required.

Unexpired notices of [intended] deposit

Since April 3, 1995, it has not been possible to apply for **13–026** registration of a new notice of [intended] deposit. However there are some titles where such entries still subsist.

By virtue of the transitional provisions in the Act, any notice of [intended] deposit entered on the register before April 3, 1995, shall, until cancelled, continue to operate as a caution against dealings under s.54 of the 1925 Act, as it has since April 3, 1995. Part 16 of the Rules contains transitional provisions regarding cautions against dealings. Anyone who has entered such a notice will, of course, have to consider their position in the light of *United Bank of Kuwait plc v Sahib* [1995] 2 W.L.R. 94 which was the case which said that s.2 of the Law of Property Act 1925 prevents the creation of a lien by mere deposit of deeds and documents including a land or charge certificate. The effect of a caution against dealings is considered in Chapter 15.

A depositee's consent to a dealing may be by way of a letter or it may be endorsed by way of reply on a notice sent by the Registry to the depositee. As for a caution against dealings, consent may be given by the depositee, or his personal representative or by a conveyancer.

When there is to be a transfer of part of the land in a title, and when a lease or rentcharge is to be granted out of registered land, a depositee of the land certificate of the parent title usually provides a letter of consent, which can then be sent to the Registry together with the application to register the transfer or grant. When necessary, the consent must refer to a plan enabling the land to which it relates to be identified on the title plan of the parent title. A transfer of whole should of course be accompanied by a withdrawal of the notice of intended deposit.

A notice of intended deposit can be "warned off" in the same way as a caution against dealings (see Chapter 15).

Forms 85A, 85B and 85C, which were the application forms for entry of notices of [intended] deposit, were completed in duplicate, and the duplicate was returned to the applicant by the Registry as an acknowledgement of the receipt of the original. Printed on the back of each duplicate is a Form 86, which is a form of application for the withdrawal of the notice. Application to withdraw the notice should be made on Form AP1 accompanied by Form 86 or the duplicate Forms 85A, B or C. Alternatively, Form WCT (application to withdraw a caution) can be used, amended to refer to the withdrawal of the notice of [intended] deposit. Consent to withdrawal may be given by the depositee or his personal representative or by a conveyancer.

No fee is payable.

Chapter 14

Rentcharges

The Rentcharges Act 1977

The preamble to the Rentcharges Act 1977 describes it as "An **14–001** Act to prohibit the creation, and provide for the extinguishment, apportionment and redemption, of certain rentcharges." Its main provisions, including ss.1, 2 and 3 referred to below, came into operation on August 22, 1977. The remainder came into operation on February 1, 1978.

Section 1 defines a rentcharge for the purposes of the 1977 Act as "any annual or other periodic sum charged on or issuing out of land except (i) rent reserved by a lease or tenancy, or (ii) any sum payable by way of interest". "Land" has the same meaning as in s.205(1) of the Law of Property Act 1925.

Section 2 prohibits the creation of any rentcharge, whether at law or in equity, after the coming into force of the section, except the classes specified in s.2(3). The specified classes comprise any rentcharge:

(a) which has the effect of making the land on which the rent is charged settled land by virtue of s.1(1)(v) of the Settled Land Act 1925;

(b) which would have that effect but for the fact that the land on which the rent is charged is already settled land or is held on trust for sale;

(c) which is an estate rentcharge;

(d) under any Act providing for the creation of rentcharges in connection with the execution of works on land (whether by way of improvements, repairs or otherwise) or the commutation of any obligation to do any such work; or

(e) by, or in accordance with the requirements of, any order of a court.

Section 2(4) and (5) define an estate rentcharge as follows:

"(4) For the purpose of this section 'estate rentcharge' means (subject to subsection (5) below) a rentcharge created for the purpose

(a) of making covenants to be performed by the owner of the land affected by the rentcharge enforceable by the rent owner against the owner for the time being of the land; or

(b) of meeting, or contributing towards, the cost of the performance by the rent owner of covenants for the provision of services, the carrying out of maintenance or repairs, the effecting of insurance or the making of any payment by him for the benefit of the land affected by the rentcharge or for the benefit of that and other land.

(5) A rentcharge of more than a nominal amount shall not be treated as an estate rentcharge for the purpose of this section unless it represents a payment for the performance by the rent owner of any such covenant as is mentioned in sub-section 4(b) above which is reasonable in relation to that covenant."

Under the transitional provisions contained in s.17 of the 1977 Act rentcharges created pursuant to agreements entered into before July 22, 1977 are excluded from the prohibition of s.2.

Section 3 of the 1977 Act, referred to in more detail below, provides (subject to exceptions) for the extinguishment of rentcharges after a period of 60 years. Sections 4 to 10 deal with apportionment and redemption (see below).

First registration of rentcharges

Rentcharges capable of being registered

14–002 A rentcharge is capable of registration under s.3 if it is a "legal rentcharge", *i.e.* a rentcharge in possession issuing out of or charged on a legal freehold or leasehold estate in land and being either perpetual or for a term of years absolute of which more than seven years are unexpired and either:

(1) it is based on a deed dated before August 22, 1977; or

(2) it is based on a deed dated on or after August 22, 1977, and its creation is not prohibited by s.2 of the Rentcharges Act 1977.

The fact that a rentcharge is subject to extinguishment in accordance with the provisions of the 1977 Act does not of itself prevent it from being "perpetual" or for a term of years "absolute" for the purposes of registration.

Rentcharges that subsist as equitable interests only, *e.g.* because of the mode of their creation or because they are informally apportioned parts of a legal or equitable rentcharge, cannot be registered but they can be protected on the register by means of a notice (see below).

Rentcharges created out of unregistered land
A legal rentcharge created out of unregistered land is not **14–003** compulsorily registrable on creation nor does it ever become compulsorily registrable on sale or transfer. If otherwise registrable (see above) it may be voluntarily registered at any time.

Where a conveyance of unregistered land lodged for registration also creates a rentcharge, the Registry will take no steps to register the rentcharge substantively unless the application for registration of the land is accompanied by a specific application for first registration of the rentcharge. The rentcharge will be noted against the title to the land without a specific application (see below).

A fee is payable in accordance with the current Fee Order.

Rentcharges created out of registered land
A legal rentcharge created out of registered land in fee simple **14–004** or for a term of more than seven years must be registered and notice of the rentcharge must be entered on the register of the title to the land out of which it issues. (s.27 and para.6 of Pt 1 of Sch.2 to the Act).

A legal rentcharge may be created as a disposition of registered land in one of two ways. It may be the subject of a deed of grant by the proprietor of the land, or it may be granted by the transferee to the transferor, out of the land transferred, in and as part of the consideration for a transfer of registered land. In both cases an application for the registration of the rentcharge should be made on Form AP1. In the latter case one AP1 can cover both registration of the land and registration of the rentcharge.

If a legal rentcharge is granted out of leasehold land registered with good leasehold title, and more than a qualified title to the rentcharge is desired, conveyancing evidence must be produced to show that the lease (and any superior lease) was validly granted.

Every deed creating a rentcharge out of registered land must contain a reference to the title number of that land and particulars, by plan if necessary, to enable the land charged to be identified on the title plan of the grantor's title.

A fee is payable in accordance with the current Fee Order.

Rentcharges which cannot be registered

14–005 Rentcharges subsisting as equitable interests only cannot be registered but must be appropriately protected on the register of the title to the land out of which they issue if that land is registered.

When an equitable rentcharge is created out of registered land, wherever the land is situated, notice of the rentcharge should be entered on the register of the title to the land out of which it issues.

If an equitable rentcharge is created (out of the land transferred) by the transferee in a transfer of registered land as the consideration or part of the consideration for the transfer, notice of it will be entered in the register of the transferee's title as a matter of course when the transfer is registered. In any other case of an equitable rentcharge created out of registered land, a separate application should be made to enter notice of the rentcharge on the register of the title out of which it issues (see below and Chapter 15).

Notice of rentcharge

14–006 When land is first registered, notices of subsisting rentcharges, whether legal or equitable, issuing out of the land and appearing on the title, with details of any apportionments and exonerations, are entered in the charges register of the title to the land as a matter of course (r.35).

On the substantive registration of a legal rentcharge created out of registered land, notice of the rentcharge is entered as a matter of course in the register of the title to the land out of which the rentcharge issues (see above).

On the creation out of registered land of a rentcharge which cannot be registered, a specific application for the entry of notice of the rentcharge on the register of the title to the land out of which the rentcharge issues will be necessary (see Chapter 15).

Dealings with registered rentcharges

14–007 A registered rentcharge can be transferred, leased, charged, etc. in the same way and subject to the same rules as registered land, so far as the nature of a rentcharge permits. The advice appearing elsewhere in this book, whilst primarily relating to registered corporeal land, applies generally to registered rentcharges.

Transfer of registered estate subject to a rentcharge

Under r.69 where the covenants set out in Pt VII (Covenants **14–008** Implied in a Conveyance for Valuable Consideration, other than a Mortgage, of the Entirety of Land Affected by a Rentcharge) or Pt VIII (Covenants Implied in a Conveyance for Valuable Consideration, other than a Mortgage, of Part of Land Affected by a Rentcharge, Subject to a Part (not Legally Apportioned) of that Rentcharge) of Sch.2 to the Law of Property Act 1925 are included in a transfer, the references to "the grantees", "the conveyance" and "the conveying parties" shall be treated as references to the transferees, the transfer and the transferors respectively.

Rules 69(2) and (3) contain provisions modifying the covenants in Pt VIII of Sch.2 to the Law of Property Act 1925 when they are included in certain transfers of parts of registered land affected by rentcharges to which s.77(1)(B) of the Law of Property Act 1925 does not apply.

Rule 69(4) provides that on a transfer of a registered title subject to a rentcharge:

(a) any covenant implied by ss.77(1)(A) or (B) of the Law of Property Act 1925 may be modified or negatived; and

(b) any covenant included in the transfer may be modified,

by adding suitable words to the transfer.

Apportionment and redemption of rentcharges

A registered title (to land or to a rentcharge) may be affected by **14–009** a ministerial order apportioning a rentcharge or by a ministerial certificate that a rentcharge has been redeemed. If it is not known whether the title to the land or rentcharge is registered, an enquiry on this point, with a request for the title number if the land or rentcharge is registered, may be made on Form SIM addressed to the appropriate office.

A fee is payable calculated in accordance with the current Fee Order.

An application should then be made to the appropriate office for effect to be given on the registered title to the order or the certificate; but where an apportionment is made conditional on the redemption of the rentcharge the application should not be made until after the redemption has taken place.

The application should be made on Form AP1. It should be supported by:

(1) an official copy of the order and/or an official copy of the certificate of redemption as appropriate; and

(2) the appropriate fee.

No fee is payable if the application is accompanied by an application upon which a scale fee is payable. It follows that no fee for the registration of the order or the certificate will be payable where the order or certificate has been obtained with a sale of the registered land or rentcharge in view and the application for the registration of the order or certificate is lodged with the application for the registration of the transfer on sale of the land or rentcharge.

Extinguishment of rentcharges

14–010 Section 3(1) of the 1977 Act provides that, subject to exceptions, every rentcharge shall (if it has not then ceased to have effect) be extinguished at the expiry of the period of 60 years beginning with:

(a) the passing of the Act (July 22, 1977); or

(b) the date on which the rentcharge first became payable,

whichever is later.

The section will not extinguish any rentcharge payable wholly or partly in lieu of tithes or of a kind referred to in s.2(3) of the 1977 Act (disregarding s.2(5)). Variable rentcharges are also excluded from extinguishment under s.3(1) of the 1977 Act; but where a variable rentcharge ceases to be variable s.3(1) will apply as if the date on which the rentcharge first became payable was the date on which it ceased to be variable.

An application following the extinguishment of a rentcharge, other than by ministerial certificate, should be made supported by appropriate evidence of extinguishment and documents as follows:

(1) *Both interests registered with absolute title:*

(a) application in Form AP1;

(b) original deed of grant or duplicate conveyance creating the rentcharge;

      (c) a fee calculated in accordance with the current Fee Order unless the application is accompanied by an application upon which a scale fee is payable, when no fee is payable.

(2) *Land only registered:*

      (a) application in Form CN1 or UN4;
      (b) all the title deeds relating to the rentcharge (including the original deed of grant or duplicate conveyance creating it);
      (c) a fee calculated as at (1)(c) above.

(3) *Rentcharge only registered:*

      (a) application in Form AP1;
      (b) original deed of grant or duplicate conveyance creating the rentcharge;
      (c) a fee calculated as at (1)(c) above.

It is assumed that in each case the rentcharge and the whole of the land out of which it is payable are held by the same person(s) in the same capacity without any intervening estate.

Adverse possession of a rentcharge

Rule 191, made pursuant to the power contained in para. 14 of **14–011** Sch.6 of the Act, applies the provisions of Sch.6 of the Act (see Chapter 6) to rentcharges but in the modified form set out in Sch.8 to the Rules.

Rule 192 contains provisions which apply where adverse possession is based on non-payment of rent and r.193 sets out provisions which prohibit recovery of rent after adverse possession of a rentcharge.

Under r.224, if title to a rentcharge was acquired by adverse possession prior to October 13, 2003, and it was held in trust under s.75(1) of the Land Registration Act 1925 immediately before that date, the beneficiary of that trust may apply either to be registered as proprietor of the rentcharge, or for the registration of the rentcharge to be cancelled.

Chapter 15

Protection of Third Party Rights

Introduction

Under the Land Registration Act 1925 there were four methods **15–001** of protecting third party interests on the register. These were cautions against dealings, inhibitions, notices and restrictions. Since October 13, 2003, only two methods of protection, notices and restrictions, have been available. Where a caution against dealings would have been used either a notice or restriction will now be appropriate. A notice will provide greater protection because if the interest the subject of the notice is valid the notice will give it priority. Where an inhibition would have been appropriate a restriction will now be used.

Entries dated before October 13, 2003, will continue in force until they are removed from the register and the ways in which that can be done are set out in this chapter.

Notices (ss.32–39)

A notice is an entry on the charges register which protects a **15–002** burden affecting the registered land or charge against which it is entered. The fact that a notice is entered in the register does not mean that the interest of which notice is given is valid but if it is valid its priority is protected.

Matters typically protected by notice are contracts for sale and agreements for lease, subjective easements, leases, rentcharges, restrictive covenants, matrimonial homes rights and orders of court, including charging orders made under the Charging Orders Act 1979 affecting the registered land itself (see below under "**Restrictions**" as to the position if the charging order is on the beneficial interest under a trust of land).

In many cases notice is entered as a matter of course, without the need for a separate application, as part of the registration process. For example, on first registration notice of existing easements and restrictive covenants is entered on the new title (s.14 and r.35); notice of new easements and restrictive covenants in a transfer of part is entered in the registers of the existing and new titles as appropriate, and on the registration of a lease granted out of registered land notice of the lease will be entered in the register of the lessor's title (s.38).

Also where the registrar is satisfied that the registered land is subject to an interest which overrides under Sch.1 of the Act (see Chapter 4) and which can be noted (see (1) to (5) below) he may enter notice of that interest (s.37) without an application being made. If the registrar enters a notice under s.37 he must give notice to the registered proprietor, unless he applied for or consents to the entry of the notice. He must also give notice to any person who appears to the registrar to be entitled to the interest protected by the notice, or whom the registrar otherwise considers appropriate, unless that person applied for or consented to the entry of the notice, or that person's name and address for service are not set out in the register in which the notice is entered.

A notice cannot be used to protect:

(1) trusts of land or interests under settlements under the Settled Land Act 1925;

(2) a lease granted for three years or less which is not required to be registered;

(3) a restrictive covenant between a lessor and lessee so far as it affects the land in the lease (see Chapter 11);

(4) an interest which can be registered under the Commons Registration Act 1965; and

(5) any interest in, rights attached to or rights of any person under ss.38, 49 or 51 of the Coal Industry Act 1994 in coal or a coal mine.

Under s.77 there is a duty, owed to any person who suffers damages as a result, not to enter a notice without reasonable cause.

Agreed notices

15–003   An agreed notice can only be entered (s.34):

(1) by or with the consent of the registered proprietor of the land or charge affected or by a person entitled to be registered as such; or

(2) by the registrar if he is satisfied that the applicant for the entry has a valid claim to the interest to which the notice relates.

Rule 80 provides that if an application is made to protect certain interests it must be for the entry of an agreed notice. Those interests are:

(a) matrimonial homes rights (see Chapter 16);

(b) inheritance tax (see Chapter 18);

(c) an order under the Access to Neighbouring Land Act 1992;

(d) variation of a lease under ss. 38 or 39(4) of the Landlord and Tenant Act 1987; and

(e) a public or customary right.

An application for the entry of an agreed notice, unless it relates to matrimonial homes rights, as to which see Chapter 16, must be made on Form AN1 accompanied by (r.81):

(1) the order or document which created the claimed interest or if there is none such details of the interest as are required by the registrar;

(2) when appropriate a Land Transaction Return certificate or a self certificate in form SDLT60 or a letter explaining why neither certificate is required (see Chapter 1);

(3) any evidence required to satisfy the registrar that the claim to the interest is valid; and

(4) if appropriate, evidence of the right to be registered or of consent (see above);

(5) the fee calculated in accordance with the current Fee Order.

The entry of the agreed notice in the charges register must give details of the interest protected and if it only affects part of the land in the title it must identify that part (r.84).
An application to cancel an agreed notice must be made on Form CN1 accompanied by evidence to satisfy the registrar that the interest has determined (r.87). The register will not show any

devolution of title to the noted interest and, where such devolution has occurred appropriate conveyancing evidence of devolution should be lodged to prove either determination of the interest or the right of the applicant to apply for the notice to be cancelled.

No fee is payable.

Unilateral notices

15–004   A unilateral notice is entered without the consent of the registered proprietor of the land or charge which it affects.

The entry must state that it is a unilateral notice and identify who is entitled to the benefit of the notice (s.35(2)). It will give such details of the interest protected as the registrar considers appropriate (r.84(5)). If it only affects part of the land in the title it must identify that part (r.84(2)).

An application for the entry of a unilateral notice (ss.34 and 35 and r.83) must be made on Form UNI. The Form incorporates a declaration or certificate to be given by the applicant or his conveyancer in which must be set out the nature of the interest claimed. If the declaration or certificate shows a prima facie interest which is capable of being noted (see s.33 and (1) to (5) under "**Notices**" above) that interest will be noted in the charges register.

A fee calculated in accordance with the current Fee Order is payable.

The registrar must, subject to the exceptions mentioned below, serve notice of the entry of a unilateral notice on the registered proprietor and on any person who appears to the registrar to be entitled to the interest protected by the notice or on whom the registrar considers it appropriate to serve notice. The registrar is not obliged to give notice to a person who would otherwise be entitled to notice if that person is the person in whose favour the notice has been entered or if that person consented to the entry being made. Nor is the registrar obliged to serve notice on any person who appears to the registrar to be entitled to the interest protected by the notice or on whom the registrar considers it appropriate to serve notice if that person's address for service does not appear on the register in which the entry is to be made.

An application to be registered as beneficiary of an existing unilateral notice (r.88) must be made on Form UN3. The application must be supported by such evidence as is necessary to satisfy the registrar that the applicant has title to the interest which is the subject of the unilateral notice. Unless the registered beneficiary has signed Form UN3 or otherwise consented or the application is by his personal representative the registrar must serve notice on the registered beneficiary before proceeding. When time under any such notice has expired and the application is approved details of the applicant will be entered in place of the registered beneficiary or jointly with the registered beneficiary as the case may require.

A fee calculated in accordance with the current Fee Order is payable.

An application to remove a unilateral notice (r.85) must be made on Form UN2. The application must be made and the Form must be signed by the registered beneficiary, by his personal representative or trustee in bankruptcy or by a conveyancer on behalf of the applicant.

No fee is payable.

An application to cancel a unilateral notice (s.36 and r.86) must be made on Form UN4 by the registered proprietor, or by someone entitled to be registered as proprietor, of the land or charge affected. If the applicant is a person entitled to be registered he must produce evidence, or a certificate by a conveyancer, that he is so entitled.

No fee is payable.

Notice of such an application must be served on the registered beneficiary allowing 15 business days for objection. The 15 day period can be extended to a period of up to 30 business days if the beneficiary applies for an extension and the registrar, after consulting the applicant for cancellation if he thinks it appropriate, agrees to allow it. The extension allowed does not have to be the extension applied for. It can be for any period the registrar thinks fit to allow up to a total period of 30 business days.

If the registered beneficiary or a person entitled to be registered as such does not object within the notice period the unilateral notice must be cancelled. Even if an objection is lodged the registrar may decide that it is groundless and cancel the notice (s.73(6)). If the objection is not held to be groundless the registrar must give notice of it to the applicant for cancellation and it cannot be cancelled until the objection is disposed of (s.73(5)). If the matter cannot be disposed of by agreement it must be referred to the Adjudicator (s.73(7) and see Chapter 22).

Cautions against dealings

Although it has not been possible to enter a new caution against **15–005** dealings since October 13, 2003, any such caution entered before, or pursuant to an application lodged before, that date continues to have effect. It will be many years before all such cautions are withdrawn or cancelled. Paragraph 2(3) of Sch.12 to the Act provides that ss.55 and 56 of the Land Registration Act 1925 shall continue to have effect in relation to such cautions.

It should be noted that, although when a cautioner has died, his personal representatives can exercise his rights under the caution, unlike a unilateral notice, the benefit of a caution cannot be transferred. If the interest protected by the caution has changed hands, the new beneficiary should register a notice or restriction as appropriate and procure the withdrawal of the caution as to which see below.

A caution against dealings which was entered by a person claiming an interest in the proceeds of sale will not be allowed to prevent the registration of a disposition by which the protected interest would be overreached (for example, under s.27 of the Law of Property Act 1925).

A cautioner against dealings is liable in damages to anyone injured as a result of his lodging a caution without reasonable cause (see s.56(3) of the Land Registration Act 1925 and para.2(3) of Sch.12 to the Act).

The effect of a caution against dealings

15–006 If a caution against dealings is on the register, the registrar cannot, without the cautioner's consent (in writing signed by the cautioner or his conveyancer (r.219)), register any dealing with the land or charge affected until notice has been served on the cautioner. As to service of such notice see below.

Unlike a unilateral notice, a caution against dealings confers no priority for nor does it give notice of the cautionable interest (see *Clark v Chief Land Registrar* [1993] 2 W.L.R. 141).

It is important to note that a caution against dealings by the proprietor of land will not affect dispositions by the proprietor of a registered charge. On registration of a transfer of the land by a registered chargee in exercise of his power of sale, any caution against dealings with the land will be cancelled automatically without the cautioner being given the opportunity to object.

Withdrawal of a caution against dealings

15–007 A caution against dealings may be withdrawn by the cautioner at any time by lodging Form WCT signed by the cautioner or his conveyancer.

No fee is payable.

Cancellation of a caution against dealings

15–008 A caution against dealings can be cancelled following service of notice by the registrar:

(1) under s.55(1) of the Land Registration Act 1925 on receipt of an application to register a dealing with the land or charge affected; or

(2) pursuant to an application in Form CCD lodged by the registered proprietor, or by someone who, but for the caution, would be entitled to be registered as proprietor, of the land or charge affected (r.223). If the applicant is a person who, but for the caution, would be entitled to be registered he must produce evidence that he is so entitled.

The notice must warn the cautioner that his caution will cease to have any effect after the expiration of a period of 15 business days (or such longer period as the registrar directs under r.218) unless the registrar makes an order to the contrary (r.221(4)).

Cautioner showing cause (r.221)
Before the expiration of the notice period the cautioner can **15–009** show cause why the registrar should not give effect to the application which led to the service of notice. To show cause the cautioner must set grounds out in writing signed by him or his conveyancer showing a fairly arguable case why the application should not take effect. If the registrar is satisfied, by reading the written submission and making whatever other enquiries he thinks necessary, that the cautioner has shown cause he must order that the caution is to continue until withdrawn or otherwise disposed of.

When such an order has been made the registrar must give notice of it to the applicant and to the cautioner. The cautioner is then treated as having objected to the application under s.73. If the matter cannot be disposed of by agreement it must be referred to the Adjudicator (s.73(7) and see Chapter 22).

If the application that led to the service of the notice is cancelled, withdrawn or otherwise does not proceed, unless the caution has been cancelled or he has already done so, the registrar must make an order that the caution will continue to have effect (r.221(6)).

Restrictions

A restriction may prohibit, in relation to registered land or a **15–010** registered charge:

(1) the entry of any disposition or of dispositions of a particular type;

(2) the making of an entry:
    (a) indefinitely;
    (b) for a specified period; or
    (c) until a specified event which may, but does not have to, be the giving of notice, the obtaining of consent or an order of the court or of the registrar (s.40).

Under s.77 there is a duty, owed to any person who suffers damages as a result, not to enter a restriction without reasonable cause.

Effect of a restriction (s.41)

15–011 If a restriction is entered then no disposition to which it applies can be entered on the register except in accordance with the terms of that restriction unless the registrar by order disapplies or modifies the restriction in relation to a specific disposition or types of disposition.

Entry of restriction by the registrar or the court (ss.42, 44 and 46)

15–012 The registrar or the court may order a restriction to be entered and will do so if necessary to protect a right or claim but cannot do so if the interest could be protected by the entry of a notice.

In the case of the registration of two or more persons as proprietors the registrar must enter such restriction or restrictions as necessary to ensure that interests which should be overreached are overreached (see Chapter 17).

Application to enter a restriction (s.43)

15–013 A registered proprietor or a person entitled to be registered as such, or a person with the consent of a registered proprietor or of a person entitled to be registered as such, may apply on Form RX1 for a restriction to be entered. If the applicant is not the registered proprietor he must produce evidence of his right to apply or a conveyancer can certify that he is entitled to be registered or can certify, where necessary, that consent has been obtained. Application may also be made on Form RX1 by a person who has sufficient interest in the registered land or charge and r.93 (as amended by r.6 of the Land Registration (Amendment) Rules 2005) contains a detailed, but not exhaustive, list of persons regarded as having such an interest.

The application must set out full details of the required restriction. A reference to the standard form for the restriction in the Rules is not sufficient and any infills in the form must be completed. Any appropriate address for service must be provided (see r.5 of the Land Registration (Amendment) Rules 2005).

A fee calculated under the current Fee Order is payable.

An application may also be incorporated into a prescribed form of Transfer, Assent or Charge or in a Charge the form of which has first been approved by the registrar (r.92(7)). In such a case no fee is payable.

Form of restriction

Schedule 4 to the Rules, which has been amended and added to 15–014 by the Land Registration (Amendment) Rules 2005, contains standard forms of restriction. The Land Registration (Amendment) Rules 2005 allow for changes to be made to the standard forms where only part of a registered estate is affected and for the words "Until . . ." followed by a calendar date to be inserted in Form L, M, N, O, P, S or T. Certain standard forms are obligatory in the circumstances set out in rr.94 and 95. Some of the more commonly used standard forms are set out in the chapters of this book in which they are mentioned. Examples of other standard forms are:

Form M (Disposition by registered proprietor of registered estate or proprietor of charge — certificate of registered proprietor of specified title number required)

"[*Until* . . .] No disposition [*or specify details*] of the [*part of the*] registered estate [*shown edged red on the attached plan (or as the case may be)*] [(other than a charge)] by the proprietor of the registered estate [or by the proprietor of any registered charge] is to be registered without a certificate signed by the proprietor for the time being of the estate registered under title number [*title number*] [(or his conveyancer *or specify appropriate details)*] or, if appropriate, signed on such proprietor's behalf by [its secretary or conveyancer *or specify appropriate details*], that the provisions of [*specify clause, paragraph or other particulars*] of [*specify details*] have been complied with."

Form N (Disposition by registered proprietor of registered estate or proprietor of charge — consent or certificate required)

"[*Until* . . .] No disposition [*or specify details*] of the [*part of the*] registered estate [*shown edged red on the attached plan (or as the case may be)*] [(other than a charge)] by the proprietor of the registered estate [or by the proprietor of any registered charge] is to be registered without a written consent [signed by [*name*] of [*address*] [or [his conveyancer] *or specify appropriate details)*]] *or*

[signed on behalf of [*name*] of [*address*] by [its secretary or conveyancer *or specify appropriate details*]].

"Note — the text of the restriction may be continued, as follows, to allow for the provision of a certificate as an alternative to the consent.

[or without a certificate

[signed by [*name*] of [*address*] [or [his conveyancer] *or specify appropriate details*]]

or

[signed on behalf of [*name*] of [*address*] by [its secretary or conveyancer *or specify appropriate details*]]

or

[signed by a conveyancer]

or

[signed by the applicant for registration [or his conveyancer]]

that the provisions of [*specify clause, paragraph or other particulars*] of [*specify details*] have been complied with.]".

Use of the standard forms is recommended if at all possible. If no standard form is available application may be made to enter a non-standard form but the registrar may only accept it if (s.43(3)):

(1) its terms are reasonable; and

(2) its application would be straightforward and would not place an unreasonable burden on the registrar.

The fee for the entry of a non-standard restriction is double that payable for the entry of a standard restriction. Care should be taken when completing the RX1 not to alter the wording of a standard form and inadvertently change it to a non-standard form.

Application to disapply or modify a restriction (r.96)

15–015 An application for an order of the registrar disapplying or modifying a restriction must be in Form RX2. Details of any modification requested must be given. The applicant must explain how he has sufficient interest to apply and why the order is required and should be made. The registrar may serve notice or make further enquiries before making an order. If an order is made it must be noted on the register.

A fee calculated under the current Fee Order is payable.

Application to cancel a restriction (r.97)
An application to cancel a restriction must be in Form RX3 **15–016**
accompanied by evidence that the restriction is no longer
required. If the registrar is satisfied with the evidence he must
cancel the restriction.
No fee is payable.

Application to withdraw a restriction (r.98)
An application to withdraw a restriction must be in Form RX4 **15–017**
accompanied by the consent as specified in r.98 or a certificate
by a conveyancer that he holds such consent.

In general, a voluntary restriction cannot be cancelled as a
matter of course when a dealing (even a transfer on sale) made
in accordance with its provisions is registered. Therefore, if it is
intended that the restriction shall not survive the registration of
the dealing, it is advisable that an express withdrawal be
obtained.

Obligatory restrictions and those entered pursuant to an order
of the registrar or of the court cannot be withdrawn.
No fee is payable.

Inhibitions

Although it has not been possible to enter a new inhibition since **15–018**
October 13, 2003, an inhibition entered before that date will
continue to have effect. Inhibitions prohibit, wholly or partially,
the exercise of a proprietor's powers of disposition. Inhibitions,
other than bankruptcy inhibitions, are very uncommon. An
application to discharge or cancel an inhibition must be made to
the court if the inhibition was originally entered pursuant to an
order of the court; otherwise it must be made to the registrar.
No fee is payable for cancellation.

Protection of non-local land charges, pending land actions, writs and orders, deeds of arrangement

Section 14(1) of the Land Charges Act 1972 (as amended by **15–019**
para.10 of Sch.11 to the Act) provides that that Act shall not
apply to instruments or matters if and so far as they affect
registered land and can be protected under the Land Registration Act 2002.

A pending land action, writ or order affecting land, or made for the purpose of enforcing a judgment, should be protected by agreed or unilateral notice or by restriction. Forms of restriction appropriate to certain types of order are specified in r.93. The form of the restriction will depend on the nature of the pending land action or the nature of the writ or order. A writ or order relating to an undivided share under a trust of land is not an interest affecting land for this purpose. Where the order has the effect of creating a trust of land the interest cannot be protected by the entry of a notice but should be protected by a restriction, normally in Form A.

If a deed of voluntary arrangement by a sole registered proprietor contains an equitable charge or any contract for sale, option or right of pre-emption in favour of the supervisor an agreed notice or unilateral notice may be entered. A restriction (normally in Form N) will be possible with the consent of the registered proprietor or where the deed contains restrictions on the registered proprietor's power to dispose of the property. In the case of a joint proprietor, an application may be made for the entry of a restriction (normally in Form A), if the deed contains a declaration of trust or an assignment or charge of the debtor's beneficial interest.

Local land charges

15–020   Rights under local land charges affecting registered land are interests which override first registration and registered dispositions (Schs.1 and 3 to the Act).

If a local land charge affecting registered land is a legal charge or a legal mortgage and is to be realised, it must be registered as a registered charge (s.55).

Searches in the registers of local land charges maintained by local authorities must be made in relation to registered land just as for unregistered land.

Chapter 16

Home Rights

[*In this chapter the husband is treated as the owner of the matrimonial home and the wife as the spouse whose rights are in need of protection. However, the text will apply equally when the roles are reversed.*

The Civil Partnership Act 2004 received Royal Assent on November 18, 2004. The Act creates a new legal relationship of civil partnership, which two people of the same sex can form by signing a registration document. It also provides same sex couples who form a civil partnership with parity of treatment, in a wide range of legal matters with those opposite sex couples who enter into a civil marriage. Section 82 and Schedule 9 to the 2004 Act amends the Family Law Act 1996 to extend to civil partners the same rights of occupation of their home as apply to a matrimonial home. The government has announced that the Act will come into force on 5 December 2005. The Land Registration (Amendment) (No.2) Rules 2005 amend the Rules, with effect from the coming into force of Schedule 9 of the 2004 Act, to take account of the provisions of that Act, so that a matrimonial home rights notice will become a home rights notice and Forms MH1, MH2 and MH3 will be replaced by Forms HR1, HR2 and HR3.]

Family Law Act 1996 ("the 1996 Act")

A wife's rights of occupation under the 1996 Act constitute a **16–001** charge on the matrimonial home which, if the home is held under a registered title, should be protected by the registration of an agreed notice (r.80).

Even if the wife is in actual occupation of the matrimonial home her rights of occupation under the 1996 Act are not an overriding interest (see s.31(10)(b) of the 1996 Act as amended by para.34 of Sch.11 to the Act).

Prior to February 14, 1983, such a charge could also be protected by registration of a caution against dealings.

No protection under the 1996 Act is necessary when the matrimonial home is held, legally and beneficially, by husband and wife jointly.

The registration of a land charge of Class F in the Land Charges Department will afford no protection in the case of registered land.

The protection of a notice (registered land) or a Class F land charge registration in the Land Charges Department (unregistered land) is only available in respect of one home at any one time (see below).

Is the matrimonial home registered?

16–002 If it is not known whether the land is registered, an application for an official search of the index map should be made on Form SIM (see Chapter 2). The top of the form should be endorsed *"This search is being made solely for the purposes of the Family Law Act 1996. Please reveal details of any registered lease."* Provided that the applicant makes it clear that the search is required for the purposes of the 1996 Act, even if no plan of the property is available, where one would normally be required, the Registry will do its best to identify the property and will not raise any point which might otherwise arise as to the precise boundaries of the property. The certificate of the result of the search will reveal what interests (if any) in the land are registered including particulars of any registered lease. If any doubt remains as to whether or not the registered title is owned by the husband an official copy of the register can be obtained by lodging Form OC1 (see Chapter 8).

Application for notice

16–003 The application should be made to the appropriate office in Form MH1. If the court has made an order by virtue of s.33(5) of the 1996 Act (see below) either an office copy of the order must accompany the application or a conveyancer must complete the form with details of the order and certify that he holds an office copy of it. No fee is payable.

The Registry will serve notice on a husband of the entry of a notice to protect his wife's rights of occupation.

Rights continued by order of court

16–004 A wife's rights of occupation will only continue so long as the marriage subsists, but the court may direct otherwise by an order under s.33(5) of the 1996 Act during the subsistence of the marriage. If the court makes an order directing that the wife's rights of occupation shall not be brought to an end by the termination of the marriage, whether by death or otherwise, and those rights have not already been protected on the register of title, an application for an agreed notice should be made, as indicated above, as soon as possible. If the court makes such an order, and the wife's rights of occupation have already been protected on the register of title, an application for renewal of the registration in respect of matrimonial home rights should be made as soon as possible.

Renewal of registration in respect of matrimonial home rights

If by virtue of s.33(5) of the 1996 Act the court makes an order **16–005** directing that the wife's rights of occupation shall not be brought to an end by the termination of the marriage, whether by death or otherwise, and those rights have already been protected on the register by a notice or, prior to February 14, 1983, by a caution against dealings, an application should be made as soon as possible for the renewal, by way of agreed notice, of the registration of the notice or the caution against dealings so that the making of the order can be recorded on the register. The application should be made to the appropriate office in Form MH2 either accompanied by an office copy of the order or a conveyancer must complete the form with details of the order and certify that he holds an office copy of it. The renewal will be effected on the register by the entry of an agreed notice referring to the order. It will not affect the priority of the wife's charge (para.4(5) of Sch.4 to the 1996 Act). No fee is payable.

The Registry will serve notice on a husband of the entry of a notice renewing the registration of a notice or caution to protect his wife's rights of occupation.

Change of matrimonial home

A wife may have protection in relation to only one home at any **16–006** one time, whether the protection is the registration of a notice or caution in respect of registered land or a registration in the register of land charges of Class F at the Land Charges Department. Accordingly, any earlier subsisting registration must be disclosed on Form MH1, and it will be cancelled when the new charge is registered (para.2 of Sch.4 to the 1996 Act).

Cancellation of notice

16–007 An application to cancel the registration or renewal of registration of an agreed notice of a wife's rights of occupation under the 1996 Act must be made on Form AP1, accompanied by the evidence required by para.4 of Sch.4 to the 1996 Act. That evidence will normally be:

(1) the death certificate or other sufficient evidence of death of either spouse (but see (5) below); or

(2) an official copy of a decree absolute of divorce or nullity; if a decree of divorce by an overseas court is lodged, additional evidence, *e.g.* as to residence, domicile or nationality, may be required; and if the decree is not in English, a notarially certified translation should be provided (but see (5) below); or

(3) an order of the court terminating the wife's rights of occupation; or

(4) a written release of her rights by the wife; and

(5) where the supporting evidence is evidence of the husband's death or a copy of a decree absolute produced in accordance with (1) or (2) above and:

    (a) by virtue of s.33(5) of the 1996 Act, the court has made an order directing that the wife's rights of occupation shall not be brought to an end by the death or other termination of the marriage; and

    (b) that order is referred to on the register,

satisfactory evidence that the order has ceased to have effect. No fee is payable.

Cancellation of caution

16–008 An application to cancel a caution against dealings protecting a wife's rights of occupation under the 1996 Act may be made in one of the following ways:

(1) by application in Form CCD by the registered proprietor or a person who, but for the caution, would be entitled to be registered as proprietor which will lead to service of notice on the cautioner (see Chapter 15); or

(2) by withdrawal of the caution on Form WCT signed by the wife or by her personal representatives or conveyancers.

No fee is payable.

Rights of occupation of a bankrupt's spouse

A wife cannot acquire rights of occupation in the period **16–009** between the presentation of a bankruptcy petition and the vesting of the bankrupt's property in a trustee (s.336(1) of the Insolvency Act 1986 (as amended by the Family Law Act 1996, s.66(1); Sch.8, para.57(2)). Any rights of occupation existing prior to the bankruptcy petition continue to subsist notwithstanding the bankruptcy (s.336(2)).

The trustee in bankruptcy may apply to the bankruptcy court at any time for an order to restrict or terminate the wife's rights. In making an order the court must have regard to all the circumstances of the case except the needs of the bankrupt. Where such an application is made one year after the date on which the bankrupt's property vested in a trustee, the court has to assume that the interests of the creditors are paramount unless there are exceptional circumstances (s.336(4) and (5)). An office copy of the court order should accompany any application based on it.

Rights of occupation of a bankrupt

Whether or not his spouse has rights of occupation, a bankrupt **16–010** who:

(1) is entitled to occupy a dwelling-house by virtue of a beneficial estate or interest;

(2) at some time occupied that dwelling-house with children under 18; and

(3) provided a home for those children under 18 at the time of the bankruptcy petition and at the time of the bankruptcy order;

has rights of occupation against his trustee in bankruptcy under the Family Law Act 1996.

If he is in occupation he has a right not to be evicted or excluded without leave of the bankruptcy court. If he is not in occupation he has a right, with leave of the bankruptcy court, to enter into occupation (s.337 of the Insolvency Act 1986 (as amended by the Family Law Act 1996, s.66(1); Sch.8, para.58)).

The bankrupt's rights are a charge which has the same priority as an equitable interest created immediately before the commencement of the bankruptcy (s.337(2)(b)). Where a bankrupt has such rights, he may protect them by entry of notice under the 1996 Act and he may enter such notice notwithstanding the fact that he is the registered proprietor. In his application he should state that he is applying pursuant to the provisions of the Insolvency Act 1986 and that the property is vested in his trustee in bankruptcy.

To restrict or terminate these rights, the trustee in bankruptcy must apply to the bankruptcy court which must have regard to the matters mentioned in "Rights of occupation of a bankrupt's spouse" above (s.337(4), (5) and (6)). An office copy should accompany any application based on such an order.

Search by mortgagees

16–011 A mortgagee of a dwelling-house who brings an action to enforce his security is obliged, under s.56 of the 1996 Act, to serve notice of the action on a spouse whose rights of occupation are protected at the relevant time by notice or caution. The proprietor of a registered charge or mortgagee of registered land may apply to the appropriate office on Form MH3 or by telephone or electronically (r.158) for an official certificate of the result of a search which will reveal if there is a notice or caution registered. The search will confer priority for a period of 15 days (s.56(5) of the 1996 Act).

A fee calculated in accordance with the current Fee Order is payable.

Chapter 17

Trusts, Charities and Settled Land

Trusts of land

The Trusts of Land and Appointment of Trustees Act 1996 **17–001** reformed the law on trusts of land and the appointment of trustees. It defines a "trust of land" as any trust of property which consists of or includes land. The definition includes a trust created before the commencement of the 1996 Act, and any description of trust so that it includes an express, implied, constructive or resulting trust as well as a trust for sale and a bare trust. "Land" now includes an undivided share in land. It is still impossible to sever the legal estate so any trust of an undivided share will exist behind another trust. If the land is registered, it must be registered in the names of the trustees of the entirety of the land. The registrar is not affected with notice of a trust (s.78). It is, of course, sometimes clear from the register that proprietors are trustees. For example, where joint proprietors are registered, either with the joint proprietorship restriction set out in Chapter 10 or without restriction, they must be trustees of land. This fact, however, does not give notice of the trust.

As with unregistered land, the number of trustees for sale cannot exceed four, and capital money must not be paid to fewer than two trustees except where a trust corporation is the sole trustee.

Observance of this rule relating to capital money is secured by means of the joint proprietorship restriction referred to above which is entered in the proprietorship register both on first registration and on dispositions of registered land where two or more persons are registered as the proprietors of the land and the application for registration does not clearly show that a sole survivor of the proprietors will be able to give a valid receipt for capital money arising on a disposition of the land. If the proprietors are joint tenants in equity, the survivor of them will be able to give a valid receipt for capital money. In those circumstances, the position should be made clear in the appropriate panel on the form of transfer or, where the application is for first registration, in panel 11 of Form FR1.

Subject to this restriction, and to any other restriction on the register, the trustees will have full powers of disposing of the land. Accordingly, if some further restriction is necessary to protect the interests of the beneficiaries, *e.g.* in the case of partnership property, the trustees should apply for it to be registered. Application must be made on Form RX1. Rule 94 sets out the circumstances when and by whom an application for a restriction must be made, *e.g.* where the powers of the trustees are limited by virtue of s.8 of the 1996 Act. Rule 92 explains how an application for a restriction is made and r.93 states who is regarded as having a sufficient interest to apply for a restriction for the purposes of s.43(1)(c). Schedule 4 to the Rules, as amended by the Land Registration (Amendment) Rules 2005, sets out standard forms of restriction which should be used. If one of the standard forms is not used, regard should be had to s.43(3) when drafting a restriction. See also Chapter 15.

A disposition (off the register) of an individual share in the proceeds of sale of registered land may be followed by a transfer of the registered land designed to bring the registered ownership into line with the beneficial ownership.

The position on the death of a joint proprietor or the survivor of joint proprietors, and the cancellation of the joint proprietorship restriction in certain circumstances, are discussed in Chapter 18.

Creation of trust of land by registered proprietor

17–002 If a registered proprietor executes a trust deed creating a trust of his land and appointing trustees, he can (subject to any entry to the contrary on the register) transfer the land to the trustees by an ordinary transfer of whole (Form TR1). The consideration panel may be completed to the effect that the transfer is not for money or anything which has a monetary value. The declaration of trust panel can be completed to the effect that the trustees are to hold the property "on the trusts of a trust deed (*or as the case may be*) dated (*etc.*)". The trust deed should not usually accompany the application.

When a transfer to trustees is delivered for registration, it should be made clear whether or not the survivor of the transferees can give a valid receipt for capital money arising on a disposition of the land. The Registry will then enter the usual joint proprietorship restriction referred to above, if appropriate, and the trustees should apply (on Form RX1) for any other restriction necessary to ensure that the interests of the beneficiaries are protected and the trusts duly executed. If any special restriction based on the trust deed is needed, the registrar may retain an original trust deed lodged with such an application but will return the original if requested to do so and if the application is accompanied by a certified copy of the deed (r.203).

A fee for registration of a transfer other than for monetary consideration is payable, calculated in accordance with the current Fee Order. No fee is payable in respect of the joint proprietorship restriction. Fees are payable in respect of additional restrictions, calculated in accordance with the current Fee Order.

Appointment and discharge of trustees

There are a number of ways of effecting the appointment and **17–003** discharge of trustees of land. If all the outgoing trustees are willing to cooperate, the simplest way is for the existing registered proprietors to execute a transfer in Form TR1 or TR5 to the continuing and new trustees. None of the statements in the consideration panel should be completed. Instead, the words "This transfer is made for the purpose of effecting an appointment of new trustees" should be inserted in the additional provisions panel. Such a transfer can be used in addition to a separate deed of appointment or discharge or on its own, instead of a deed of appointment. If a deed of appointment is used as well, the Registry will not usually need to see it but words such as "This transfer is made pursuant to a deed of appointment of new trustees dated today" should be inserted in the additional provisions panel of the transfer.

Under s.40 of the Trustee Act 1925, some deeds of appointment or retirement automatically vest trust property in new and continuing trustees. If the tust property includes a registered estate or registered charge, the transfer by operation of law must be completed by registration in accordance with s.27(5) of the 2002 Act. On application in Form AP1 and on the production of the deed of appointment, the Registry will give effect on the register to any express or implied vesting declaration in the deed (r.161). There must be lodged with the application the deed and either a certificate from the conveyancer acting for the persons making the appointment that they are entitled to do so, or such other evidence (*e.g.* copy trust instrument or statutory declaration proving the relevant facts) to satisfy the registrar that the persons making the appointment are entitled to do so.

Such a deed of appointment may be the best way to proceed where, *e.g.* a trustee has been replaced under s.36(1) of the Trustee Act 1925, on the grounds that he has remained out of the United Kingdom for more than 12 months, or refuses or is unfit to act in the trust, or is incapable of doing so.

Fees are payable, calculated in accordance with the current Fee Order.

Sole trustees

17–004 If a sole trustee applies to be registered as proprietor of land (whether on first registration or otherwise) it is his duty to apply for a restriction or restrictions, as may be necessary, to protect the interests of the beneficiaries and to ensure that the trust is properly carried out. If he is a sole trustee of land or the sole survivor of trustees of land, he should apply for the entry of a restriction to prevent him from dealing with the land for value until an additional trustee has been appointed to act jointly with him. The joint proprietorship restriction referred to above can be used for this purpose. The registrar is under no obligation to enter such a restriction automatically on registering a sole or last surviving trustee as proprietor of land. The trustee should also apply for the entry of any other restriction necessary to protect the beneficiaries' interests. Application must be made on Form RX1. Reference should be made to the standard forms of restriction set out in Sch.4 to the Rules.

No fee will be payable for the entry of a Form A (joint proprietorship) restriction. Fees are payable in respect of other restrictions, calculated in accordance with the current Fee Order.

Charities

17–005 Under the Charities Act 1993 ("the 1993 Act") dispositions of land on or after August 1, 1993:

(1) to a charity must contain a statement as to whether the charity is an exempt charity (*i.e.* free from the restrictions on disposition imposed by s.36 of the 1993 Act); and

(2) by a charity must contain similar statements and in the case of a non-exempt charity a certificate by the charity trustees as to whether the sanction of the Charity Commissioners or the court has been obtained or is not required.

The statements enable the Registry to enter an appropriate form of restriction on registering a charity and to decide whether the restriction has been complied with when registering a disposition by a charity.

The 1993 Act does not apply to land held for the charitable purposes of the Church of England although it does catch land held by some Church of England bodies (*e.g.* the Church Commissioners and Diocesan Boards of Finance).

Dispositions to charities

A transfer, lease or other disposition of registered land to a **17–006** charity and a conveyance or assignment or lease of unregistered land which will lead to compulsory registration must contain one of the following statements (r.179), either:

> "The land transferred (*or as the case may be*) will, as a result of this transfer (*or as the case may be*), be held by (*or* in trust for) (*charity*), an exempt charity."

or

> "The land transferred [*or as the case may be*] will, as a result of this transfer [*or as the case may be*], be held by (*or* in trust for) (*charity*), a non-exempt charity and the restrictions on disposition imposed by section 36 of the Charities Act 1993 will apply to the land (subject to section 36(9) of that Act)."

The statements set out above are not required to be included in any charge in favour of a charity.

Where the disposition is to an exempt charity the registrar does not have to enter a restriction. Application for an appropriate restriction must be made if such a restriction is required because of limitations on the powers of the charity.

In the event of a voluntary application for first registration by a non-exempt charity, where the conveyance or other instrument will not contain one of the above statements, r.176 provides that the application must be accompanied by an application for entry of the appropriate restriction in Form E (Sch.4 to the Rules) (see below). Application for a restriction must be made on Form RX1. Application for the appropriate restriction must also be made where application is made to register a transfer which does not contain the necessary statement set out above or application is made under r.161 to register the vesting of a registered estate in a person other than the proprietor of that estate.

Where the charity trustees are incorporated as a body corporate under Pt VII of the 1993 Act any disposition of registered land in their favour must describe the trustees as:

"a body corporate under Part VII of the Charities Act 1993".

Applications by charities

17–007 Where application is made for registration of the Official Custodian for Charities as proprietor the application must enclose:

(1) an order of court made under s.21(1) of the 1993 Act; or

(2) an order of the Charity Commissioners made under s.16 or 18 of the 1993 Act.

In addition, where land is vested in the Official Custodian (other than by virtue of an order under s.18 of the Charities Act 1993) the address of the charity trustees must be supplied (the address of the Official Custodian may also be given as an alternative address for service). The address of the Official Custodian will be entered as the address for service if the land is vested in him by virtue of an order under s.18 of the 1993 Act and the application must be accompanied by an application for a restriction in Form F (see below).

Where the applicant is a body incorporated under Pt VII of the 1993 Act the certificate granted by the Charity Commissioners under s.50 of that Act must be lodged with the application. Where the charity is a body corporate incorporated under a statute or charter other than the 1993 Act this should be stated.

Where the disposition is in favour of an exempt charity, the document creating the charitable trust should be lodged. Otherwise no evidence of the charity's constitution or trusts should be lodged save for where the charity is incorporated otherwise than under the 1993 Act or under the Companies Act when such documentation should be lodged.

Entry of proprietor

17–008 The normal limit of four owners of a legal estate does not apply to charities.

Where charity trustees are individuals the Registry will, if requested, enter the name of the charity as a description after the names and addresses of the trustees. If the charity trustees have been incorporated under Pt VII of the 1993 Act this fact will be stated in the proprietorship entry.

Where land has been transferred to the Official Custodian for Charities the proprietorship entry will read:

"Proprietor(s): The Official Custodian for Charities on behalf of [*name of charity*] of [*address of charity*]".

In the past the Registry registered the trustees of some unincorporated charities collectively as, *e.g.* "The trustees of the charity known as the Oldbridge Trust". This practice has been discontinued. The Registry will accept a certificate from the secretary or conveyancer of the charity as to the identity of the present trustees where trustees so registered are being dealt with. The names of all the individual trustees will be entered on the register at the next available opportunity.

Schedule 4 to the Rules prescribes two restrictions for charities. They are:

Form E (Non-exempt charity — certicate required)

"No disposition by the proprietor of the registered estate to which section 36 or section 38 of the Charities Act 1993 applies is to be registered unless the instrument contains a certificate complying with section 37(2) or section 39(2) of that Act as appropriate."

Form F (Land vested in official custodian on trust for non-exempt charity — authority required)

"No disposition executed by the trustees of [*charity*] in the name and on behalf of the proprietor shall be registered unless the transaction is authorised by an order of the court or of the Charity Commissioners, as required by section 22(3) of the Charities Act 1993."

If a charity is subject to other limitations on its powers it should request on Form RX1 that appropriate restrictions are entered. A joint proprietorship restriction (see above) will be entered by the registrar when registering joint proprietors in these circumstances.

Dispositions by charities
The 1993 Act requires non-exempt charities to take certain **17–009** prescribed steps before disposing of land. Provided those steps are taken and they have power under the trusts of the charity to make the disposal, the charity trustees can dispose of the land

(but not to a connected person) without an order of the Charity Commissioners or the court. As has been stated above, when a non-exempt charity is registered as proprietor of registered land that status is reflected in a restriction in the proprietorship register. In accepting a disposition for registration the Registry must ensure that the terms of the restriction have been complied with and that the disposition contains the prescribed statements.

(1) *Compliance with the restriction* — In the case of a Form E (non-exempt charities) restriction the disposition should include a certificate as follows:

> "The [transferors (*or as the case may be*)]/[chargors] certify that this [disposition]/[charge] has been sanctioned by an order of the [court]/[Charity Commissioners]."

or

> "The [transferors (*or as the case may be*)]/[chargors] certify that as charity trustees they have power under the trusts of the charity to effect this disposition and that they have [complied with the provisions of section 36 of the Charities Act 1993 so far as applicable to it]/[obtained and considered such advice as is mentioned in subsection (2) of section 38 of the Charities Act 1993]."

The certificate must be given by the charity trustees. Even if they are not the registered proprietors of the land they must join in the disposition to give these certificates.

No certificate is required in a transfer to appoint new trustees as it is not a sale, lease or other disposal by the charity.

In the case of other restrictions the Registry will require evidence that the restriction has been complied with.

Where unregistered land is held on charitable trusts the powers of disposal are restricted just as they are if the land is registered. When examining a title on first registration the Registry will require appropriate evidence that the disposition is permitted as if the appropriate restriction had applied. The disposition will, of course, contain the certificate referred to at the beginning of this section.

(2) *Statements required in the disposition* — All dispositions, of registered land and of unregistered land which must be registered, by a charity (exempt or non-exempt) must include the appropriate one of the following statements (r.180):

"The land [transferred (*or as the case may be*)]/[charged] is held by [(*proprietors*) in trust for] (*charity*), an exempt charity."

or

"The land [transferred (*or as the case may be*)]/[charged] is held by [(*proprietors*) in trust for] (*charity*), a non-exempt charity, but this transfer (*or as the case may be*)]/[charge (*or mortgage*)] is one falling within paragraph [(a),(b) *or* (c) *as the case may be*] of section 36(9)/[section 38(5)] of the Charities Act 1993."

or

"The land [transferred (*or as the case may be*)]/[charged] is held by [(*proprietors*) in trust for] (*charity*), a non-exempt charity, and this [transfer (*or as the case may be*)] [charge (*or mortgage*)] is not one falling within paragraph (a), (b) or (c) of section 36(9) of the Charities Act 1993, so the restrictions [on disposition imposed by section 36]/[imposed by section 38] of that Act apply [to the land]."

Where the disposition is by a non-exempt charity and is a charge triggering first registration under s.4(1)(g) of the Act, it must also state that "The restrictions on disposition imposed by section 36 of the Charities Act 1993 also apply to the land (subject to section 36(9) of that Act)".

(3) *Disposition of charity land registered before 1993 or between 1993 and 2003* — Proprietorship of the land of a non-exempt charity registered before 1993 will be subject to old forms of restriction. On disposition the old restrictions will be treated as if they were in one of the new forms and one of the certificates set out at (1) should be included in the deed. One of the statements set out at (2) will, of course, also be required. The same will be true of proprietorship of such land registered between 1993 and 2003.

Execution by charities Section 82 of the 1993 Act allows charity trustees to delegate to no fewer than two of them a general authority to execute on behalf of all of them any deed which gives effect to a transaction to which the trustees are a party. The Registry will not require any evidence of delegation if the transfer, charge or other disposition states that it has been executed pursuant to s.82 and the disposition is for money or money's worth and there is no reason to doubt the good faith of the person in whose favour it is made. In the absence of a delegation under s.82 all the trustees must execute the deed using the form of execution appropriate to an individual.

If the charity trustees have been incorporated under Part VII of the 1993 Act, the body corporate can execute by affixing its common seal (if it has one) in the presence of appropriate officers of the charity. If the charity chooses not to use or does not have a common seal two other methods of execution are provided by the 1993 Act. These are:

(1) by a majority of the individual charity trustees and expressed to be executed by the body (*e.g.* "This Transfer is executed by [*names of trustees*] being a majority of the incorporated trustees of [*name of the charity*] under the provisions of section 60(3)(a) of the Charities Act 1993") — the Registry will require evidence that those executing are a majority; or

(2) pursuant to a general or limited authority conferred on any two or more trustees to execute in the name and on behalf of the body corporate (s.60(4) of the 1993 Act) — the Registry will require evidence of the authority.

If charity land is registered in the name of the Official Custodian for Charities he does not execute deeds personally. All the charity trustees must execute or they may adopt one of the methods of execution outlined above just as if they were registered as owners.

Settled land

17–010 The Trusts of Land and Appointment of Trustees Act 1996 provided that no new settlements under the Settled Land Act 1925 could be created after the commencement of the 1996 Act. As far as existing settlements are concerned, s.89 of the Act provides that rules may make provision for the purposes of the Act in relation to the application to registered land of the enactments relating to settlements under the Settled Land Act 1925. The relevant provisions of the Rules are r.186 and Sch.7.

Settled land is registered in the name of the tenant for life, statutory owner or special personal representatives in whom the legal estate would be vested if the land were unregistered. The successive or other interests created by or arising under a settlement and capable of being overridden under the Settled Land Act 1925 or any other statute do not appear on the register. The rights of the persons beneficially interested in the land are, however, protected by restrictions entered in the proprietorship register.

Three restrictions are prescribed by the Rules. They are set out in Sch.4 and are as follows:

Form G (Tenant for life as registered proprietor, where there are trustees of the settlement)

> "No disposition is to be registered unless authorised by the **17–011** Settled Land Act 1925, or by any extension of those statutory powers in the settlement, and no disposition under which capital money arises is to be registered unless the money is paid to (*name*) of (*address*) and (*name*) of (*address*), (the trustees of the settlement, who may be a sole trust corporation or, if individuals, must number at least two but not more than four) or into court."

If applicable under the terms of the settlement, a further provision may be added that no transfer of the mansion house (shown on an attached plan or otherwise adequately described to enable it to be fully identified on the Ordnance Survey Map or title plan) is to be registered without the consent of the named trustees or an order of the court.

Form H (Statutory owners as trustees of the settlement and registered proprietors of settled land)

> "No disposition is to be registered unless authorised by the **17–012** Settled Land Act 1925, or by any extension of those statutory powers in the settlement, and, except where the sole proprietor is a trust corporation, no disposition under which capital money arises is to be registered unless the money is paid to at least two proprietors."

This restriction does not apply where the statutory owners are not the trustees of the settlement.

Form I (Tenant for life as registered proprietor of settled land no trustees of the settlement)

> "No disposition under which capital money arises, or which is **17–013** not authorised by the Settled Land Act 1925 or by any extension of those statutory powers in the settlement, is to be registered."

The restrictions may be modified on application or as the registrar sees fit according to the circumstances. Where one of the prescribed restrictions should have been entered in the register and has not been, any person who has an interest in the settled land can apply for such restriction (modified if appropriate) to be entered. The persons interested under the settlement may wish to apply for any additional restriction necessitated by the provisions of the settlement.

Except in the instances referred to in para.8 of Sch.7 to the Rules (proprietor ceasing in his lifetime to be the tenant for life) and para.14 (discharge of registered land from beneficial interests and powers under a settlement) the restrictions bind the proprietor in his lifetime but do not affect dispositions by his personal representatives.

Fees are payable in respect of restrictions, calculated in accordance with the current Fee Order.

On the first registration of settled land, the application must be accompanied by an application in Form RX1 for entry of a restriction in Form G, H, or I as appropriate.

When registered land is settled land the proprietor or, if there is no proprietor, the personal representatives of a deceased proprietor must apply to the registrar in Form RX1 for the entry of any appropriate restrictions, in addition to a restriction in Form G, H or I. The application must state that the restrictions are required for the protection of the beneficial interests and powers under the settlement.

When registered land is transferred into settlement, the transfer must include the appropriate provisions set out in para.4 of Sch.7 to the Rules. The application for registration of the transfer must be accompanied by an application in Form RX1 for entry of the appropriate restriction.

Where registered land is brought into a settlement and the existing registered proprietor is the tenant for life, the registered proprietor must make a declaration in Form 6 (Sch.3 to the Rules) and apply in Form RX1 for the entry of a restriction in Form G, modified as appropriate.

Where registered land is bought with capital money the transfer must be in one of the forms prescribed by r.206 (Sch.1 forms) and include the appropriate provisions set out in para.6 of Sch.7 to the Rules. The application for registration must be accompanied by an application in Form RX1 for the appropriate restriction.

During a minority the personal representatives under a will or intestacy of a person who died before January 1, 1997, under which a settlement of registered land is created or arises must be registered as proprietors and will have all the powers conferred by the Settled Land Act 1925 on a tenant for life and on the trustees of the settlement. When the minor becomes beneficially entitled to an estate in fee simple or a term of years absolute in registered land or would, if he were of full age, be or have the powers of a tenant for life, the personal representatives must (unless they are the statutory owner) during the minority give effect on the register to the directions of the statutory owner. The statutory owner must direct the personal representatives to apply for a restriction in Form H. The registrar is under no duty to call for any information regarding why an application is made, or the terms of the will or devolution under the intestacy, or the directions of the statutory owner. Instead the registrar can assume that the personal representatives are acting according to the directions given and that the directions were given and were correct. A disponee dealing with the personal representatives who complies with the Form H restriction is not concerned to see or enquire whether any directions have been given by the statutory owner with regard to the disposition to him.

If a minor becomes entitled in possession to registered land otherwise than on a death (or will be so entitled on attaining full age) the statutory owner during the minority is entitled to have the land transferred to them and to be registered as proprietor. The transfer must be in form TR1 and must not refer to the settlement. An application to register the transfer must be accompanied by an application in Form RX1 for a restriction in Form H.

Paragraph 11 of Sch.7 to the Rules deals with registration of special personal representatives where the land was settled before the death of the sole or last surviving joint registered proprietor and not by his will and the settlement continues after death.

As changes take place under a settlement of registered land, the registered proprietor or his personal representatives must execute the instruments necessary to give effect to the changes on the register and must apply for any necessary changes in the restrictions appearing on the register. An appropriate Sch.1 form should be used, modified where necessary according to the facts, *e.g.* in accordance with para.12 of Sch.7 to the Rules.

New trustees are appointed in the usual way. Where, however, a restriction in Form G appears on the register, an application to modify the restriction by substituting the new names is necessary. This should be made in Form RX2 signed by any continuing trustees and the new trustees or their respective conveyancers. Deaths of trustees must be proved by death certificates. A fee is payable, calculated in accordance with the current Fee Order.

When the settlement ends on the death of the tenant for life, an application to register a transfer by the personal representative to the person entitled must be accompanied by the grant of probate or letters of administration of the deceased proprietor if the personal representative is not already registered and Form

RX3 for cancellation of the restriction relating to the settlement. A fee is payable, calculated in accordance with the current Fee Order. If the settlement ends because the tenant for life becomes absolutely entitled, free from all interests under the settlement, the trustees may release the land from the interests under the settlement by a deed of release. If this is lodged at the Registry with a certified copy, and a request in Form RX3 for the cancellation of any restriction, the restriction will be cancelled. No fee is payable for the cancellation of a restriction.

Chapter 18

Death

Death of sole or sole surviving proprietor

Registration of the personal representative(s)

On the death of a sole or sole surviving proprietor, his personal **18–001** representative(s) may apply to be registered as proprietor(s) in place of the deceased proprietor on production of:

- the grant of probate or letters of administration of the estate of the sole or sole surviving proprietor; or

- a court order appointing the applicant as the deceased's personal representative; or

- a certificate from the conveyancer acting for the applicant that he holds the original or an office copy of the grant, letters of administration or court order (r.163(2)).

There are exceptions. Where the register states that the deceased was the administrator of the estate of a deceased person, a grant of letters of administration de bonis non to the estate of the first deceased person must be obtained, and the administrators de bonis non can then apply to be registered as proprietors. Similarly, when the register states that the deceased was the executor of a deceased person, but the executor has died intestate, his administrator is not entitled to be registered in the deceased executor's place: a grant of letters of administration de bonis non to the estate of the original testator is necessary, and the administrators de bonis non can then apply to be registered as proprietors.

Such an application should be lodged under cover of a Form AP1 and accompanied by the fee payable under the current Fee Order under Scale 2.

On the completion of the registration, the personal representative(s) will be described on the register as "executor *or* executrix (*or* administrator *or* administratrix) of [name] deceased" and will have full powers of disposition, subject to any entry to the contrary on the register. They will however still be bound by the joint proprietorship restriction referred to in Chapter 10. This restriction will not be cancelled automatically by the Registry as a matter of course on the registration of the personal representatives as proprietors in the place of a proprietor to whom the restriction applied. The personal representatives may be able to make an application for cancellation of the restriction if they are able to show that the deceased had become legally and beneficially entitled to the whole of the land (see below).

Transfer by personal representatives

18–002   The personal representatives may deal with the property in accordance with their powers, subject to any entry to the contrary on the register, without being registered as proprietors. A disadvantage of this is that the register remains out of date longer than it would if the personal representatives were registered as proprietors as soon as the grant of probate or letters of administration was made. Whilst the register is out of date, any notice sent by the Registry and addressed to the deceased registered proprietor may go astray, to the detriment of the interests of the beneficiaries.

If the joint proprietorship restriction referred to above appears on the register in relation to the deceased proprietor when the disposition by his personal representatives is registered, it will be cancelled by the Registry if the transfer is by two or more personal representatives. However, if the transfer is by a sole personal representative of a sole surviving proprietor the application will be considered as if it were an application to register a transfer on sale by the deceased. Unless the Registry is satisfied that the equities have been overreached it will be necessary to appoint a new trustee to receive and give a receipt for the purchase money or for evidence of the equitable title to be lodged with the beneficiaries' consent to the registration.

Whether the personal representatives have been registered as proprietors or not, a transfer by them will be in the usual appropriate form as prescribed by r.58 and r.116, *e.g.* Form TR1 (transfer of the whole of the land in a registered title), Form AS1 (assent of whole), Form TR3 (transfer of charge), Form AS2 (assent of charge), Form TP1 (transfer of part) or Form AS3 (assent of part). An application to register such a dealing should be lodged at the appropriate office and be accompanied by:

(1) a completed application Form AP1;

(2) the original or official copy of the grant of probate or letters of administration unless the personal representatives are already the registered proprietors of the land or charge; and

(3) the appropriate fee payable under the current Fee Order.

For settled land reference should be made to Chapter 17.

Rule 162(2) places responsibility on the personal representatives and their advisers in relation to registered interests forming part of the deceased's estate. It provides that "the registrar shall not be under a duty to investigate the reasons a transfer of registered land by a personal representative of a deceased sole proprietor or last surviving joint proprietor is made nor to consider the contents of the will and, provided the terms of any restriction on the register are complied with, he must assume, whether he knows of the terms of the will or not, that the personal representative is acting correctly and within his powers".

Application for any restriction appropriate following the dealing by the personal representatives should be made with the application to register the dealing.

Death of a joint proprietor not being the survivor of joint proprietors

When one of two or more joint proprietors of a registered estate **18–003** dies, the registered estate will vest by survivorship in the remaining proprietors or proprietor, who should apply for the register to be altered by the removal of the name of the deceased joint proprietor. Such an application must be accompanied by evidence of death (r.164), *i.e.* death certificate, grant of probate or letters of administration. Form AP1 can be used but is not required (r.13(2)). No fee is payable. Such an application can also be lodged electronically by conveyancers via Land Registry Direct. The conveyancer must certify that the appropriate evidence has been seen.

On completion of the application, the surviving proprietors or proprietor can deal with the land or charge, subject to any entry on the register.

It often happens that a sole survivor of joint proprietors remains as proprietor of land with the joint proprietorship restriction referred to above. If he is a trustee for himself and/or others, (a) new trustee(s) can be appointed and registered as proprietor(s) jointly with him as indicated in Chapter 17 and the restriction will remain.

It may be, however, that the sole surviving joint proprietor has become legally and beneficially entitled to the whole of the land; and if this is the case, he can apply for the cancellation of the restriction. The application (on Form RX3) should be supported by evidence of the equitable title showing that the survivor can give a valid receipt for capital money arising on a disposition of the land. Usually the Registry will accept a statutory declaration by the survivor, or a certificate by a conveyancer with personal knowledge of the facts, that:

- in stated circumstances, *e.g.* under the will of a deceased joint proprietor, the survivor has become legally and beneficially entitled to the whole of the land in the registered title;

- he has not incumbered his share in any way; and

- he has not received notice of any incumbrance of the share of any deceased proprietor.

The declaration or certificate should be accompanied by any available documentary evidence, *e.g.* an assent relating to an undivided share. No fee is payable for the cancellation of the restriction.

The circumstances in which the joint proprietorship restriction is entered on the register are discussed in Chapter 10 in relation to transfers of registered land. The same principles apply to first registrations.

The restriction has sometimes been entered when it did not apply, simply because the conveyancer did not complete the appropriate panel on the first registration application form or, in the case of a transfer of registered land, did not supply the necessary information. In such cases, an application for the cancellation of the restriction may be made on the lines indicated above.

Inheritance tax: capital transfer tax: death duties

18–004 The Finance Act 1975 (see now the Inheritance Tax Act 1984 ("IHTA 1984") — also known as the Capital Transfer Tax Act 1984 — which consolidated the existing provisions) abolished estate duty in respect of deaths occurring after March 12, 1975, and (subject to exceptions) imposed a charge of capital transfer tax on lifetime transfers of capital made after March 26, 1974, and on deaths occurring after March 12, 1975. The charge on death extended to gifts inter vivos made before March 27, 1974, but within seven years of the donor's death. The Finance Act 1986 changed the name of capital transfer tax to inheritance tax (s.100) and abolished the charge on most lifetime gifts between individuals occurring at least seven years before the transferor's death (s.101).

On first registration or upgrading of title the Registry will consider whether the land may be liable to an Inland Revenue charge for death duty (in practice, only estate duty), inheritance tax or capital transfer tax and will register a notice relating to such liability if appropriate. On occasions other than first registration and upgrading of title, a notice will be registered only on application by the Inland Revenue.

As to deaths on or before March 12, 1975, a notice in the original Form 60 (death duties) will be cancelled when application is made to register a transfer of the registered estate on sale or other disposition for value. Also, an application for cancellation of a notice in the original Form 60 can be made at any time by lodging Form CN1 completed by the Commissioners of Inland Revenue. No fee is payable for the cancellation of the notice.

As to inheritance tax or capital transfer tax claims on deaths after March 12, 1975, and on lifetime transfers after March 26, 1974, s.31 of the Act, provides that the effect of a disposition of a registered estate or charge on a charge under s.237 of the IHTA 1984 is to be determined not in accordance with ss.28 to 30 of the Act (see Chapter 9), but in accordance with ss.237(6) and 238 of the IHTA 1984 (under which a purchaser in good faith for money or money's worth takes free from the charge in the absence of registration). A disposition of the property therefore takes subject to a subsisting Inland Revenue charge unless:

(1) the disposition is in favour of a purchaser within the meaning of the IHTA 1984; and

(2) the charge is not, at the time of registration of the disposition, protected by a notice on the register.

When a charge for inheritance tax or capital transfer tax is protected by notice on the register, the notice will be cancelled on the production to the appropriate office of Form CN1 completed by the Commissioners for Inland Revenue. If Form CN1 states that the application for cancellation is only to take

effect on registration of a disposition to a purchaser, the
Registry will only remove the entry when Form CN1 is lodged
with an application to register the transfer or other specified
disposition to the purchaser. No fee is payable for the cancellation of the notice.

Although a notice in relation to *death duties* is cancelled as a
matter of course (without a Form CN1 completed by the Inland
Revenue) when a disposition in favour of a purchaser is
registered, a notice of a charge for *inheritance tax* or *capital
transfer tax* will not be automatically cancelled. Accordingly, a
Form CN1 completed by the Inland Revenue is always necessary
for the cancellation of a notice of a charge for inheritance tax or
capital transfer tax.

Chapter 19

Insolvency

Bankruptcy

Entry of creditors' notice and/or bankruptcy inhibition prior to October 13, 2003

Prior to October 13, 2003, when the Act came into force, **19–001** whenever a bankruptcy petition was presented, the officials of the court informed the Land Charges Department, and the petition was then registered in the register of pending actions kept at that Department. Details of the registration were passed from the Land Charges Department to the Registry, which then entered a creditors' notice against the title of any proprietor of any registered land or charge which appeared to be affected. Where it appeared that the title of the proprietor of land was affected, the creditors' notice was entered in the proprietorship register as follows:

> "CREDITORS' NOTICE entered under section 61(1) of the Land Registration Act 1925 to protect the rights of all creditors, as the title of the proprietor of the land appears to be affected by a petition in bankruptcy against [*name of debtor*], presented in the [*name*] Court (Court Reference Number   ] (Land Charges Reference Number PA   )."

Where it appeared that the title of the proprietor of a registered charge was affected, the creditors' notice, in a similar form, was entered in the charges register.

When a bankruptcy order was registered in the register of writs and orders affecting land, kept at the Land Charges Department, details were passed to the Registry and a bankruptcy inhibition was entered against the title of any proprietor of any registered land or charge which appeared to be affected. Where it appeared that the title of the proprietor of land was affected, the bankruptcy inhibition was entered in the proprietorship register as follows:

> "BANKRUPTCY INHIBITION entered under section 61(3) of the Land Registration Act 1925, as the title of the proprietor of the land appears to be affected by a bankruptcy order made by the [*name*] Court (Court Reference Number   ) against [*name of debtor*] (Land Charges Reference Number WO   ).
> No disposition by the proprietor of the land or transmission is to be registered until the trustee in bankruptcy of the property of the bankrupt is registered."

Where it appeared that the title of the proprietor of a registered charge was affected, the bankruptcy inhibition, in a similar form, was entered in the charges register.

Entry of bankruptcy notice and/or restriction after October 13, 2003

19–002 The new legislation contains very similar provisions and similar procedures now operate when a bankruptcy petition is presented or a bankruptcy order is made. Section 86 places an obligation on the registrar to make appropriate entries on the register in relation to bankruptcy petitions and orders where it appears to him that a registered estate or charge is affected.

A creditors' notice is now called a bankruptcy notice. Rule 165 provides that a bankruptcy notice in relation to a registered estate will be entered in the proprietorship register and a notice in relation to a registered charge will be entered in the charges register. The form of the notice is as follows:

> "BANKRUPTCY NOTICE entered under section 86(2) of the Land Registration Act 2002 in respect of a pending action, as the title of the [proprietor of the registered estate] *or* [the proprietor of the charge dated   referred to above] appears to be affected by a petition in bankruptcy against [*name of debtor*], presented in the [*name*] Court (Court Reference Number   ) (Land Charges Reference Number PA   )."

The new legislation does not allow the entry of any new inhibitions. As a result, the entry which is made following the making of a bankruptcy order is now a bankruptcy restriction. Rule 166 sets out the form of wording of the restriction which is entered in the proprietorship or charges register as appropriate:

"BANKRUPTCY RESTRICTION entered under section 86(4) of the Land Registration Act 2002, as the title of [the proprietor of the registered estate] *or* [the proprietor of the charge dated   referred to above] appears to be affected by a bankruptcy order made by the [*name*] Court (Court Reference Number   ) against [*name of debtor*] (Land Charges Reference Number WO   ). [No disposition of the registered estate] *or* [No disposition of the charge] is to be registered until the trustee in bankruptcy of the property of the bankrupt is registered as the proprietor of the [registered estate] *or* [charge]."

The registrar must give notice of the entry of a bankruptcy notice or restriction to the proprietor of the registered estate or charge to which it relates.

If any doubt arises as to the identity of the debtor or the bankrupt, the registrar will make such inquiries and serve such notices as he considers necessary or desirable before deciding whether to enter a bankruptcy notice or restriction.

Where there is doubt as to whether the debtor or bankrupt is the same person as the proprietor of the registered estate or charge in respect of which a notice or restriction has been entered, the registrar must, as soon as practicable, take such action as he considers necessary to resolve the doubt.

Section 86(5) provides that where a debtor has been made bankrupt, a disponee in good faith is protected. The title of the trustee in bankruptcy is void against a person to whom a registrable disposition is made if it is for valuable consideration, the disponee is acting in good faith and at the time of the disposition no bankruptcy entry is on the register and the disponee has no notice of the petition or order.

Neither a bankruptcy notice nor a bankruptcy restriction will be entered in relation to one of two or more joint proprietors. If the debtor has a beneficial interest in the land, his trustee in bankruptcy may apply for the entry of a restriction in Form A and/or J set out in Sch.4 to the Rules (see Chapter 14) as follows:

Form A — "No disposition by a sole proprietor of the registered estate (except a trust corporation) under which capital money arises is to be registered unless authorised by an order of the court."

Form J — "No disposition of the [registered estate *or* registered charge dated [*date*]] is to be registered without a certificate signed by the applicant for registration or his conveyancer that written notice of the disposition was given to

> [*name of trustee in bankruptcy*] (the trustee in
> bankruptcy of [*name of bankrupt person*]) at
> [*address for service*]."

Registration of the official receiver or trustee in bankruptcy

19–003 All the property, including registered property, vested in the
bankrupt beneficially at the date of the bankruptcy order
automatically vests either in the trustee in bankruptcy when his
appointment takes effect or in the official receiver on his
becoming trustee (s.306 of the Insolvency Act 1986).

Rule 168 sets out the requirements for registration of the
official receiver or trustee in bankruptcy in place of the
bankrupt.

The official receiver can be registered as proprietor in place
of the bankrupt on production of:

(1) the bankruptcy order; and

(2) a certificate by the official receiver that the land or
charge is comprised in the bankrupt's estate; and

(3) a certificate by the official receiver that he is the
trustee.

The trustee in bankruptcy can be registered as proprietor in
place of the bankrupt on production of the evidence required in
the case of the official receiver specified at (1) and (2) above
(but in the case of the certificate at (2) signed by the trustee)
and either:

(a) his certificate of appointment as trustee by the meeting
of the bankrupt's creditors; or

(b) his certificate of appointment as trustee by the Secretary
of State; or

(c) the order of the court appointing him trustee.

The application should be made on Form AP1.

A fee calculated in accordance with the current Fee Order, is
payable.

On the registration of the official receiver or the trustee in
bankruptcy as the proprietor of the bankrupt's registered estate
or interest, the bankruptcy notice and restriction will be
cancelled.

Transfer by the official receiver or trustee in bankruptcy

19–004 If the official receiver or trustee wishes to transfer the registered
estate or interest without himself being registered as proprietor,
the transfer must be lodged for registration accompanied by the

evidence required for registration of the official receiver or trustee, as the case may be, mentioned at para.19–003 above. The bankruptcy notice and restriction will be cancelled when the transfer is registered.

Cancellation of the bankruptcy notice or bankruptcy restriction
A bankruptcy notice will not be cancelled on the production of **19–005** an order of the court which simply authorises the cancellation of the registration of the bankruptcy petition as a pending action in the Land Charges Department. Similarly a bankruptcy restriction will not be cancelled on the production of an order of the court which simply authorises the cancellation of the registration of the bankruptcy order in the register of writs and orders affecting land at the Land Charges Department. Such an order does not re-vest property in a bankrupt which has automatically vested in his trustee in bankruptcy. Such property will remain vested in the trustee in bankruptcy. Rule 167 provides that a bankruptcy notice or bankruptcy restriction will be cancelled if the registrar is satisfied that:

(1) the bankruptcy order has been annulled; or

(2) the bankruptcy proceedings have been dismissed or withdrawn with the court's permission; or

(3) the bankruptcy proceedings do not affect or have ceased to affect the registered estate or charge in relation to which the bankruptcy notice or restriction has been entered on the register.

Neither an automatic discharge under the provisions of s.279 of the Insolvency Act 1986 (as amended by the Enterprise Act 2002) nor an order for discharge under s.280 of the said Act operates to revest the bankrupt's property. Production of evidence of discharge is not, therefore, sufficient to enable a bankruptcy notice or restriction to be cancelled. Section 261 of the Enterprise Act 2002 introduces a new s.283A into the 1986 Act. Where property comprised in a bankrupt's estate consists of an interest in a dwelling house which at the date of the bankruptcy was the sole or principal residence of the bankrupt, his spouse or former spouse, at the end of three years from the date of the bankruptcy that interest ceases to be comprised in the bankrupt's estate and re-vests in the bankrupt without conveyance, assignment or transfer, unless, within that period, the trustee in bankruptcy realises the interest, applies to court for an order for sale or possession or charging order or reaches agreement with the bankrupt. The three year period for the automatic re-vesting started to run from April 1, 2004. The trustee can make an appropriate application to the Registry to remove any relevant restriction and bankruptcy notice when an automatic re-vesting has occurred.

No fee is payable for the cancellation of a bankruptcy notice or restriction.

The application for cancellation should be made on Form AP1. Where application for cancellation is made in the circumstances referred to at (1) and (2) above, it must be accompanied by an office copy of the relevant court order which must expressly authorise the cancellation of the pending action and/or the bankruptcy order in the register of writs and orders at the Land Charges Department under the reference number set out in the bankruptcy notice and/or bankruptcy restriction.

Charge on bankrupt's home

19–006 Where a dwelling-house occupied by a bankrupt or his spouse or former spouse forms part of the bankrupt's estate and the trustee is unable to realise it, he can apply to the court for a charging order on the property. Any such order shall provide for the property to revest in the bankrupt subject to the charge and any prior charges (s.313 of the Insolvency Act 1986). Where such an order is made, an office copy or certified copy should be lodged so that the bankruptcy notice and/or bankruptcy restriction can be cancelled, any other entry necessary to reflect the vesting provisions can be made and the charging order can be noted. Where the bankrupt is the sole registered proprietor and does not hold as trustee, the trustee in bankruptcy can apply for an agreed or unilateral notice in respect of the court order (see Chapter 15).

Where there are joint proprietors a restriction in Form K as follows will be the appropriate method of protection:

> "No disposition of the [registered estate *or* registered charge dated [*date*]] is to be registered without a certificate signed by the applicant for registration or his conveyancer that written notice of the disposition was given to [*name of person with the benefit of the charging order*] at [*address for service*], being the person with the benefit of [an interim] [a final] charging order on the beneficial interest of (*name of judgment debtor*) made by the (*name of court*) on (*date*) (*Court reference*   )."

Rights of occupation of a bankrupt and of a bankrupt's spouse

19–007 The effect of bankruptcy on a spouse's statutory rights of occupation under the Family Law Act 1996 and the rights of occupation of a bankrupt who has occupied a dwelling-house with a person under 18 are considered in Chapter 16.

Bankruptcy of a joint proprietor

When one of two or more joint proprietors is made bankrupt **19–008** and a trustee in bankruptcy is appointed, the legal estate in the land or charge affected does not automatically vest in the trustee. Property held by a bankrupt on trust for another, whether or not the debtor also holds it on trust for himself, does not form part of the bankrupt's estate. No bankruptcy entries will therefore be made. Any subsequent transfer of the property needs to be executed by all the joint proprietors in the usual way and not by the trustee on behalf of the bankrupt proprietor.

Liquidation

The liquidator of a company may have notice of his appoint- **19–009** ment entered on the register, but the company will remain the registered proprietor. Rules 184(4) and (5) apply. The application should be made on Form AP1 and should be accompanied by the order, appointment by the Secretary of State or resolution under which the liquidator was appointed and such other evidence as the registrar may require. The evidence which will be required will depend upon the type of liquidation:

(1) If the liquidation is by order of the court, a certified copy of the winding up order; and:

    (a) a certified copy of the resolution passed at the creditors' meeting appointing the liquidator; or

    (b) a certified copy of the resolution passed at the contributories' meeting appointing the liquidator and a certificate by the liquidator (or his conveyancer) that the meeting of the creditors was duly held at which either the appointment of the liquidator by the contributories' meeting was confirmed or no resolution nominating a liquidator was passed; or

    (c) a certified copy of the order of the court appointing the liquidator; or

    (d) a certified copy of the appointment by the Secretary of State of the liquidator.

(2) If the winding-up is a members' voluntary winding-up:

    (a) a certificate by the secretary or conveyancer of the company or by the liquidator or his conveyancer that a statutory declaration of solvency complying with the requirements of s.89 of the Insolvency Act 1986 has been filed with the Registrar of Companies; and

    (b) a certified copy of the resolution passed by the general meeting of the company appointing the liquidator.

(3) If the winding-up is a creditors' voluntary winding-up, a certified copy of the resolution passed at the company's general meeting that the company be wound up, and appointing a liquidator; and:

    (a) a certified copy of a resolution passed at the creditors' meeting appointing the liquidator; or

    (b) a certificate by the liquidator (appointed at the company's meeting) or his conveyancer that the meeting of the creditors was duly held in accordance with s.98(1) of the Insolvency Act 1986 at which either the appointment of the liquidator by the company's meeting was confirmed or no resolution nominating a liquidator was passed.

A fee is payable, calculated in accordance with the current Fee Order.

When notice of the appointment is entered in the register, consideration should be given as to whether application should be made for any appropriate restriction to be entered.

If a transfer by a company in liquidation is lodged for registration and notice of the appointment has not previously been entered, evidence as at (1), (2) or (3) above will be required. A disposition by a company in liquidation should be executed by the liquidator affixing the company seal and signing the document to attest that the seal has been affixed in his presence or by him signing the document as a deed in his name and on behalf of the company.

Rule 185 provides that where a registered proprietor company has been dissolved the registrar may enter a note of that fact in the proprietorship register or charges register, as appropriate.

Administration orders

19–010 Where an administration order is made under the provisions of s.8 of the Insolvency Act 1986, the property of the company remains vested in the company but the administrator may have notice of the order and the appointment of the administrator entered on the register. Rule 184(2) applies. The application should be made on Form AP1 and should be accompanied by the administration order. Where the administrator has been appointed out of court, the application should be accompanied by a certificate by the administrator that the requirements of Sch.B1 to the Insolvency Act 1986 have been complied with and the date on which that was done and certified copies of the notice of appointment, statutory declaration by the appointor and statement by the administrator filed at court pursuant to paras.18 or 29 of Sch.B1.

A fee is payable, calculated in accordance with the current Fee Order.

On a disposal by the administrator, the application should be accompanied by the documentation referred to above unless the administration order has already been noted. If the administrator disposes of a property free from a floating charge which is entered as an agreed notice, or noted by the registrar on first registration or under the provisions of the Land Registration Act 1925, a Form CN1 should be supplied, signed by the administrator, stating in panel 12 that the disposal is "pursuant to s.15 of the Insolvency Act 1986". Where the floating charge has been entered as a unilateral notice the application should be accompanied by a Form UN2 signed by the administrator and a certificate from the administrator that the property has been transferred free from the floating charge pursuant to s.15 of the Insolvency Act 1986. If the disposal is made free from a fixed charge, an office copy of the court order authorising the disposal as if the property were not subject to the charge in question (s.15(2) of the Insolvency Act 1986) should be lodged with the application.

Where a company subject to an administration order acquires land, the following entry will be made in the charges register:

"The registered estate is subject to such security or securities as may exist and affect the same by virtue of the provisions of section 15(4) of the Insolvency Act 1986."

This entry will be cancelled, without fee, on production of a certificate from the administrator that there are no such securities affecting the land or, on a transfer, that such securities have been discharged.

Company receivership

Although the court has power to appoint a receiver of a **19–011** company ("a receiver") it is a power which is rarely exercised and it is not considered here. The Law of Property Act 1925 authorises the holder of a mortgage over a company's property to appoint a receiver in specified circumstances whether the mortgage contains such a power or not. These statutory powers will usually be extended by express provisions in a debenture and this section deals with the points which the Registry will need to consider in registering a disposition by a receiver appointed under a debenture.

Throughout this section the word "debenture" is used to mean the mortgage or charge, whether legal or equitable, by a company under which the receiver has been appointed.

Sections 28 to 49 of the Insolvency Act 1986 contain provisions which regulate the appointment and conduct of receivers generally and also designate certain receivers "administrative receivers" with statutory powers and duties. An "administrative receiver" is either the receiver of the whole (or substantially the whole) of a company's property appointed under a floating charge, or under such a charge and one or more other securities, or a person who would have been such a receiver but for the appointment of some other person as receiver of part of the company's property (s.29(2) of the 1986 Act). Unless otherwise stated the Registry's requirements in relation to receivers set out in this section apply equally to administrative receivers. The statutory powers of an administrative receiver are covered below. Consideration should also be given to the effect of the Enterprise Act 2002 (see below).

The debenture under which the receiver is appointed

19–012 Every application based on a disposition by a receiver should be accompanied by the original or certified copy of the debenture under which the receiver was appointed unless it is already registered or noted against an identified registered title. The debenture must be valid and enforceable. In particular it must be duly executed and registered at the Companies Registry under s.395 of the Companies Act 1985 and must contain the appropriate provisions to allow the receiver to be appointed and to carry out the disposition.

The appointment of the receiver

19–013 The statutory power of appointing a receiver will normally be extended by the debenture. The appointment of a receiver does not have the effect of vesting the company's property in the receiver and no note of such an appointment may be entered on the register. Evidence that the power of appointment has arisen should be lodged. This will normally be in the form of a certificate by or on behalf of the chargee. The instrument of appointment of the receiver or a certified copy of it should also accompany the application. Application may be made for the entry of a restriction to the effect that no disposition of the registered estate by the proprietor is to be registered without a written consent signed by the receiver or his conveyancer.

Powers of the receiver

Whatever the nature of the transaction it must be clearly **19–014** established that the receiver has power to carry it out. Unless he is an administrative receiver (see below) his statutory powers are very limited (see s.109 of the Law of Property Act 1925) but they will usually be extended by the debenture. If the receiver, other than an administrative receiver, is to dispose of property then he must be given an express power to do so by the debenture. A non-administrative receiver's leasing powers, which must be given to him expressly by the debenture or be delegated to him by the chargee, give rise to complex questions which will require careful consideration if met in practice. As to execution of deeds in receivership cases, see para.19–016 and below.

In exercising his powers the receiver will normally be acting as agent of the mortgagor and not as agent of the mortgagee. This is expressly provided in relation to the statutory powers by s.109(2) of the Law of Property Act 1925 and s.44 of the Insolvency Act 1986 and it is standard practice for a debenture to contain a statement to this effect. The receiver will not, therefore, be exercising the mortgagee's powers, and will not be in a position to release the land from the debenture. It follows that a person dealing with a receiver should obtain an express release both from the debenture and from any prior or subsequent mortgages and charges.

Effect of liquidation on receiver's powers

On the commencement of a winding-up the receiver ceases to **19–015** be agent of the mortgagor but continues to have powers to act for the purposes of holding and disposing of the property comprised in the debenture including power to use the company name for that purpose (see *Sowman v David Samuel Trust Ltd* [1978] 1 W.L.R. 22; [1978] 1 All E.R. 616 and the authorities therein mentioned). In a winding-up by the court any disposition of the company's property made after the commencement of the winding-up is void under s.127 of the Insolvency Act 1986 unless sanctioned by an order of the court. However, where a debenture has been created prior to the winding-up, the disposition for the purposes of s.127 is the debenture, and any subsequent disposition by the debenture-holder or his receiver under powers contained in the debenture does not require an order of the court.

The provisions of ss.238 to 241, 244 and 245 of the Insolvency Act 1986 in relation to transactions at an undervalue, preferences, extortionate credit transactions and the avoidance of certain floating charges may have the effect of invalidating the debenture wholly or in part.

In appropriate cases the Registry may require evidence that the purchaser had no express notice of any pending court proceedings for the making of an administration order or for the winding-up of the company (see s.5(7) of the Land Charges Act 1972).

In appropriate cases, the Registry will serve notice of an application, based on a disposition by a receiver, on the liquidator to enable him to consider whether he accepts its validity. Applicants should therefore include details of the name and address of the liquidator in all cases where it is known that the company is being wound up. Any challenge by the liquidator to the validity of the debenture should be disclosed to the Registry when the application is lodged.

As to the effect of liquidation on a power of attorney given to the receiver in the debenture see below.

Execution of deeds in receivership cases

19–016 In all cases it appears that the receiver should personally execute the deed so as to signify that the transaction is being carried out with his authority. The deed must also be executed by or on behalf of the company and this can be done in a number of ways:

(1) By affixing the company's seal in the presence of its duly authorised officers, if available, or in the presence of the liquidator where the company is being wound up (ss.165–167 of and para.7 of Pt III of Sch.4 to the Insolvency Act 1986), or by signing as a deed by a director and secretary or by two directors of the company, at the direction of the receiver. Unlike a liquidator, other than an administrative receiver (see below), a receiver is not authorised to affix the company's seal (although it does seem theoretically possible for him to be authorised to do so by the company's articles of association).

(2) By the chargee or by the receiver as attorney for the company where so appointed by the debenture. It is usual for a debenture to appoint both the chargee and any receiver or receivers appointed by him as attorney for the company. A power of attorney must be granted by an instrument under seal (s.1 of the Powers of Attorney Act 1971). It follows that if a chargee or receiver derives his appointment as attorney from a debenture that debenture must be by deed. Since the appointment as attorney derives from the debenture, which is an instrument under seal, the fact that the instrument of appointment of the receiver by the chargee is under hand is immaterial.

Where the chargee is so appointed *his* appointment will be a security power (see s.4(1) of the Powers of Attorney Act 1971) and will not be revoked by liquidation.

However, it has been held in *Barrows v Chief Land Registrar* (reported in *The Times* on October 20, 1977) that a power of attorney given to a *receiver* by a company under a debenture is not a security power as it does not secure a proprietary interest of the donee or the performance of an obligation owing to him. A power of attorney given to a receiver in these circumstances would cease on the commencement of the liquidation of the company.

If, therefore, it is sought to rely upon an instrument executed by a receiver as attorney, the application should in all cases be supported either by a statutory declaration by the applicant (or in the case of a company applicant by its director or secretary) or by a certificate by the applicant's conveyancer in Form 1 or 2 as set out in Sch.3 to the Rules, as appropriate.

The form of execution pursuant to a power of attorney is discussed in Chapter 9.

(3) In the case of *Barrows v Chief Land Registrar* (see above) it was held that, notwithstanding the revocation of a power of attorney given in a debenture to a receiver by reason of the winding-up of the donor company, a power given to him in the same instrument to sell, convey, *etc.* in the name and on behalf of the company should be treated as a power in the nature of a contractual right which would survive liquidation. Such a power would have to be clearly stated in the debenture and would only be exercisable in relation to those of the receiver's powers for which it was expressly granted. The execution in such a case should clearly show that the receiver is acting in the name and on behalf of the company under powers expressly given to him for that purpose in the debenture. A suggested form of execution where the receiver is relying on his contractual powers is as follows:

SIGNED as a deed by (*name of company*)
[in liquidation] by (*name of receiver*) its receiver,   (*name of company*)
pursuant to powers granted to [him][her] by   by (*name of receiver*)
clauses (*relevant clause numbers*) of a   its receiver
debenture dated (*date*) in favour of   (*name of lender*)
in the presence of:

It would seem in a purchaser's interest to insist, wherever possible, upon the receiver executing a deed under a power of attorney rather than under a contractual power so as to obtain the protection of s.5 of the Powers of Attorney Act 1971.

Administrative receivers

19–017 Certain receivers, as defined above, are designated by the Insolvency Act 1986 as administrative receivers. Unless otherwise indicated, all the requirements set out above in relation to receivers generally will apply also to administrative receivers.

The effect of the Enterprise Act 2002, which came into force on September 15, 2003, is that (subject to exceptions for particular types of company) an administrative receiver cannot be appointed under powers contained in a floating charge entered into on or after September 15, 2003. After that date, an existing administrative receiver must vacate office if an administration order is made by the court. A Law of Property Act 1925 receiver may be required to vacate office by an administrator appointed on or after that date.

The powers conferred on an administrative receiver by the debenture(s) under which he is appointed are deemed to include the statutory powers set out in Sch.1 to the Insolvency Act 1986 unless the statutory powers are inconsistent with any of the provisions of the debenture(s). The statutory powers include powers to sell, to use the company's seal, to execute in the name and on behalf of the company and to grant and accept the surrender of and to take a lease. Under s.42 of the Insolvency Act 1986, a person dealing with an administrative receiver in good faith and for value is not concerned to inquire whether the receiver is acting within his powers.

Under s.43 of the 1986 Act, the court may authorise a disposition by an administrative receiver free from a charge having priority to the charge under which the administrative receiver has been appointed. Any application based on a disposition so authorised should be supported by an office copy of the court order.

Inspection of the register on insolvency

19–018 This is covered in Chapter 8.

Chapter 20

Building Estates

The Registry's Practice Guide 41 (and its six supplements) is a **20–001** general guide for developers of building estates, buyers, legal advisers and surveyors. Developers are encouraged to bring this leaflet to the attention of buyers. It provides information about the registration of developing estates and in particular the relevant services the Registry offers. Those services are:

- estate boundary approval;
- estate plan approval;
- approval of draft transfers and leases;
- pre and post registration services on plot sales.

The aim of those services is to ensure the early identification and resolution of registration problems so that the process of estate development and plot sales takes place as smoothly and as cost effectively as possible. This is of benefit to all parties involved in the process. There are no fees for any of these services. Further details of the services available and the procedures involved are set out below. This information relates equally to developments by way of transfers on sale and to those by way of long leases and commonhold developments (see Chapter 12). Where appropriate, therefore, "transfer" includes "lease" and "seller" and "buyer" have corresponding meanings. "Estate plan" includes a plan showing flat or maisonette development.

Estate boundary approval

This service is for use before design of the estate layout. It **20–002** ensures that the developer's initial site survey plan corresponds with the extent of the developer's registered title. Any discrepancies between the registered extent and the proposed or actual physical external boundaries can be identified and resolved. Advice can also be given on easements intended to be granted. The initial site survey plans showing the extent of the land included in the development should be sent to the Registry.

Estate plans

20–003 As early as possible before the first transfer of part is likely to be lodged for registration, the developer's conveyancer should send to the appropriate office two copies of the estate plan for approval of its use in connection with official searches of the register and official certificates of inspection of the title plan (see below). The estate plan should show the final layout of the proposed development and must show sufficient detail to enable it to be accurately related to the title plan of the developer's title and the surrounding boundary features. It must be drawn to a suitable scale, usually 1/500; its true scale and orientation must be shown and it must clearly and precisely define each plot or property and identify it by a plot number or other reference. Plans marked "For identification only" or with some similar phrase are not acceptable. Where a property comprises more than one parcel *(e.g.* a house and separate garage) each parcel must be distinguished on the estate plan by means of a separate number. If two or more floors of a purpose-built block of flats are co-extensive, and the layout of the flats on each floor is identical, it is usually sufficient to lodge the plan of a single floor, but this plan must show the reference numbers distinguishing each flat on each floor. Common areas should be identified. All buildings, drives and pathways should be shown in their correct positions. The Registry is always willing to advise as to the plan to be used for any particular estate.

When approved, one copy of the plan will be retained in the Registry. The other, marked as officially approved, will be returned to the developer's conveyancer. The advantages of this approved plan are that:

(1) negotiations for the sale of individual plots can proceed without an official copy of the title plan (see below);

(2) applications for official searches of the register and for official certificates of inspection of the title plan may describe the land being purchased by reference to the plot number(s) on the approved plan, so avoiding the need to provide separate plans (see below); and

(3) the approved plan, or extracts from it, can form the basis of transfer or lease plans, ensuring consistency throughout the transaction.

Much trouble can be avoided if, before contract, builders and surveyors check the position of fences against the approved plan. Conveyancers should ask the developers to notify them immediately of any change in the layout of the estate and should return the duplicate approved plan to the Registry with a new plan (in duplicate) showing the changes. Failure to do this will probably lead to the withdrawal of approval of the obsolete part of the plan and to the cancellation of application for searches and may lead to difficulties for the registration of transfers based on the obsolete part.

The Registry should be told of the progress of the development periodically so that new surveys can be made.

Surveys

Land Registry plans are based on the Ordnance Survey Map **20–004** and in the case of building estates are normally drawn to a scale of 1/1250. Surveys of developing estates are made at frequent intervals and the Registry's plans are then revised to show all new buildings, fences, roads and other physical features. The registration of transfers is facilitated if the Registry is notified, when the layout plan is lodged for approval, of the areas in which new roads are being laid out and development is proceeding. The Registry should again be notified when more roads are being constructed and fences or other boundary structures are being erected.

Sales off in plots

When a developer requires official copies of the register or **20–005** certificates of inspection of the title plan for providing to buyers he should apply for them in batches as the development proceeds. This will avoid the disadvantages of using out of date official copies or certificates of inspection in the later stages of the development.

Verifications and searches by purchasers

A developer can apply for official copies of the register to hand **20–006** over to buyers, or buyers can apply themselves.

The fees payable for official copies are covered in Chapter 8.

Under s.67, official copies are admissible in evidence to the same extent as the originals. Official copies issued on developing estates, particularly leasehold estates, are frequently backdated. This is because an official copy must be dated prior to the earliest application pending against the title. Problems should not arise as the result of an official search of part made by reference to the official copies guarantees that the plot in question remains within the title and provides details of any adverse entries made or to be made since the date of the official copies.

Where the estate plan has been officially approved by the Registry and the buyer is satisfied that his plot is or will be fenced in accordance with it, it only remains for him to satisfy himself of two things. Initially he wishes to know that his plot is in the developer's title and whether any references on the title plan affect it; and, just before completion, he wants to know that the plot is still in the title, that it is not subject to any prior pending application and that no adverse entry affecting it has been made in the register since the date of issue of the official copy of the register. These details are obtained as follows:

Proof that a plot being purchased is in the seller's title — Application should be made in Form OC1 to the appropriate office for a certificate of official inspection of the title plan in Form CI (see also Chapter 8).

A fee calculated in accordance with the current Fee Order, is payable.

An adequate, verbal description of the property being purchased must be given in the application as well as the plot number on the approved estate plan. In the case of a property which comprises more than one parcel, all relevant plot numbers must be quoted. If there is no approved estate plan or if there is but the applicant does not wish to rely on it, the application must be accompanied by a plan (in duplicate) of a kind that would be appropriate to an application for an official search in Form OS2 (see Chapter 8).

If the application is in order, the certificate in Form CI will be issued without delay. It will certify that the property is in the title and whether or not it is affected by any colour or other reference shown on the title plan and referred to in the entries in the register. The certificate's accuracy is guaranteed, but it confers no priority.

If he has this certificate, a buyer does not need to inspect an official copy of the title plan of the developer's title because he is given the information that he would obtain by such an inspection.

The use of certificates of official inspection of title plans is designed to save the delay and expense of numerous applications for official copies of the title plans of registered developing building estates.

If a draft transfer is approved for use for the estate (see below) the Registry will supply a letter to the developer confirming that if easements are granted in the approved form they will be entered as appurtenant to the buyer's title. This avoids the need to inspect the title plan to ensure than the developer has power to grant the easements proposed. Alternatively it may be possible to arrange with the Registry to confirm on the Form CI that a particular road, for example, over which rights of way are to be granted is within the developer's title.

Ascertaining whether any adverse entry has been made in the register affecting the plot since the date of issue of the official copy — This is done by applying for an official search of the register in Form OS2 (see Chapter 8).

Sometimes a plot is served by an approach road or by other easements to be granted over land owned by the same developer but in another registered title. In such a case, one Form OS2 may be used for a search against both titles. The printed wording must be appropriately modified; and, in particular, if the official copies of the two registers were issued on different dates, both dates must be shown on the Form OS2.

It is unnecessary, however, to refer on the Form OS2 to interests and rights to be transferred or granted over land in the same title as the corporeal land that is being transferred, because the priority under the certificate of search will extend to those interests and rights.

Instrument plans

Each transfer must be accompanied by a plan of the property **20–007** concerned. Mere reference to plot numbers on the estate plan in a transfer of part or similar instrument is not sufficient. Transfer plans may be drawn to any suitable scale. The scales most commonly used range between 1/500 and 1/1250 but the true scale and orientation must be shown. It is recommended that an extract from the approved estate plan is used for the transfer plan, but if this is not done the transfer plan should show not only the land being dealt with but also sufficient adjacent details to enable its position to be ascertained on the seller's title plan. These details should include figured dimensions tying the position of the land to the nearest road, corner or other physical feature and also the dimensions of the land itself. A plan "for identification only" is unacceptable. In the case of a flat or maisonette, the transfer must identify the precise position and extent of the parcel(s) that make up the premises in the building and the floor(s) on which they are situated. Care should be taken to ensure that 'T' marks and other plan references mentioned in the body of the transfer appear on the transfer plan.

To comply with r.213, the transfer plan must be signed by the developer. If the developer is a company or corporation the plan should be executed in the same way as the transfer.

The above remarks apply equally to the plans in leases of part.

Discharges

20–008 This is covered in Chapter 13. A Form DS3 must be accompanied by a suitable plan identifying the land which is released, which ideally should be an exact copy of the transfer plan. When a standard form of transfer, previously approved by the Registry, is being used, the discharge need not refer to easements of the usual kinds granted by the transfer. But if the easements granted are peculiar to the particular plot, the discharge should specifically refer to them.

Draft transfers

20–009 A draft of the proposed form of transfer or lease (with plan) for general use may be sent to the appropriate office for approval. This will often help to avoid difficulties in connection with easements and the development generally. The draft and plan must be lodged in duplicate. No fee will be charged for the consideration and approval of the draft.

Restrictions

20–010 It is possible to apply for a standard form of restriction in the additional provisions panel of Form TP1 or TP2, or on Form RX1. Form RX1 must be used for a non-standard restriction application. Neither a standard nor a non-standard restriction can be applied for in a lease — Form RX1 must be used.

Absolute leasehold title

20–011 When a developer registered with absolute title grants leases of part, lessees' solicitors are advised to apply for registration of their clients' leases with absolute leasehold title and to supply any necessary consents.

Chapter 21

Upgrading Title

Introduction

Section 62 of the Act gives the registrar power to upgrade title **21–001** and r.124 provides details as to how an application for a title to be upgraded should be made. The only persons who can apply for a title to be upgraded are:

(1) the proprietor of the title to which the application relates;

(2) a person entitled to be registered as the proprietor of that title;

(3) the proprietor of a registered charge affecting that title; and

(4) a person interested in a registered title which derives from that title.

Upgrading possessory titles

The registrar may upgrade a possessory title, in the case of **21–002** freehold land to absolute or in the case of leasehold land to good leasehold, if:

(1) satisfied as to title (s.62(1) and s.62(3)(a)); or

(2) the land has been registered with possessory title for at least 12 years and the registrar is satisfied that the proprietor is in possession (s.62(4) and s.62(5)).

If an upgrade is sought under (1), the application must be supported by such documents as will satisfy the registrar as to the title (r.124(2)). If an upgrade is sought under (2), the applicant must state who is in physical possession of the land in the title and, if this is not the registered proprietor, how his relationship with the person(s) in physical possession means that the registered proprietor is to be treated as being in possession. In both cases (1) and (2) confirmation is required that no claim adverse to the title of the proprietor has been made by virtue of an estate, right or interest whose enforceability is preserved by virtue of the existing entry about the class of title. If any adverse claim has been made upgrading cannot take place until it has been disposed of (s.62(6)). The Lord Chancellor may by order substitute for the 12 year period mentioned such number of years as the order may provide (s.62(9)).

Upgrading possessory leasehold or good leasehold to absolute leasehold

21–003 The registrar may upgrade a good leasehold title to absolute if he is satisfied as to the superior title (s.62(2)). It must be established that the lessor had power to grant the lease. An application must therefore be accompanied by (r.124(3)):

(1) such documents as will satisfy the registrar as to any superior title which is not registered;

(2) where any superior title is registered with possessory, qualified or good leasehold title, such evidence as will satisfy the registrar that that title qualifies for upgrading to absolute title; and

(3) evidence of any consent to the grant of the lease required from any chargee of any superior title, and any superior lessor.

Since the effect of registration with an absolute title is to confer an absolute title to any easements granted in the lease, the title of the lessor to grant the easements should be shown. Where the Registry is not satisfied on this point, an entry may be made on the register excluding the easement concerned from the registration.

Confirmation is required that no claim adverse to the title of the proprietor has been made by virtue of an estate, right or interest whose enforceability is preserved by virtue of the existing entry about the class of title. If any adverse claim has been made upgrading cannot take place until it has been disposed of.

It follows from the above that the registrar may upgrade a possessory leasehold title to absolute if he is satisfied both as to the title to the estate and the superior estate (s.62(3)(b)). Such documents as will satisfy the registrar as to the title, as well as the documents listed at (1), (2) and (3), must accompany an application for such upgrading (r.123(4)).

Upgrading qualified titles

The registrar may upgrade a qualified title, in the case of **21–004** freehold land to absolute and in the case of leasehold land to good leasehold (or absolute leasehold — see above) if satisfied as to title (s.62(1) and s.62(3)).

Inquiries before upgrading

Before approving an application for upgrading, the registrar **21–005** may require the production of further documents or evidence, or serve such notices, as he considers necessary or desirable.

Effect of upgrading of title

When title is upgraded to absolute, the proprietor no longer **21–006** holds the estate subject to any estate, right or interest whose enforceability was preserved by virtue of the previous entry about the class of title. The same is true where the title is upgraded to good leasehold save that the upgrading does not affect or prejudice the enforcement of any estate, right or interest affecting, or in derogation of, the title of the lessor to grant the lease.

Application form and fees

All applications for upgrading of title must be made in Form **21–007** UT1.

A fixed fee calculated in accordance with the current Fee Order, is payable but no fee is payable where the application is accompanied by an application upon which a scale fee is payable.

The applicant must state in what capacity he is entitled to apply for upgrading of title. If the applicant is entitled to be registered as the proprietor of the title to which the application relates evidence of that entitlement must accompany the application (r.124(5)). If the applicant is interested in a registered title which derives from the title to which the application relates details of that interest and such evidence of the applicant's interest as satisfies the registrar must accompany the application.

Chapter 22

Alteration, Adjudication and Indemnity

Alteration

An alteration may or may not be a rectification. A rectification **22–001** is defined as an alteration of the register which:

(1) involves the correction of a mistake; and

(2) prejudicially affects the title of a registered proprietor.

Alteration by the court or by the registrar

The court may make an order for alteration of or the registrar **22–002** may alter the register to:

(1) correct a mistake;

(2) bring the register up to date; or

(3) give effect to any estate, right or interest excepted from the effect of registration (Sch.4 to the Act).

The registrar may also remove a superfluous entry (para.5(d) of Sch.4 to the Act).

But where a freehold estate in land is registered in error as a freehold estate in commonhold land, the register may not be altered by the registrar under Sch.4 (s.6(2) of the Commonhold and Leasehold Reform Act 2002). In such a case the court may grant a declaration that the freehold estate should not have been registered as a freehold estate in commonhold land and make any order which appears to it to be appropriate. The order may provide for alteration of the register.

If the court makes an order for alteration the registrar must give effect to it when it is served on him (para.2(2) of Sch.4 to the Act).

If the alteration is a rectification, no order or alteration can be made without the proprietor's consent in relation to land in his possession unless:

(a) he has by fraud or lack of proper care caused or substantially contributed to the mistake; or

(b) it would for any other reason be unjust for the alteration not to be made (paras.3 and 6 of Sch.4 to the Act).

Under s.131 land is in the possession of a proprietor if it is physically in his possession, or in that of a person who is entitled (other than as an adverse possessor under Sch.6 to the Act) to be registered as the proprietor of the registered estate. In the following cases land which is (or is treated as being) in the possession of the second-mentioned person is to be treated for these purposes as in the possession of the first-mentioned person:

• landlord and tenant;

• mortgagor and mortgagee;

• licensor and licensee;

• trustee and beneficiary.

Where there is power to do so the court must make an order for alteration unless there are exceptional circumstances which justify not doing so (para.3 of Sch.4 to the Act and r.126). Where he has power to do so the registrar must approve any application for rectification made to him unless there are exceptional circumstances which justify his not making the alteration (para.6 of Sch.4 to the Act).

Applications for alteration by the registrar

22–003   Whenever a case for alteration arises, an application should be submitted to the appropriate office at the first opportunity. The application should be in Form AP1 supported by a statement of the facts and of any legal arguments on which it is based and by all available evidence.

The application may be submitted without a fee and the Registry will requisition for payment of any fee which may be appropriate.

Any alteration made by the registrar for the purpose of correcting a mistake in any application or accompanying document will have effect as if made by the applicant or other interested party or parties:

- in the case of a mistake of a clerical or like nature, in all circumstances; but
- in the case of any other mistake, only if the applicant and every other interested party has requested, or consented to, the alteration (r.130).

Except for mistakes covered by the last paragraph, unless he is satisfied that such notice is unnecessary the registrar must make such enquiries as he thinks fit and give notice of a proposed alteration to:

- the registered proprietor of the land and of any charge; and
- any person who appears to the registrar to be entitled to an interest protected by a notice and whose name and address for service is set out in the register in which the notice is entered (r.128).

If any objection cannot be disposed of by agreement it must be referred to the Adjudicator (see below).

Adjudication

Before October 13, 2003, objections and disputes were referred **22–004** to the Solicitor to HM Land Registry and he continues to deal with such matters where the objection was lodged before that date.

The Act created a new post of Adjudicator to Her Majesty's Land Registry (s.107) to determine:

(1) objections referred to him under s.73(7); and

(2) appeals under para.4 of Sch.5 to the Act relating to e-conveyancing network access agreements.

Also, the Adjudicator may make any order which the High Court could make for the rectification or setting aside of a document which effects a registrable disposition or is a contract to make one or effects a disposition which creates an interest which may be the subject of a notice in the register (s.108).

Hearings before the Adjudicator shall be held in public, except where he is satisfied that exclusion of the public is just and reasonable (s.109(1)).

On a reference under s.73(7), the Adjudicator may, instead of deciding a matter himself, direct a party to the proceedings to commence proceedings in the court within a specified time (s.110).

A person aggrieved by a decision of the Adjudicator may appeal to the High Court but in the case of a decision relating to a network access agreement an appeal can only be on a point of law.

Objections

22–005 An objection, whether to a notice or otherwise, must be in writing signed by the objector or his conveyancer and must be delivered to the appropriate office, or, if different, to the office specified in the notice to which it is a response. It must state that the objector objects to the application, state the grounds for the objection and give the full name of the objector and an address to which communications may be sent (r.19).

When an objection is received, unless the registrar decides that it is groundless, the application to which it relates cannot proceed until it is withdrawn or it is disposed of by agreement or by a decision of the Adjudicator or of the court (s.73).

Notice of any objection must be given to the applicant (s.73(5)). The notice will invite him to either withdraw his application or indicate that he intends to proceed. If the applicant does not respond to the notice it will be assumed that he does not wish to proceed.

If the applicant indicates that he intends to proceed the parties will be allowed time to negotiate. This will be done by inviting them to complete Form 737 or Form 737A. If they indicate at any time that they do not wish to negotiate, or fail to respond to Form 737 or 737A or it appears that negotiations are not progressing the matter will be referred to the Adjudicator (s.73(7)).

Reference to the Adjudicator is by means of a Case Summary prepared by the registrar. It contains the names and addresses of the parties, details of their legal or other representatives, a summary of the core facts, details of the disputed application, details of the objection, any other information the registrar considers appropriate and a list of any documents that will be copied to the Adjudicator. The purpose of the case summary is to give the Adjudicator brief details of the case being referred to him to allow him to make an initial decision as to whether he will hear the case himself or direct one of the parties to start court proceedings. The case summary does not form part of the pleadings in the proceedings before the Adjudicator and it does not set out the parties' detailed arguments or evidence. The parties will be allowed to comment on the Case Summary before it is referred to the Adjudicator but they are not entitled to insist on it being amended.

When the Case Summary has been finalised the registrar will send it, with copies of the documents listed in it, to the Adjudicator under cover of a written notice informing him that the matter is referred. At the same time the parties will be informed in writing that the matter has been referred to the Adjudicator and will be sent a copy of the case summary and documents.

Indemnity

Under Sch.8 to the Act indemnity is payable by the registrar **22–006** where a person suffers loss by reason of:

(1) rectification of the register;

(2) a mistake whose correction would involve rectification of the register;

(3) a mistake in an official search;

(4) a mistake in an official copy;

(5) a mistake in a document kept by the registrar which is not an original and is referred to in the register;

(6) the loss or destruction of a document lodged at the Registry for inspection or safe custody;

(7) a mistake in the cautions register; or

(8) failure by the registrar to give notice of an overriding statutory charge as required under s.50.

A mistake means anything mistakenly omitted as well as anything mistakenly included (para.11 of Sch.8 to the Act).

A proprietor claiming in good faith under a forged disposition is, where the register is rectified, regarded as having suffered loss by reason of such rectification as if the disposition had not been forged (para.1(2) of Sch.8 to the Act).

No indemnity is payable:

(a) under (2) above until a decision has been made about whether to alter the register for the purpose of correcting the mistake and the loss suffered by reason of the mistake is to be determined in the light of that decision (para.1(3) of Sch.8 to the Act);

(b) on account of any mines or minerals or the right to work or get them unless the title specifically includes mines or minerals (para.2 of Sch.8 to the Act);

(c) on account of any loss suffered by a claimant wholly or partly as a result of his own fraud or wholly as a result of his own lack of proper care. Where any loss is suffered by a claimant partly as a result of his own lack of proper care, any indemnity payable to him is to be reduced to such extent as is fair having regard to his share in the responsibility for the loss (para.5 of Sch.8 to the Act).

Indemnity payable as a result of rectification of the register cannot exceed the value of the property immediately before rectification. Indemnity payable in the case of a mistake, the correction of which would involve rectification of the register is not to exceed the value of the property at the time when the mistake which caused the loss was made (para.6 of Sch.8 to the Act).

For the purposes of the Limitation Act 1980 a liability to pay indemnity is a simple contract debt, and the cause of action arises at the time when the claimant knows, or but for his own default might have known, of the existence of his claim (para.8 of Sch.8 to the Act).

Rule 195 contains provisions which govern the payment of interest on indemnity.

The registrar is entitled to recover indemnity:

- from any person who caused or substantially contributed to the loss by his fraud; or

- by enforcing rights of action which the claimant would have been entitled to enforce had the indemnity not been paid, and where the register has been rectified, any right of action which the person in whose favour the register has been rectified would have been entitled to enforce had it not been rectified (para.10 of Sch.8 to the Act).

If the court grants a declaration that a freehold estate should not have been registered as a freehold estate in commonhold land, then, under s.6(6)(g) of the Commonhold and Leasehold Reform Act 2002, the court may by order apply, disapply or modify a provision of Sch.8 to the Act.

Costs and expenses

Claimants entitled to be indemnified will be paid their reason- **22–007**
able costs and expenses properly incurred in relation to the
matter even if no other indemnity is payable (para.3 of Sch.8 to
the Act).

Particular attention is directed to the provisions of para.3(1)
of Sch.8 to the Act, which provides that a claimant can only be
indemnified against costs and expenses incurred with the consent of the registrar. If such consent is required, application
should be made by letter to the appropriate office at the earliest
possible opportunity.

The need for consent does not apply where:

(1) the costs or expenses must be incurred urgently; and

(2) it is not reasonably practicable to apply for the registrar's
consent (para.3(2) of Sch.8 to the Act).

The registrar may approve costs or expenses after they have
been incurred in which case they are treated as having been
incurred with his consent (para.3(3) of Sch.8 to the Act).

If the register is altered in a case not involving rectification,
the registrar may pay such amount as he thinks fit in respect of
any costs or expenses reasonably incurred, with the consent of
the registrar, in connection with the alteration. As above it is
important that such consent is sought at the earliest opportunity.
The registrar may make a payment notwithstanding the absence
of consent if it appears to him that the costs or expenses had to
be incurred urgently, and either it was not reasonably practicable to apply for his consent, or he has subsequently approved
the incurring of the costs or expenses (para.9 of Sch.4 to the
Act).

Claims for payment of indemnity

A claim for indemnity should normally be submitted by letter, **22–008**
supported by relevant valuations, calculations and accounts, to
the appropriate office.

Almost all claims for indemnity are settled by agreement but
if agreement cannot be reached, whether as to the right to or to
the amount of indemnity, the question will be determined by the
court. It is not necessary to obtain the registrar's consent to the
costs of court proceedings relating to indemnity (para.7 of Sch.8
to the Act).

APPENDIX I

Postal and document exchange addresses and telephone and fax numbers of Land Registry Offices

Head Office
Lincoln's Inn Fields
London WC2A 3PH
DX No. 1098 London/Chancery
Lane WC2
Tel: 020 7917 8888
Fax No: 020 7955 0110

Croydon Office
Sunley House
Bedford Park
Croydon CR9 3LE
DX No. 2699 Croydon (3)
Tel: 020 8781 9100
Fax No: 020 8781 9110

Birkenhead (Old Market) Office
Old Market House
Hamilton Street
Birkenhead
Merseyside CH41 5FL
DX No. 14300 Birkenhead (3)
Tel: 0151 473 1110
Fax No: 0151 473 0251

Durham (Boldon) Office
Boldon House
Wheatlands Way
Pity Me
Durham DH1 5GJ
DX No. 60860 Durham (6)
Tel: 0191 301 2345
Fax No: 0191 301 2300

Birkenhead (Rosebrae) Office
Rosebrae Court
Woodside Ferry Approach
Birkenhead
Merseyside CH41 6DU
DX No. 24270 Birkenhead (4)
Tel: 0151 472 6666
Fax No: 0151 472 6789

Durham (Southfield) Office
Southfield House
Southfield Way
Durham DH1 5TR
DX No. 60200 Durham (3)
Tel: 0191 301 3500
Fax No: 0191 301 0020

Coventry Office
Leigh Court
Torrington Avenue
Tile Hill
Coventry CV4 9XZ
DX No. 18900 Coventry (3)
Tel: 024 7686 0860
Fax No: 024 7686 0021

Gloucester Office
Twyver House
Bruton Way
Gloucester GL1 1DQ
DX No. 7599 Gloucester (3)
Tel: 01452 511 111
Fax No: 01452 510050

Harrow Office
Lyon House
Lyon Road
Harrow
Middlesex HA1 2EU
DX No. 4299 Harrow (4)
Tel: 020 8235 1181
Fax No: 020 8862 0176

Kingston Upon Hull Office
Earle House
Colonial Street
Hull HU2 8JN
DX No. 26700 Hull (4)
Tel: 01482 223244
Fax No: 01482 224278

Lancashire Office
Wrea Brook Court
Lytham Road
Warton
Preston PR4 1TE
DX No. 721560 Lytham (6)
Tel: 01772 836700
Fax No: 01772 836970

Leicester Office
Westbridge Place
Leicester LE3 5DR
DX No. 11900 Leicester (5)
Tel: 0116 265 4000
Fax No: 0116 265 4008

Lytham Office
Birkenhead House
East Beach
Lytham St Annes
Lancs FY8 5AB
DX No. 14500
Lytham St Annes (3)
Tel: 01253 849849
Fax No: 01253 840001

Nottingham (East) Office
Robins Wood Road
Nottingham NG8 3RQ
DX No. 716126 Nottingham (26)
Tel: 0115 906 5353
Fax No: 0115 936 0036

Nottingham (West) Office
Chalfont Drive
Nottingham NG8 3RN
DX No. 10298 Nottingham (3)
Tel: 0115 935 1166
Fax No: 0115 935 0038

Peterborough Office
Touthill Close
City Road
Peterborough PE1 1XN
DX No.12598 Peterborough (4)
Tel: 01733 288288
Fax No: 01733 280022

Plymouth Office
Plumer House
Tailyour Road
Crownhill
Plymouth PL6 5HY
DX No.8299 Plymouth (4)
Tel: 01752 636000
Fax No: 01752 636161

Portsmouth Office
St Andrew's Court
St Michael's Road
Portsmouth
Hants PO1 2JH
DX No.83550 Portsmouth (2)
Tel: 023 9276 8888
Fax No: 023 9276 8768

Stevenage Office
Brickdale House
Swingate
Stevenage
Herts SG1 1XG
DX No.6099 Stevenage (2)
Tel: 01438 788888
Fax No: 01438 785 460

Swansea Office
Ty Bryn Glas
High Street
Swansea SA1 1PW
DX No. 33700 Swansea (2)
Tel: 01792 458877
Fax No: 01792 473236

Telford Office
Parkside Court
Hall Park Way
Telford TF3 4LR
DX No. 28100 Telford (2)
Tel: 01952 290355
Fax No: 01952 290356

Tunbridge Wells Office
Forest Court
Forest Road
Tunbridge Wells TN2 5AQ
DX No. 3999 Tunbridge Wells
(2)
Tel: 01892 510015
Fax No: 01892 510032

Wales Office
Ty Cwm Tawe
Phoenix Way
Llansamlet
Swansea SA7 9FQ
DX No. 82800 Swansea (2)
Tel: 01792 355000
Fax No: 01792 355055

Weymouth Office
Melcombe Court
1 Cumberland Drive
Weymouth
Dorset DT4 9TT
DX No. 8799 Weymouth (2)
Tel: 01305 363636
Fax No: 01305 363646

York Office
James House
James Street
York YO10 3YZ
DX No. 61599 York (2)
Tel: 01904 450000
Fax No: 01904 450086

APPENDIX II

List of administrative areas and the Land Registry Offices which are responsible for them

ABERCONWY	Wales Office
ADUR	Portsmouth Office
ALLERDALE	Durham (Boldon) Office
ALNWICK	Durham (Southfield) Office
ALYN AND DEESIDE	Wales Office
AMBER VALLEY	Nottingham (West) Office
ARFON	Wales Office
ARUN	Portsmouth Office
ASHFIELD	Nottingham (East) Office
ASHFORD	Tunbridge Wells Office
AYLESBURY VALE	Leicester Office
BABERGH	Kingston Upon Hull Office
BARKING AND DAGENHAM	Stevenage Office
BARNET	Swansea Office
BARNSLEY	Nottingham (East) Office
BARROW-IN-FURNESS	Durham (Boldon) Office
BASILDON	Peterborough Office
BASINGSTOKE AND DEANE	Weymouth Office
BASSETLAW	Nottingham (East) Office
BATH	Plymouth Office
BATH AND NORTH EAST SOMERSET	Plymouth Office
BEDFORD	Peterborough Office
BEDFORDSHIRE	Peterborough Office
BERWICK-UPON-TWEED	Durham (Southfield) Office
BEXLEY	Croydon Office
BIRMINGHAM	Coventry Office
BLABY	Leicester Office
BLACKBURN	Lancashire Office
BLACKBURN WITH DARWEN	Lancashire Office
BLACKPOOL	Lancashire Office
BLAENAU GWENT	Wales Office
BLYTH VALLEY	Durham (Southfield) Office
BOLSOVER	Nottingham (West) Office
BOLTON	Lytham Office
BOOTHFERRY	Kingston Upon Hull Office
BOSTON	Kingston Upon Hull Office
BOURNEMOUTH	Weymouth Office
BRACKNELL	Gloucester Office

BRACKNELL FOREST	Gloucester Office
BRADFORD	Nottingham (West) Office
BRAINTREE	Peterborough Office
BRECKLAND	Kingston Upon Hull Office
BRECKNOCK	Wales Office
BRENT	Harrow Office
BRENTWOOD	Peterborough Office
BRIDGEND	Wales Office
BRIDGNORTH	Telford Office
BRIGHTON	Portsmouth Office
BRIGHTON AND HOVE	Portsmouth Office
BRISTOL	Gloucester Office
BROADLAND	Kingston Upon Hull Office
BROMLEY	Croydon Office
BROMSGROVE	Coventry Office
BROXBOURNE	Stevenage Office
BROXTOWE	Nottingham (East) Office
BRYHER	Plymouth Office
BUCKINGHAMSHIRE	Leicester Office
BURNLEY	Lancashire Office
BURY	Lytham Office
CAERPHILLY	Wales Office
CALDERDALE	Nottingham (West) Office
CAMBRIDGE	Peterborough Office
CAMBRIDGESHIRE	Peterborough Office
CAMDEN	Harrow Office
CANNOCK CHASE	Birkenhead (Old Market) Office
CANTERBURY	Tunbridge Wells Office
CARADON	Plymouth Office
CARDIFF	Wales Office
CARDIGANSHIRE	Wales Office
CARLISLE	Durham (Boldon) Office
CARMARTHEN	Wales Office
CARMARTHENSHIRE	Wales Office
CARRICK	Plymouth Office
CASTLE MORPETH	Durham (Southfield) Office
CASTLE POINT	Peterborough Office
CEREDIGION	Wales Office
CHARNWOOD	Leicester Office
CHELMSFORD	Peterborough Office
CHELTENHAM	Gloucester Office
CHERWELL	Gloucester Office
CHESHIRE	Birkenhead (Rosebrae) Office
CHESTER	Birkenhead (Rosebrae) Office
CHESTERFIELD	Nottingham (West) Office
CHESTER-LE-STREET	Durham (Southfield) Office
CHICHESTER	Portsmouth Office
CHILTERN	Leicester Office
CHORLEY	Lancashire Office
CHRISTCHURCH	Weymouth Office
CITY OF BRISTOL	Gloucester Office
CITY OF DERBY	Nottingham (West) Office

CITY OF KINGSTON UPON HULL	Kingston Upon Hull Office
CITY OF LONDON	Harrow Office
CITY OF NOTTINGHAM	Nottingham (East) Office
CITY OF PETERBOROUGH	Peterborough Office
CITY OF PLYMOUTH	Plymouth Office
CITY OF WESTMINSTER	Harrow Office
CLEETHORPES	Kingston Upon Hull Office
COLCHESTER	Peterborough Office
COLWYN	Wales Office
CONGLETON	Birkenhead (Rosebrae) Office
CONWY	Wales Office
COPELAND	Durham (Boldon) Office
CORBY	Leicester Office
CORNWALL	Plymouth Office
COTSWOLD	Gloucester Office
COVENTRY	Coventry Office
CRAVEN	York Office
CRAWLEY	Portsmouth Office
CREWE AND NANTWICH	Birkenhead (Rosebrae) Office
CROYDON	Croydon Office
CUMBRIA	Durham (Boldon) Office
CYNON VALLEY	Wales Office
DACORUM	Stevenage Office
DARLINGTON	Durham (Southfield) Office
DARTFORD	Tunbridge Wells Office
DAVENTRY	Leicester Office
DELYN	Wales Office
DENBIGHSHIRE	Wales Office
DERBY	Nottingham (West) Office
DERBYSHIRE	Nottingham (West) Office
DERBYSHIRE DALES	Nottingham (West) Office
DERWENTSIDE	Durham (Southfield) Office
DEVON	Plymouth Office
DINEFWR	Wales Office
DONCASTER	Nottingham (East) Office
DORSET	Weymouth Office
DOVER	Tunbridge Wells Office
DUDLEY	Coventry Office
DURHAM	Durham (Southfield) Office
DWYFOR	Wales Office
EALING	Swansea Office
EASINGTON	Durham (Southfield) Office
EAST CAMBRIDGESHIRE	Peterborough Office
EAST DEVON	Plymouth Office
EAST DORSET	Weymouth Office
EAST HAMPSHIRE	Portsmouth Office
EAST HERTFORDSHIRE	Stevenage Office
EAST LINDSEY	Kingston Upon Hull Office
EAST NORTHAMPTONSHIRE	Leicester Office
EAST RIDING OF YORKSHIRE	York Office
EAST STAFFORDSHIRE	Birkenhead (Old Market) Office

EAST SUSSEX	Portsmouth Office
EAST YORKSHIRE	Kingston Upon Hull Office
EASTBOURNE	Portsmouth Office
EASTLEIGH	Weymouth Office
EDEN	Durham (Boldon) Office
ELLESMERE PORT AND NESTON	Birkenhead (Rosebrae) Office
ELMBRIDGE	Durham (Boldon) Office
ENFIELD	Swansea Office
EPPING FOREST	Peterborough Office
EPSOM AND EWELL	Durham (Boldon) Office
EREWASH	Nottingham (West) Office
ESSEX	Peterborough Office
EXETER	Plymouth Office
FAREHAM	Weymouth Office
FENLAND	Peterborough Office
FLINTSHIRE	Wales Office
FOREST HEATH	Kingston Upon Hull Office
FOREST OF DEAN	Gloucester Office
FYLDE	Lancashire Office
GATESHEAD	Durham (Southfield) Office
GEDLING	Nottingham (East) Office
GILLINGHAM	Tunbridge Wells Office
GLANFORD	Kingston Upon Hull Office
GLOUCESTER	Gloucester Office
GLOUCESTERSHIRE	Gloucester Office
GLYNDWR	Wales Office
GOSPORT	Weymouth Office
GRAVESHAM	Tunbridge Wells Office
GREAT GRIMSBY	Kingston Upon Hull Office
GREAT YARMOUTH	Kingston Upon Hull Office
GREATER MANCHESTER	Lytham Office
GREENWICH	Telford Office
GUILDFORD	Durham (Boldon) Office
GWYNEDD	Wales Office
HACKNEY	Stevenage Office
HALTON	Birkenhead (Rosebrae) Office
HAMBLETON	York Office
HAMMERSMITH AND FULHAM	Birkenhead (Rosebrae) Office
HAMPSHIRE	Weymouth Office
HARBOROUGH	Leicester Office
HARINGEY	Swansea Office
HARLOW	Peterborough Office
HARROGATE	York Office
HARROW	Harrow Office
HART	Weymouth Office
HARTLEPOOL	Durham (Southfield) Office
HASTINGS	Portsmouth Office
HAVANT	Portsmouth Office
HAVERING	Stevenage Office
HEREFORD	Telford Office

HEREFORDSHIRE	Telford Office
HERTFORDSHIRE	Stevenage Office
HERTSMERE	Stevenage Office
HIGH PEAK	Nottingham (West) Office
HILLINGDON	Swansea Office
HINCKLEY AND BOSWORTH	Leicester Office
HOLDERNESS	Kingston Upon Hull Office
HORSHAM	Portsmouth Office
HOUNSLOW	Swansea Office
HOVE	Portsmouth Office
HUNTINGDONSHIRE	Peterborough Office
HYNDBURN	Lancashire Office
INNER AND MIDDLE TEMPLES	Harrow Office
IPSWICH	Kingston Upon Hull Office
ISLE OF ANGLESEY	Wales Office
ISLE OF WIGHT	Portsmouth Office
ISLES OF SCILLY	Plymouth Office
ISLINGTON	Harrow Office
ISLWYN	Wales Office
KENNET	Weymouth Office
KENSINGTON AND CHELSEA	Birkenhead (Rosebrae) Office
KENT	Tunbridge Wells Office
KERRIER	Plymouth Office
KETTERING	Leicester Office
KING'S LYNN AND WEST NORFOLK	Kingston Upon Hull Office
KINGSTON UPON HULL	Kingston Upon Hull Office
KINGSTON UPON THAMES	Croydon Office
KINGSWOOD	Gloucester Office
KIRKLEES	Nottingham (West) Office
KNOWSLEY	Birkenhead (Old Market) Office
LAMBETH	Telford Office
LANCASHIRE	Lancashire Office
LANCASTER	Lancashire Office
LANGBAURGH-ON-TEES	Durham (Southfield) Office
LEEDS	Nottingham (West) Office
LEICESTER	Leicester Office
LEICESTERSHIRE	Leicester Office
LEOMINSTER	Telford Office
LEWES	Portsmouth Office
LEWISHAM	Telford Office
LICHFIELD	Birkenhead (Old Market) Office
LINCOLN	Kingston Upon Hull Office
LINCOLNSHIRE	Kingston Upon Hull Office
LIVERPOOL	Birkenhead (Old Market) Office
LLANELLI	Wales Office
LLIW VALLEY	Wales Office
LUTON	Peterborough Office
MACCLESFIELD	Birkenhead (Rosebrae) Office
MAIDSTONE	Tunbridge Wells Office
MALDON	Peterborough Office

MALVERN HILLS	Coventry Office
MANCHESTER	Lytham Office
MANSFIELD	Nottingham (East) Office
MEDINA	Tunbridge Wells Office
MEDWAY	Tunbridge Wells Office
MEDWAY TOWNS	Tunbridge Wells Office
MEIRIONNYDD	Wales Office
MELTON	Leicester Office
MENDIP	Weymouth Office
MERSEYSIDE	Birkenhead (Old Market) Office
MERTHYR TYDFIL	Wales Office
MERTON	Croydon Office
MID BEDFORDSHIRE	Peterborough Office
MID DEVON	Plymouth Office
MID SUFFOLK	Kingston Upon Hull Office
MID SUSSEX	Portsmouth Office
MIDDLESBROUGH	Durham (Southfield) Office
MILTON KEYNES	Leicester Office
MOLE VALLEY	Durham (Boldon) Office
MONMOUTH	Wales Office
MONMOUTHSHIRE	Wales Office
MONTGOMERYSHIRE	Wales Office
NEATH	Wales Office
NEATH PORT TALBOT	Wales Office
NEW FOREST	Weymouth Office
NEWARK AND SHERWOOD	Nottingham (East) Office
NEWBURY	Gloucester Office
NEWCASTLE UPON TYNE	Durham (Southfield) Office
NEWCASTLE-UNDER-LYME	Birkenhead (Old Market) Office
NEWHAM	Stevenage Office
NEWPORT	Wales Office
NORFOLK	Kingston Upon Hull Office
NORTH BEDFORDSHIRE	Peterborough Office
NORTH CORNWALL	Plymouth Office
NORTH DEVON	Plymouth Office
NORTH DORSET	Weymouth Office
NORTH EAST DERBYSHIRE	Nottingham (West) Office
NORTH EAST LINCOLNSHIRE	Kingston Upon Hull Office
NORTH HERTFORDSHIRE	Stevenage Office
NORTH KESTEVEN	Kingston Upon Hull Office
NORTH LINCOLNSHIRE	Kingston Upon Hull Office
NORTH NORFOLK	Kingston Upon Hull Office
NORTH NORTHAMPTONSHIRE	Peterborough Office
NORTH SHROPSHIRE	Telford Office
NORTH SOMERSET	Plymouth Office
NORTH TYNESIDE	Durham (Southfield) Office
NORTH WARWICKSHIRE	Gloucester Office
NORTH WEST LEICESTERSHIRE	Leicester Office
NORTH WILTSHIRE	Weymouth Office
NORTH YORKSHIRE	York Office

NORTHAMPTON	Leicester Office
NORTHAVON	Gloucester Office
NORTHUMBERLAND	Durham (Southfield) Office
NORWICH	Kingston Upon Hull Office
NOTTINGHAMSHIRE	Nottingham (East) Office
NUNEATON AND BEDWORTH	Gloucester Office
OADBY AND WIGSTON	Leicester Office
OGWR	Wales Office
OLDHAM	Lytham Office
OSWESTRY	Telford Office
OXFORD	Gloucester Office
OXFORDSHIRE	Gloucester Office
PEMBROKESHIRE	Wales Office
PENDLE	Lancashire Office
PENWITH	Plymouth Office
PETERBOROUGH	Peterborough Office
PLYMOUTH	Plymouth Office
POOLE	Weymouth Office
PORT TALBOT	Wales Office
PORTSMOUTH	Portsmouth Office
POWYS	Wales Office
PRESELI	Wales Office
PRESELI PEMBROKESHIRE	Wales Office
PRESTON	Lancashire Office
PURBECK	Weymouth Office
RADNOR	Wales Office
RADNORSHIRE	Wales Office
READING	Gloucester Office
REDBRIDGE	Stevenage Office
REDCAR AND CLEVELAND	Durham (Southfield) Office
REDDITCH	Coventry Office
REIGATE AND BANSTEAD	Durham (Boldon) Office
RESTORMEL	Plymouth Office
RHONDDA	Wales Office
RHONDDA CYNON TAFF	Wales Office
RHUDDLAN	Wales Office
RHYMNEY VALLEY	Wales Office
RIBBLE VALLEY	Lancashire Office
RICHMOND UPON THAMES	Telford Office
RICHMONDSHIRE	York Office
ROCHDALE	Lytham Office
ROCHESTER UPON MEDWAY	Tunbridge Wells Office
ROCHFORD	Peterborough Office
ROSSENDALE	Lancashire Office
ROTHER	Portsmouth Office
ROTHERHAM	Nottingham (East) Office
RUGBY	Gloucester Office
RUNNYMEDE	Durham (Boldon) Office
RUSHCLIFFE	Nottingham (East) Office
RUSHMOOR	Weymouth Office
RUTLAND	Leicester Office
RYEDALE	York Office

SALFORD	Lytham Office
SALISBURY	Weymouth Office
SANDWELL	Coventry Office
SCARBOROUGH	York Office
SCUNTHORPE	Kingston Upon Hull Office
SEDGEFIELD	Durham (Southfield) Office
SEDGEMOOR	Plymouth Office
SEFTON	Birkenhead (Old Market) Office
SELBY	York Office
SEVENOAKS	Tunbridge Wells Office
SHEFFIELD	Nottingham (East) Office
SHEPWAY	Tunbridge Wells Office
SHREWSBURY AND ATCHAM	Telford Office
SHROPSHIRE	Telford Office
SLOUGH	Gloucester Office
SOLIHULL	Coventry Office
SOMERSET	Plymouth Office
SOUTH BEDFORDSHIRE	Peterborough Office
SOUTH BUCKS	Leicester Office
SOUTH CAMBRIDGESHIRE	Peterborough Office
SOUTH DERBYSHIRE	Nottingham (West) Office
SOUTH GLOUCESTERSHIRE	Gloucester Office
SOUTH HAMS	Plymouth Office
SOUTH HEREFORDSHIRE	Telford Office
SOUTH HOLLAND	Kingston Upon Hull Office
SOUTH KESTEVEN	Kingston Upon Hull Office
SOUTH LAKELAND	Durham (Boldon) Office
SOUTH NORFOLK	Kingston Upon Hull Office
SOUTH NORTHAMPTONSHIRE	Leicester Office
SOUTH OXFORDSHIRE	Gloucester Office
SOUTH PEMBROKESHIRE	Wales Office
SOUTH RIBBLE	Lancashire Office
SOUTH SHROPSHIRE	Telford Office
SOUTH SOMERSET	Weymouth Office
SOUTH STAFFORDSHIRE	Birkenhead (Old Market) Office
SOUTH TYNESIDE	Durham (Southfield) Office
SOUTH WIGHT	Tunbridge Wells Office
SOUTH YORKSHIRE	Nottingham (East) Office
SOUTHAMPTON	Weymouth Office
SOUTHEND-ON-SEA	Peterborough Office
SOUTHWARK	Telford Office
SPELTHORNE	Durham (Boldon) Office
ST AGNES	Plymouth Office
ST ALBANS	Stevenage Office
ST EDMUNDSBURY	Kingston Upon Hull Office
ST HELENS	Birkenhead (Old Market) Office
ST MARTIN'S	Plymouth Office
ST MARY'S	Plymouth Office
STAFFORD	Birkenhead (Old Market) Office
STAFFORDSHIRE	Birkenhead (Old Market) Office

STAFFORDSHIRE MOORLANDS	Birkenhead (Old Market) Office
STEVENAGE	Stevenage Office
STOCKPORT	Lytham Office
STOCKTON-ON-TEES	Durham (Southfield) Office
STOKE-ON-TRENT	Birkenhead (Old Market) Office
STRATFORD-ON-AVON	Gloucester Office
STROUD	Gloucester Office
SUFFOLK	Kingston Upon Hull Office
SUFFOLK COASTAL	Kingston Upon Hull Office
SUNDERLAND	Durham (Southfield) Office
SURREY	Durham (Boldon) Office
SURREY HEATH	Durham (Boldon) Office
SUTTON	Croydon Office
SWALE	Tunbridge Wells Office
SWANSEA	Wales Office
SWINDON	Weymouth Office
TAFF-ELY	Wales Office
TAMESIDE	Lytham Office
TAMWORTH	Birkenhead (Old Market) Office
TANDRIDGE	Durham (Boldon) Office
TAUNTON DEANE	Plymouth Office
TEESDALE	Durham (Southfield) Office
TEIGNBRIDGE	Plymouth Office
TENDRING	Peterborough Office
TEST VALLEY	Weymouth Office
TEWKESBURY	Gloucester Office
THAMESDOWN	Weymouth Office
THANET	Tunbridge Wells Office
THE EAST YORKSHIRE BOROUGH OF BEVERLEY	Kingston Upon Hull Office
THE VALE OF GLAMORGAN	Wales Office
THE WREKIN	Telford Office
THREE RIVERS	Stevenage Office
THURROCK	Peterborough Office
TONBRIDGE AND MALLING	Tunbridge Wells Office
TORBAY	Plymouth Office
TORFAEN	Wales Office
TORRIDGE	Plymouth Office
TOWER HAMLETS	Stevenage Office
TRAFFORD	Lytham Office
TRESCO	Plymouth Office
TUNBRIDGE WELLS	Tunbridge Wells Office
TYNE AND WEAR	Durham (Southfield) Office
TYNEDALE	Durham (Southfield) Office
UTTLESFORD	Peterborough Office
VALE OF GLAMORGAN	Wales Office
VALE OF WHITE HORSE	Gloucester Office
VALE ROYAL	Birkenhead (Rosebrae) Office
WAKEFIELD	Nottingham (West) Office
WALSALL	Coventry Office

WALTHAM FOREST	Stevenage Office
WANDSWORTH	Telford Office
WANSBECK	Durham (Southfield) Office
WANSDYKE	Plymouth Office
WARRINGTON	Birkenhead (Rosebrae) Office
WARWICK	Gloucester Office
WARWICKSHIRE	Gloucester Office
WATFORD	Stevenage Office
WAVENEY	Kingston Upon Hull Office
WAVERLEY	Durham (Boldon) Office
WEALDEN	Portsmouth Office
WEAR VALLEY	Durham (Southfield) Office
WELLINGBOROUGH	Leicester Office
WELWYN HATFIELD	Stevenage Office
WEST BERKSHIRE	Gloucester Office
WEST DEVON	Plymouth Office
WEST DORSET	Weymouth Office
WEST LANCASHIRE	Lancashire Office
WEST LINDSEY	Kingston Upon Hull Office
WEST MIDLANDS	Coventry Office
WEST OXFORDSHIRE	Gloucester Office
WEST SOMERSET	Plymouth Office
WEST SUSSEX	Portsmouth Office
WEST WILTSHIRE	Weymouth Office
WEST YORKSHIRE	Nottingham (West) Office
WEYMOUTH AND PORTLAND	Weymouth Office
WIGAN	Lytham Office
WILTSHIRE	Weymouth Office
WINCHESTER	Weymouth Office
WINDSOR AND MAIDENHEAD	Gloucester Office
WIRRAL	Birkenhead (Old Market) Office
WOKING	Durham (Boldon) Office
WOKINGHAM	Gloucester Office
WOLVERHAMPTON	Coventry Office
WORCESTERSHIRE	Coventry Office
WORTHING	Portsmouth Office
WREKIN	Telford Office
WREXHAM	Wales Office
WREXHAM MAELOR	Wales Office
WYCHAVON	Coventry Office
WYCOMBE	Leicester Office
WYRE	Lancashire Office
WYRE FOREST	Coventry Office
YNYS MON-ISLE OF ANGLESEY	Wales Office
YORK	York Office

APPENDIX III

List of Forms

Schedule 1 Forms

Application for approval of a standard form of charge deed and allocation of official Land Registry Reference	ACD
Application for registration of a person in adverse possession under Sch. 6 to the Act	ADV1
Application to be registered as a person to be notified of an application for adverse possession	ADV2
Application to enter an agreed notice	AN1
Application to change the register	AP1
Assent of whole of registered title(s)	AS1
Assent of charge	AS2
Assent of part of registered title(s)	AS3
Entry of a note of consolidation of charges	CC
Application to cancel a caution against dealings	CCD
Application to cancel a caution against first registration	CCT
Legal charge of a registered estate	CH1
Application to enter an obligation to make further advances	CH2
Application to note agreed maximum amount of security	CH3
Certificate of inspection of title plan	CI
Application in connection with court proceedings, insolvency and tax liability	CIT
Application to register a freehold estate in commonhold land	CM1
Application for the freehold estate to cease to be registered as a freehold estate in commonhold land during the transitional period	CM2
Application for the registration of an amended commonhold community statement and/or altered memorandum and articles of association	CM3
Application to add land to a commonhold registration	CM4
Application for the termination of a commonhold registration	CM5
Application for the registration of a successor commonhold association	CM6
Application to cancel a notice (other than a unilateral notice)	CN1
Notification of change of extent of a commonhold unit over which there is a registered charge	COE
Consent to the registration of land as commonhold land	CON1

Consent to an application for the freehold estate to cease to be registered as a freehold estate in commonhold land during the transitional period	CON2
Application for registration with unit holders	COV
Continuation sheet for use with application and disposition forms	CS
Caution against first registration	CT1
Application to determine the exact line of a boundary	DB
Disclosable overriding interests	DI
Application to remove from the register the name of a deceased registered proprietor	DJP
List of documents	DL
Cancellation of entries relating to a registered charge	DS1
Application to cancel entries relating to a registered charge	DS2
Release of part of the land from a registered charge	DS3
Application for the registrar to designate a document as an exempt information document	EX1
Reasons for exemption in support of an application to designate a document as an exempt information document	EX1A
Application for official copy of an exempt information document	EX2
Application to remove the designation of a document as an exempt information document	EX3
First registration application	FR1
Application for copies of historical edition(s) of the register/title plan held in electronic form	HC1
Application for registration of a notice of home rights	HR1
Application for renewal of registration in respect of home rights	HR2
Application by mortgagee for official search in respect of home rights	HR3
Evidence of identity for a private individual	ID1
Evidence of identity for a corporate body	ID2
Evidence of identity for use with FR1 only	ID3
Notice to the registrar in respect of an adverse possession application	NAP
Application for official copies of register/plan or certificate in Form CI	OC1
Application for official copies of documents only	OC2
Application by purchaser for official search with priority of the whole of the land in a registered title or a pending first registration application	OS1
Application by purchaser for official search with priority of part of the land in a registered title or a pending first registration application	OS2
Application for official search without priority of the land in a registered title	OS3
Application for a personal inspection under s.66	PIC
Application for a search in the Index of Proprietors' Names	PN1
Request for the production of documents	PRD1

Notice to produce a document, s.75 and r.201	PRD2
Request for the return of an original document(s)	RD1
Application to enter a restriction	RX1
Application for an order that a restriction be disapplied or modified	RX2
Application to cancel a restriction	RX3
Application to withdraw a restriction	RX4
Application for noting the overriding priority of a statutory charge	SC
Application for an official search of the index of relating franchises and manors	SIF
Application for an official search of the index map	SIM
Notice of surrender of development right(s)	SR1
Transfer of part of registered title(s)	TP1
Transfer of part of registered title(s) under power of sale	TP2
Transfer of portfolio of titles	TP3
Transfer of whole of registered title(s)	TR1
Transfer of whole of registered title(s) under power of sale	TR2
Transfer of charge	TR3
Transfer of a portfolio of charges	TR4
Transfer of portfolio of whole titles	TR5
Application to enter a unilateral notice	UN1
Application to remove a unilateral notice	UN2
Application to be registered as beneficiary of an existing unilateral notice	UN3
Application for the cancellation of a unilateral notice	UN4
Application for upgrading of title	UT1
Application to withdraw a caution	WCT

Schedule 3 Forms

Certificate as to execution of power of attorney (r.61)	Form 1
Statutory declaration/certificate as to non-revocation for powers more than 12 months old at the date of the disposition for which they are used (r.62)	Form 2
Statutory declaration/certificate in support of power delegating trustees' functions to a beneficiary (r.63)	Form 3
Certificate as to Vesting in an Incumbent or other Ecclesiastical Corporation (r.174) Form 4	
Certificate as to Vesting in the Church Commissioners, etc. (r.175)	Form 5
Transfer where the Tenant for Life is already registered as proprietor (r.186 and para.5 of Sch.7 to the Rules)	Form 6

APPENDIX IV

Land Registration, England and Wales

The Land Registration Fee Order 2004
(SI 2004 No. 595)

Made - - - - - - - - - - - - *3 March 2004*
Laid before Parliament - - - - - *9 March 2004*
Coming into force - - - - - - - - *1 April 2004*

The Lord Chancellor, with the advice and assistance of the Rule Committee appointed in pursuance of section 127 of the Land Registration Act 2002,[1] and with the consent of the Treasury, in exercise of the powers conferred on him by section 102 of that Act, hereby makes the following Order:

PART 1

General

Citation, commencement and interpretation

1.—(1) This Order may be cited as the Land Registration Fee Order 2004 and shall come into force on 1st April 2004.

(2) In this Order unless the context otherwise requires—

"account holder" means a person or firm holding a credit account,

"the Act" means the Land Registration Act 2002,

"charge" includes a sub-charge,

"credit account" means an account authorised by the registrar under article 14(1),

"large scale application" is as defined in article 6(1),

"monetary consideration" means a consideration in money or money's worth (other than a nominal consideration or a consideration consisting solely of a covenant to pay money owing under a mortgage),

"premium" means the amount or value of any monetary consideration given by the lessee as part of the same transaction in which a lease is granted by way of fine, premium or otherwise, but, where a registered leasehold estate of substantially the same land is surrendered on the grant of a new lease, the premium for the new lease shall not include the value of the surrendered lease,

"profit" means a profit à prendre in gross,

"rent" means the largest amount of annual rent the lease reserves within the first five years of its term that can be quantified at the time an application to register the lease is made,

"the rules" means the Land Registration Rules 2003,[2] and a rule referred to by number means the rule so numbered in the rules,

"Scale 1" means Scale 1 in Schedule 1,

"Scale 2" means Scale 2 in Schedule 2,

"scale fee" means a fee payable in accordance with a scale set out in Schedule 1 or 2 whether or not reduced in accordance with article 2(6),

"scale fee application" means an application which attracts a scale fee, or which would attract such a fee but for the operation of article 6,

"share", in relation to land, means an interest in that land under a trust of land,

"surrender" includes a surrender not made by deed,

"voluntary application" means an application for first registration (other than for the registration of title to a rentcharge, a franchise or a profit) which is not made wholly or in part pursuant to section 4 of the Act (when title must be registered).

(3) Expressions used in this Order have, unless the contrary intention appears, the meaning which they bear in the rules.

PART 2

Scale fees

Applications for first registration and applications for registration of a lease by an original lessee

2.—(1) The fee for an application for first registration of an estate in land is payable under Scale 1 on the value of the estate in land comprised in the application assessed under article 7 unless the application is—

  (a) for the registration of title to a lease by the original lessee or his personal representative, where paragraph (2) applies,

  (b) a voluntary application, where paragraph (6) applies, or

  (c) a large scale application, where article 6 applies.

(2) The fee for an application for the registration of title to the grant of a lease by the original lessee or his personal representative is payable under Scale 1—
  (a) on an amount equal to the sum of the premium and the rent, or
  (b) where
      (i) there is no premium and
      (ii) either there is no rent or the rent cannot be quantified at the time the application is made,
    on the value of the lease assessed under article 7 subject to a minimum fee of £40,
unless either of the circumstances in paragraph (3) applies.

(3) Paragraph (2) shall not apply if the application is—
  (a) a voluntary application, where paragraph (6) applies, or
  (b) a large scale application, where article 6 applies.

(4) The fee for an application for the first registration of a rentcharge is £40.

(5) The fee for an application for the first registration of a franchise or a profit is payable under Scale 1 on the value of the franchise or the profit assessed under article 7.

(6) The fee for a voluntary application is the fee which would otherwise be payable under paragraphs (1) and (2) for applications to which those paragraphs apply reduced by 25 per cent and, where the reduced fee would be a figure which includes pence, the fee must be adjusted to the nearest £10.

(7) In paragraph (2) "lease" means—
  (a) a lease which grants an estate in land whether or not the grant is a registrable disposition, or
  (b) a lease of a franchise, profit or manor the grant of which is a registrable disposition.

Transfers of registered estates for monetary consideration, etc.

3.—(1) Subject to paragraphs (2), (3) and (4), the fee for an application for the registration of—
  (a) a transfer of a registered estate for monetary consideration,
  (b) a transfer for the purpose of giving effect to a disposition for monetary consideration of a share in a registered estate,
  (c) a surrender of a registered leasehold estate for monetary consideration, other than a surrender to which paragraph (3) of Schedule 4 applies,
is payable under Scale 1 on the amount or value of the consideration.

(2) Paragraph (1) shall not apply if the application is—

(a) a large scale application, where article 6 applies, or

(b) for the registration of a transfer of a matrimonial home made pursuant to an order of the court, where article 4(1)(h) applies.

(3) Where a sale and sub-sale of a registered estate are made by separate deeds of transfer, a separate fee is payable for each deed of transfer.

(4) Where a single deed of transfer gives effect to a sale and a sub-sale of the same registered estate a single fee is assessed upon the greater of the monetary consideration given by the purchaser and the monetary consideration given by the sub-purchaser.

(5) The fee for an application to cancel an entry in the register of notice of an unregistered lease which has determined is payable under Scale 1 on the value of the lease immediately before its determination under article 7.

Transfers of registered estates otherwise than for monetary consideration, etc.

4.—(1) Unless the application is a large scale application (where article 6 applies), the fee for an application for the registration of—

(a) a transfer of a registered estate otherwise than for monetary consideration (unless paragraph (2) applies),

(b) a surrender of a registered leasehold estate otherwise than for monetary consideration,

(c) a transfer of a registered estate by operation of law on death or bankruptcy, of an individual proprietor,

(d) an assent of a registered estate (including a vesting assent),

(e) an appropriation of a registered estate,

(f) a vesting order or declaration to which section 27(5) of the Act applies,

(g) an alteration of the register, or

(h) a transfer of a matrimonial home (being a registered estate) made pursuant to an order of the Court,

is payable under Scale 2 on the value of the registered estate which is the subject of the application, assessed under article 7, but after deducting from it the amount secured on the registered estate by any charge subject to which the registration takes effect.

(2) Where a transfer of a registered estate otherwise than for monetary consideration is for the purpose of giving effect to the disposition of a share in a registered estate, the fee for an application for its registration is payable under Scale 2 on the value of that share.

Charges of registered estates or registered charges

5.—(1) The fee for an application for the registration of a charge is payable under Scale 2 on the amount of the charge assessed under article 8 unless it is an application to which paragraphs (2), (3) or (4) apply.

(2) No fee is payable for an application to register a charge lodged with or before the completion of a scale fee application ("the primary application") that will result in the chargor being registered as proprietor of the registered estate included in the charge unless—

(a) the charge includes a registered estate which is not included in the primary application, where paragraph (4) applies, or

(b) the primary application is a voluntary application, in which case this paragraph shall apply only if the application to register the charge accompanies the primary application.

(3) No fee is to be paid for an application to register a charge made by a predecessor in title of the applicant that is lodged with or before completion of an application for first registration of the estate included in the charge.

(4) Where a charge also includes a registered estate which is not included in the primary application ("the additional property") any fee payable under Scale 2 is to be assessed on an amount calculated as follows:

$$\frac{\text{Value of the additional property}}{\text{Value of all the property included in the charge}} \times \text{Amount secured by the charge}$$

(5) The fee for an application for the registration of—

(a) the transfer of a registered charge for monetary consideration, or

(b) a transfer for the purpose of giving effect to the disposition for monetary consideration of a share in a registered charge,

is payable under Scale 2 on the amount or value of the consideration.

(6) The fee for an application for the registration of the transfer of a registered charge otherwise than for monetary consideration is payable under Scale 2 on—

(a) the amount secured by the registered charge at the time of the transfer or,

(b) where the transfer relates to more than one charge, the aggregate of the amounts secured by the registered charges at the time of the transfer.

(7) The fee for an application for the registration of a transfer for the purpose of giving effect to a disposition otherwise than for monetary consideration of a share in a registered charge is payable under Scale 2 on—

(a) the proportionate part of the amount secured by the registered charge at the time of the transfer or,

(b) where the transfer relates to more than one charge, the proportionate part of the aggregate of the amounts secured by the registered charges at the time of the transfer.

(8) This article takes effect subject to article 6 (large scale applications).

Large scale applications, etc.

6.—(1) In this article—

(a) "land unit" means—

(i) the land registered under a single title number other than, in the case of an application to register a charge, any estate under any title number which is included in a primary application within the meaning of article 5(2), or

(ii) on a first registration application, a separate area of land not adjoining any other unregistered land affected by the same application.

(b) "large scale application" means a scale fee application which relates to 20 or more land units, other than a low value application,

(c) "low value application" means a scale fee application, other than an application for first registration, where the value of the land or the amount of the charge to which it relates (as the case may be) does not exceed £30,000.

(2) The fee for a large scale application is the greater of—

(a) the scale fee, and

(b) a fee calculated on the following basis—

(i) where the application relates to not more than 500 land units, £10 for each land unit, or

(ii) where the application relates to more than 500 land units, £5,000 plus £5 for each land unit in excess of 500, up to a maximum of £40,000.

(3) If a large scale application is a voluntary application, the fee payable under this article is reduced in accordance with article 2(6).

PART 3

Valuation

Valuation (first registration and registered estates)

7.—(1) The value of the estate in land, franchise, profit, manor or share is the maximum amount for which it could be sold in the open market free from any charge—
  (a) in the case of a surrender, at the date immediately before the surrender, and
  (b) in any other case, at the date of the application.
  (2) As evidence of the amount referred to in paragraph (1), the registrar may require a written statement signed by the applicant or his conveyancer or by any other person who, in the registrar's opinion, is competent to make the statement.
  (3) Where an application for first registration is made on—
  (a) the purchase of a leasehold estate by the reversioner,
  (b) the purchase of a reversion by the leaseholder, or
  (c) any other like occasion,
and an unregistered interest is determined, the value of the land is the combined value of the reversionary and determined interests assessed in accordance with paragraphs (1) and (2).

Valuation (charges)

8.—(1) On an application for registration of a charge, the amount of the charge is—
  (a) where the charge secures a fixed amount, that amount,
  (b) where the charge secures further advances and the maximum amount that can be advanced or owed at any one time is limited, that amount,
  (c) where the charge secures further advances and the total amount that can be advanced or owed at any one time is not limited, the value of the property charged,
  (d) where the charge is by way of additional or substituted security or by way of guarantee, an amount equal to the lesser of—
     (i) the amount secured or guaranteed, and
     (ii) the value of the property charged,
  (e) where the charge secures an obligation or liability which is contingent upon the happening of a future event ("the obligation"), and is not a charge to which sub-paragraph (d) applies, an amount equal to—
     (i) the maximum amount or value of the obligation, or

(ii) if that maximum amount is greater than the value of the property charged, or is not limited by the charge, or cannot be calculated at the time of the application, the value of the property charged.

(2) Where a charge of a kind referred to in paragraph (1)(a) or (1)(b) is secured on unregistered land or other property as well as on a registered estate or registered charge, the fee is payable on an amount calculated as follows—

$$\frac{\text{Value of the registered estate or registered charge}}{\text{Value of all the property charged}} \times \text{Amount of the charge}$$

(3) Where one deed contains two or more charges made by the same chargor to secure the same debt, the deed is to be treated as a single charge, and the fee for registration of the charge is to be paid on the lesser of—

(a) the amount of the whole debt, and

(b) an amount equal to the value of the property charged.

(4) Where one deed contains two or more charges to secure the same debt not made by the same chargor, the deed is to be treated as a separate single charge by each of the chargors and a separate fee is to be paid for registration of the charge by each chargor on the lesser of—

(a) the amount of the whole debt, and

(b) an amount equal to the value of the property charged by that chargor.

(5) In this article "value of the property charged" means the value of the registered estate or the amount of the registered charge or charges affected by the application to register the charge, less the amount secured by any prior registered charge.

PART 4

Fixed Fees and Exemptions

Fixed fees

9.—(1) Subject to paragraph (2) and to article 10, the fees for the applications and services specified in Schedule 3 shall be those set out in that Schedule.

(2) The fee for an application under rule 140 shall be the aggregate of the fees payable for the services provided, save that the maximum fee for any one application shall be £200.

Exemptions

10. No fee is payable for any of the applications and services specified in Schedule 4.

PART 5

General and Administrative Provisions

Cost of surveys, advertisements and special enquiries

11. The applicant is to meet the costs of any survey, advertisement or other special enquiry that the registrar requires to be made or published in dealing with an application.

Applications not otherwise referred to

12. Upon an application for which no other fee is payable under this Order and which is not exempt from payment, there shall be paid a fee of £40.

Method of payment

13.—(1) Except where the registrar otherwise permits, every fee shall be paid by means of a cheque or postal order crossed and made payable to the Land Registry.

(2) Where there is an agreement with the applicant, a fee may be paid by direct debit to such bank account of the Land Registry as the registrar may from time to time direct.

(3) Where the amount of the fee payable on an application is immediately quantifiable, the fee shall be payable on delivery of the application.

(4) Where the amount of the fee payable on an application is not immediately quantifiable, the applicant shall pay the sum of £40 towards the fee when the application is made and shall lodge at the same time an undertaking to pay on demand the balance of the fee due, if any.

(5) Where an outline application is made, the fee payable shall be the fee payable under paragraph (9) of Part 1 of Schedule 3 in addition to the fee otherwise payable under this Order.

Credit accounts

14.—(1) Any person or firm may, if authorised by the registrar, use a credit account in accordance with this article for the payment of fees for applications and services of such kind as the registrar shall from time to time direct.

(2) To enable the registrar to consider whether or not a person or firm applying to use a credit account may be so authorised, that person or firm shall supply the registrar with such information and evidence as the registrar may require to satisfy him of the person or firm's fitness to hold a credit account and the ability of the person or firm to pay any amounts which may become due from time to time under a credit account.

(3) To enable the registrar to consider from time to time whether or not an account holder may continue to be authorised to use a credit account, the account holder shall supply the registrar, when requested to do so, with such information and evidence as the registrar may require to satisfy him of the account holder's continuing fitness to hold a credit account and the continuing ability of the account holder to pay any amounts which may become due from time to time under the account holder's credit account.

(4) Where an account holder makes an application where credit facilities are available to him, he may make a request, in such manner as the registrar directs, for the appropriate fee to be debited to the account holder's credit account, but the registrar shall not be required to accept such a request where the amount due on the account exceeds the credit limit applicable to the credit account, or would exceed it if the request were to be accepted.

(5) Where an account holder makes an application where credit facilities are available to him, and the application is accompanied neither by a fee nor a request for the fee to be debited to his account, the registrar may debit the fee to his account.

(6) A statement of account shall be sent by the registrar to each account holder at the end of each calendar month or such other interval as the registrar shall direct.

(7) The account holder must pay any sums due on his credit account before the date and in the manner specified by the registrar.

(8) The registrar may at any time and without giving reasons terminate or suspend any or all authorisations given under paragraph (1).

(9) In this article "credit limit" in relation to a credit account authorised for use under paragraph (1) means the maximum amount (if any) which is to be due on the account at any time, as notified by the registrar to the account holder from time to time, by means of such communication as the registrar considers appropriate.

Revocation

15. The Land Registration Fee Order 2003[3] is revoked.

Signed by the authority of the Lord Chancellor

David Lammy
Parliamentary Under Secretary of State, Department for Constitutional Affairs

Dated 27th February 2004

Jim Murphy

John Heppell
Two of the Lord Commissioners of Her Majesty's Treasury

Dated 3rd March 2004

| SCHEDULE 1 | Articles 2 & 3 |

SCALE 1

NOTE 1: Where the amount or value is a figure which includes pence, it may be rounded down to the nearest £1.
NOTE 2: The third column, which sets out the reduced fee payable where article 2(6) (voluntary registration: reduced fees) applies, is not part of the scale.

Amount or value	Fee	Reduced fee where article 2(6) (voluntary registration: reduced fees) applies
£	£	£
0–50,000	40	30
50,001–80,000	60	45
80,001–100,000	100	75
100,000–200,000	150	110
200,001–500,000	220	165
500,001–1,000,000	420	315
1,000,001 and over	700	525

SCHEDULE 2 Articles 4 & 5

SCALE 2

NOTE: Where the amount or value is a figure which includes pence, it may be rounded down to the nearest £1.

Amount or value £	Fee £
0–100,000	40
100,001–200,000	50
200,001–500,000	70
500,001–1,000,000	100
1,000,001 and over	200

SCHEDULE 3 Articles 9 & 13

PART 1

FIXED FEE APPLICATIONS

Fee

(1) To register:
   (a) a standard form of restriction contained in Schedule 4 to the rules, or
   (b) a notice (other than a notice to which section 117(2)(b) of the Act applies), or
   (c) a new or additional beneficiary of a unilateral notice
       — total fee for up to three registered titles affected............................... £40
       — additional fee for each subsequent registered title affected £20

Provided that no such fee is payable if, in relation to each registered title affected, the application is accompanied by a scale fee application or another application which attracts a fee under this paragraph.

(2) To register a restriction in a form not contained in Schedule 4 to the rules
       — for each registered title £80

(3) To register a caution against first registration (other than a caution to which section 117(2)(a) of the Act applies)..................................... £40

(4) To alter a cautions register — for each individual cautions register £40

(5) To close or partly close a registered leasehold or a registered rentcharge title other than on surrender — for each registered title closed or partly closed £40

Provided that no such fee is payable if the application is accompanied by a scale fee application.

(6) To upgrade from one class of registered title to another £40

Provided that no such fee is payable if the application for upgrading is accompanied by a scale fee application.

(7) To cancel an entry in the register of notice of an unregistered rentcharge which has determined — for each registered title affected £40

Provided that no such fee is payable if the application is accompanied by a scale fee application.

(8) To enter or remove a record of a defect in title pursuant to section 64(1) of the Act £40

Provided that no such fee is payable if the application is accompanied by a scale fee application.

(9) An outline application made under rule 54:

   (a) where delivered directly to the registrar's computer system by means of a remote terminal £2

   (b) where delivered by any other means £4

Such fee is payable in addition to any other fee which is payable in respect of the application.

(10) For an order in respect of a restriction under section 41(2) of the Act — for each registered title affected £40

(11) To register a person in adverse possession of a registered estate — for each registered title affected... £100

(12) For registration as a person entitled to be notified of an application for adverse possession — for each registered title affected £40

(13) For the determination of the exact line of a boundary under rule 118 — for each registered itle affected £80

PART 2

SERVICES — INSPECTION AND COPYING

(1) Inspection of the following, including in each case the making of a copy, on any one occasion when a person gains access to the registrar's computer system by means of a remote terminal by virtue of rule 132:

   (a) for each individual register £2

   (b) for each title plan £2

(c) for any or all of the documents referred to in an individual register (other than the documents referred to in paragraph (7)) £2
(d) for each individual caution register £2
(e) for each caution plan £2
(f) for any other document kept by the registrar which relates to an application to him — for each document £2

(2) Inspection (otherwise than under paragraph (1)):
(a) for each individual register £4
(b) for each title plan £4
(c) for any or all of the documents referred to in an individual register (other than the documents referred to in paragraph (7)) £4
(d) for each individual caution register £4
(e) for each caution plan £4
(f) for any other document kept by the registrar which relates to an application to him — for each document £4

(3) Official copy in respect of a registered title:
(a) for each individual register
    (i) where an official copy in electronic form is requested from a remote terminal by virtue of a notice under rule 132............... £2
    (ii) where an official copy in paper form is requested by any permitted means £4
(b) for each title plan
    (i) where an official copy in electronic form is requested from a remote terminal by virtue of a notice under rule 132............... £2
    (ii) where an official copy in paper form is requested by any permitted means £4

(4) Official copy in respect of the cautions register
(a) for each individual caution register
    (i) where an official copy in electronic form is requested from a remote terminal by virtue of a notice under rule 132............... £2
    (ii) where an official copy in paper form is requested by any permitted means £4
(b) for each caution plan
    (i) where an official copy in electronic form is requested from a remote terminal by virtue of a notice under rule 132............... £2
    (ii) where requested by any other permitted means £4

(5) Official copy of any or all of the documents referred to in an individual register (other than documents referred to in paragraph (7)) — for each registered title

    (a) where an official copy in electronic form is requested from a remote terminal by virtue of a notice under rule 132........................ £2

    (b) where requested by any other permitted means   £4

(6) Official copy of any other document kept by the registrar which relates to an application to him — for each document

    (a) where an official copy in electronic form is requested from a remote terminal by virtue of a notice under rule 132........................ £2

    (b) where an official copy in paper form is requested by any permitted means £4

(7) Where permitted (being unavailable as of right) inspection or official copy (or both) of a transitional period document — for each document £8

(8) Copy of an historical edition of a registered title (or of part of the edition where rule 144(4) applies) — for each title £8

(9) Subject to paragraph (14) of Schedule 4, application to the registrar to ascertain the title number or numbers (if any) under which the estate is registered where the applicant seeks to inspect or to be supplied with an official copy of an individual register or of a title plan and the applicant has not supplied a title number, or the title number supplied does not relate to any part of the land described by the applicant — for each title number in excess of ten disclosed.......... £4

PART 3

SERVICES — SEARCHES

(1) An official search of an individual register or of a pending first registration application made to the registrar by means of a remote terminal communicating with the registrar's computer system by virtue of rule 132 — for each title £2

(2) An official search of an individual register by a mortgagee for the purpose of section 56(3) of the Family Law Act 1996[4] made to the registrar by means of a remote terminal communicating with the registrar's computer system by virtue of rule 132 — for each title £2

(3) An official search of an individual register or of a pending first registration application other than as described in paragraphs (1) and (2) — for each title ..   £4

(4) The issue of a certificate of inspection of a title plan — for each registered title affected £4

(5) Subject to paragraph (15) of Schedule 4, an official search of the index map — for each registered title in excess of ten in respect of which a result is given.......................................   £4

(6) Search of the index of proprietors' names — for each name £10

(7) An official search of the index of relating franchises and manors — for each administrative area:

(a) where the application is made by means of a remote terminal communicating with the registrar's computer system by virtue of rule 132 ....   £2

(b) where the application is made by any other permitted means £4

PART 4

SERVICES — OTHER INFORMATION

(1) Application to be supplied with the name and address of the registered proprietor of a registered title identified by its postal address — for each application £4

(2) Application for return of a document under rule 204 ....   £8

(3) Application that the registrar designate a document an exempt information document £20

(4) Application for an official copy of an exempt information document under rule 137 ....   £40

SCHEDULE 4   Article 10

EXEMPTIONS

No fee is payable for:

(1) reflecting a change in the name, address or description of a registered proprietor or other person referred to in the register, or in the cautions register, or changing the description of a property,

(2) giving effect in the register to a change of proprietor where the registered estate or the registered charge, as the case may be, has become vested without further assurance (other than on the death or bankruptcy of a proprietor) in some person by the operation of any statute (other than the Act), statutory instrument or scheme taking effect under any statute or statutory instrument,

(3) registering the surrender of a registered leasehold estate where the surrender is consideration or part consideration for the grant of a new lease to the registered proprietor of substantially the same premises as were comprised in the surrendered lease and where a scale fee is paid for the registration of the new lease,

(4) registering a discharge of a registered charge,

(5) registering a matrimonial home rights notice, or renewal of such a notice, or renewal of a matrimonial home rights caution under the Family Law Act 1996,

(6) entering in the register the death of a joint proprietor,

(7) cancelling the registration of a notice, (other than a notice in respect of an unregistered lease or unregistered rentcharge), caution against first registration, caution against dealings, including a withdrawal of a deposit or intended deposit, inhibition, restriction, or note,

(8) the removal of the designation of a document as an exempt information document,

(9) approving an estate layout plan or any draft document with or without a plan,

(10) an order by the registrar (other than an order under section 41(2) of the Act),

(11) deregistering a manor,

(12) an entry in the register of a note of the dissolution of a corporation,

(13) registering a restriction in form A in Schedule 4 to the rules,

(14) an application to ascertain the title number or numbers (if any) under which the estate is registered where the applicant seeks to inspect or to be supplied with an official copy of an individual register or of a title plan and the applicant has not supplied a title number, or the title number supplied does not relate to any part of the land described by the applicant, provided the number of registered titles supplied does not exceed ten,

(15) an official search of the index map where either no part of the land to which the search relates is registered, or, where the whole or part is registered, the number of registered titles disclosed does not exceed ten,

(16) an application for day list information on any one occasion when a person gains access to the registrar's computer system by means of a remote terminal communicating with the registrar's computer system by virtue of rule 132,

(17) an application to lodge a caution against first registration or to make a register entry where in either case the application relates to rights in respect of the repair of a church chancel.

Notes
[1] 2002 c.9.
[2] SI 2003/1417.
[3] SI 2003/2092.
[4] 1996 c.27.

Index

THE COMPANION CD

Instructions for Use

Introduction

These notes are provided for guidance only. They should be read and interpreted in the context of your own computer system and operational procedures. It is assumed that you have a basic knowledge of Microsoft Windows. However, if there is any problem please contact our help line on 020 7393 7266 who will be happy to help you.

CD Format and Contents

To run this CD you need at least:

- IBM compatible PC with Pentium processor
- 8MB RAM
- CD-ROM drive
- Microsoft Windows 95

The CD contains data files of the clauses in this book. It does not contain software or commentary.

Installation

The following instructions make the assumption that you will copy the data files to a single directory on your hard disk (e.g. **C:\Wontners Guide to Land Registry Practice**).

Open your **CD ROM drive**, select and double click on **setup.exe** and follow the instructions. The files will be unzipped to your **C drive** and you will be able to open them up from the new **C:\Wontners Guide to Land Registry Practice** folder there.

LICENCE AGREEMENT

Definitions

1. The following terms will have the following meanings:
"The PUBLISHERS" means SWEET & MAXWELL LIMITED, incorporated in England & Wales under the Companies Acts (Registered No. 28096) whose registered office is 100 Avenue Road, London NW3 3PF, (which expression shall, where the context admits, include the PUBLISHERS' assigns or successors in business as the case may be) of the other part (on behalf of Thomson Legal & Regulatory Europe Limited incorporated in England & Wales under the Companies Acts (Registered No. 1679046) whose registered office is 100 Avenue Road, London NW3 3PF)
"The LICENSEE' means the purchaser of the work containing the Licensed Material.
"Licensed Material" means the data included on the disk;
"Licence" means a single user licence;
"Computer" means an IBM-PC compatible computer.

Grant of Licence; Back-up Copies

2. (1) The PUBLISHERS hereby grant to the LICENSEE, a non-exclusive, non-transferable licence to use the Licensed Material in accordance with those terms and conditions.

(2) The LICENSEE may install the Licensed Material for use on one computer only at any one time.

(3) The LICENSEE may make one back-up copy of the Licensed Material only, to be kept in the LICENSEE's control and possession.

Proprietary Rights

3. (1) All rights not expressly granted herein are reserved.

(2) The Licensed Material is not sold to the LICENSEE who shall not acquire any right, sale or interest in the Licensed Material or in the media upon which the Licensed Material is supplied.

(3) The LICENSEE, shall not erase, remove, deface or cover any trademark, copyright notice, guarantee or other statement on any media containing the Licensed Material.

(4) The LICENSEE shall only use the Licensed Material in the normal course of its business and shall not use the Licensed Material for the purpose of operating a bureau or similar service or any online service whatsoever.

(5) Permission is hereby granted to LICENSEES who are members of the legal profession (which expression does not include individuals or organisations engaged in the supply of services to the legal profession) to reproduce, transmit and store small quantities of text for the purpose of enabling them to provide legal advice to or to draft documents or conduct proceedings on behalf of their clients.

(6) The LICENSEE shall not sublicense the Licensed Material to others and this Licence Agreement may not be transferred, sublicensed, assigned or otherwise disposed of in whole or in part.

(7) The LICENSEE shall inform the PUBLISHERS on becoming aware of any unauthorised use of the Licensed Material.

Warranties

4. (1) The PUBLISHERS warrant that they have obtained all necessary rights to grant this licence.

(2) Whilst reasonable care is taken to ensure the accuracy and completeness of the Licensed Material supplied, the PUBLISHERS make no representations or warranties, express or implied, that the Licensed Material is free from errors or omissions.

(3) The Licensed Material is supplied to the LICENSEE on an "as is" basis and has not been supplied to meet the LICENSEE's individual requirements. It is the sole responsibility of the LICENSEE to satisfy itself prior to entering this Licence Agreement that the Licensed Material will meet the LICENSEE's requirements and be compatible with the LICENSEE's hardware/software configuration. No failure of any part of the Licensed Material to be suitable for the LICENSEE's requirements will give rise to any claim against the PUBLISHERS.

(4) In the event of any material inherent defects in the physical media on which the licensed material may be supplied, other than caused by accident abuse or misuse by the LICENSEE, the PUBLISHERS will replace the defective original media free of charge provided it is returned to the place of purchase within 90 days of the purchase date. The PUBLISHERS' entire liability and the LICENSEE's exclusive remedy shall be the replacement of such defective media.

(5) Whilst all reasonable care has been taken to exclude computer viruses, no warranty is made that the Licensed Material is virus free. The LICENSEE shall be responsible to ensure that no virus is introduced to any computer or network and shall not hold the PUBLISHERS responsible.

(6) The warranties set out herein are exclusive of and in lieu of all other conditions and warranties, either express or implied, statutory or otherwise.

(7) All other conditions and warranties, either express or implied, statutory or otherwise, which relate in the condition and fitness for any purpose of the Licensed Material are hereby excluded and the PUBLISHERS shall not be liable in contract, delict or in tort for any loss of any kind suffered by reason of any defect in the Licensed Material (whether or not caused by the negligence of the PUBLISHERS).

Limitation of Liability and Indemnity

5. (1) The LICENSEE shall accept sole responsibility for and the PUBLISHERS shall not be liable for the use of the Licensed Material by the LICENSEE, its agents and employees and the LICENSEE shall hold the PUBLISHERS harmless and fully indemnified against any claims, costs, damages, loss and liabilities arising out of any such use.

(2) The PUBLISHERS shall not be liable for any indirect or consequential loss suffered by the LICENSEE (including without limitation loss of profits, goodwill or data) in connection with the Licensed Material howsoever arising.

(3) The PUBLISHERS will have no liability whatsoever for any liability of the LICENSEE to any third party which might arise.

(4) The LICENSEE hereby agrees that

    (a) the LICENSEE is best placed to foresee and evaluate any loss that might be suffered in connection with this Licence Agreement,

    (b) that the cost of supply of the Licensed Material has been calculated on the basis of the limitations and exclusions contained herein; and

    (c) the LICENSEE will effect such insurance as is suitable having regard to the LICENSEE's circumstances.

(5) The aggregate maximum liability of the PUBLISHERS in respect of any direct loss or any other loss (to the extent that such loss is not excluded by this Licence Agreement or otherwise) whether such a claim arises in contract or tort shall not exceed a sum equal to that paid at the price for the title containing the Licensed Material.

Termination

6. (1) In the event of any breach of this Agreement including any violation of any copyright in the Licensed Material, whether held by the PUBLISHERS or others in the Licensed Material, the Licence Agreement shall automatically terminate immediately, without notice and without prejudice to any claim which the PUBLISHERS may have either for moneys due and/or damages and/or otherwise.

(2) Clauses 3 to 5 shall survive the termination for whatsoever reason of this Licence Agreement.

(3) In the event of termination of this Licence Agreement the LICENSEE will remove the Licensed Material.

Miscellaneous

7. (1) Any delay or forbearance by the PUBLISHERS in enforcing any provisions of this License Agreement shall not be construed as a waiver of such provision or an agreement thereafter not to enforce the said provision.

(2) This Licence Agreement shall be governed by the laws of England and Wales. If any difference shall arise between the Parties touching the meaning of this Licence Agreement or the rights and liabilities of the parties thereto, the same shall be referred to arbitration in accordance with the provisions of the Arbitration Act 1996, or any amending or substituting statute for the time being in force.

Learning Resources
Centre